KAZAKHSTAN

Coming of Age

KAZAK

Michael Fergus
with **Janar Jandosova**

**STACEY
INTERNATIONAL**

HSTAN

Coming of Age

The Publishers wish to thank wholeheartedly the following:

For invaluable guidance and multifarious assistance in the assembly of this work:
Adel Abishev, Murat Auezov, Oljas Auyezov, Sacha Baradanov, Bakijan Bektenov, Jean-Marc Deom, Ulukbek Ibagimov, Eduard Kaplan, Jazira Kazembayeva, Vitaliy Krotov, Nina Lobanov-Rostovski, Guljan Mamirova, Shawki Nasser Eldien, Zhanai Omarov, Igor Pikalnet, Armands Pupols, Renato Sala, Maira Sarybay,

For textual contributions in draft, or otherwise:
Zifa Auezova (literature), Tulegan Baitukenov (film), Bayan Barmankulova (art), Jean-Marc Deom (archaeology and history), Vladimir Filatov (art), Ian Green (botany), Saule Kalikova (education), Ksenia Kaspari (rural affairs), Carol Kervan (anthropology), Alas Ordobayev (architecture), Renato Sala (archaeology and history), Maira Sarybay (music).

For their outstanding gifts as photographers and personal generosity:
Renato Sala, Alexei Senin, Shamil Zhumatov.

PHOTOGRAPHIC CREDITS:
Sergei Bondarenko: 9, 12(3), 12-13c, 14c, 14-15b, 15c, 16-17b, 17t, 150bl, 151(3), 154; *V Budnevic:* 145(2), 147, 150br; *Igor Burgadenov:*155bc, 246tl; *Carol Kerven:* 94cl, 94-95t, 95cr; *Central Museum, Almaty:* 81bl, 126br, 127bc, 135br, 139bl&br; *Consolidated Contractors Co:* 82bl&br, 82-83C, 83bl&br. *Michael Fergus:* 168t&br, 169tr, 231bc, 234cr, 248cl&bl, 250br; *Fotobank, Almaty (Oleg Belyalov):* 48lc, 51(4), 54(2), 55br, 57tl, cr&br, 58bl; *(also) Eugeny Soldatkin :* 174tr, 187tr; *Yuri Galov:* 1, 2, 3, 64-65cb, 64-65ct, 65tr, 128bl, 156cl&cr, 176-177tc, 176bl, 177c, 189tr, 230b(3), 231t(3), 234cl; *Ian Green:* 60cl, 60-61c, 61(3); *Ricarda Künzel:* 227br; *Nina Lobanov-Rostovski:* 180, 228bl; *Kasteyev Museum* 212l, 212-213t, 213r&bl; *National Museum Astana:* 102(5), 103(4), 107c, 108tc, 114c, 130br, 131(8), 133(2), 134(2), 138(2), 139bl&br, 141bl&br, 143br, 144(1), 216tc,bl&bc, 217(2nd)c&(3rd)c, 221tl; *Reuters (Zhumatov):* 4, 89, 157cr, 182-183tc, 184-185ct, 185br; *Renato Sala/Jean-Marc Deom:* 5, 19, 22bl, 22-23, 26-27, 28tr, 28-29b, 34tl, 38c, 42-43c, 43cr, 46tl, 47c&tr, 49c, 50t&br, 55bl, 58br&cr, 78bl, 90-91b, 92tc&bc, 93tc, cr&br, 97tc, 98cl&cr, 99tc&bl, 100bl, ct&cb, 102cr, 104cr&b, 106c, 108br, 110bl, 112bl, 112-113c, 113bl&br, 114tl, tr, cl,cr&br, 118tl&cl, 119tl, 159, 223tr; *Alexei Senin:* 20(2), 21l, 21l&r, 24(2), 25(2), 29tl&tr, 30-31, 33(2), 33-34c, 34c&br, 35br, 36(2) 36-37c, 38tl&bl, 39(2), 40br, 42cl, 46(2ndl), 50bl, 52-53, 56(2), 60,tl&bl, 73b, 78tr, 79tl, 87tr, 88tc, 92c, 93cl&bl, 95bl, 99br, 103cl, 104tl&tr, 105tl&tr, 160-161ct, 181(4), 196tc&(3), 197ct(2), 201(3rd)r &br, 207cr, 214tl, br&bc, 215br, 216r, 217tl,tc&tr, 221tr, 223br&bc, 224(3), 225; *Vladimir Simakov:* 80br, 81tr; *Soros Foundation:* 170tl&bl, 171(3), 172tl, 173br; *Tom Stacey:* 64bl, 65br, 66cr, 75(5), 76tl&bl, 76-77c, 76-77b, 77(3), 79bl, bc&br, 80tr, 81br, 84bl&br, 85bl&br, 149, 158bl&br, 159bl, 160tl&br, 160-161(2nd c), 160tc,cl,bl&br, 162tl&bl, 164-65bc, 166-67(11), 168br, 169tl, 170cr, 172cl&bl, 175br, 176bl, 177br, 199cr, 212cr, 215bl, cr&cl, 217bl,c&r, 226br, 227tl, 242-243c, 250tr, 251br; *Vladimir Suslin:* 40-41t, 86-87c, 119tr&cr, 179cl, 190-191ct, 191bl&br, 201(3rd)r&bl, 227tc, 228cr, 229bl&br, 244, 245, 246tr, 249tl; *Anatoly Ustinenko:* 10, 13c, 14t, 15t, 44-45c, 45cr, 46(3rdl), 46bl, 47br, 68-69, 72br, 88bc, 140bl, 174bl&br, 181tr, 185bl, 186bl, 188 bl&br (2), 189bl, 190bl, 190-91c, 191br, 192bl, 196-97bc, 199cl&c, 200l,201-l2,l3,l4,tr&tl, 208(4l)&2r, 208-98bc,233, 237, 242l, 243l 246tr, 247tr&bl, 248cr; *Shamil Zhumatov:* 157tc&cl, 158tl, 159tr, 162c, 163(2), 164tl&tr, 164-165ct, 173tr 176tr,bl&c(2), 178cl&cr, 182(3), 183bc, 184bl, 188-189c, 200bl&br, 222-223, 236cr, 238(3), 241(3), 247tl&cr, 248tl, 249tr.

Title page picture shows the capital's principal bridge across the Ishym river, dominated by the triple-juz unity arch.

Half title picture shows Astana's outstanding landmark, the 97-metre Baiterek Tower.

Stacey International
128 Kensington Church Street
London W8 4BH
Tel: 44 (0)207 221 7166
E-mail: enquiries@stacey-international.co.uk
www.stacey-international.co.uk
ISBN: 1 900988 615
© Stacey International 2003
Printed & Bound in Dubai by Oriental Press
Designer: Sam Crooks
Project Manager: Kitty Carruthers
Assistant: Jacqui Currie
Copy Editor: Caroline Singer

A LINGUISTIC NOTE

Kazakh is a Turkic language, and Russian a Slavic one. They differ in sounds and word-formation. Under colonisation, Kazakh names were Russified, and orthographized to fit the Cyrillic alphabet. Kazakh instinct, and to some extent policy, is to restore the centrality of Kazkh as the national language. This work is sensitive to re-assertion of Kazakh usages and orthography, in the contemporary context, while remaining loyal to such usages and orthography in their historical setting. Hence, we write of Karaganda in pre-independent historical contexts, and of Karagandy in modern and general contexts. Likewise Ust-Kamenogorsk and Oskemen, Aktyubinsk and Aktobe, Semipalatinsk and Semey, and so on.

As to sounds, we have opted to transliterate the Russified *Zh* to *J* whenever the word or name is Kazakh, except where the name is irreversibly or professionally established in the *Zh* formation. Hence, the mining town annotated on most Western maps as Zhezkazgan becomes Jezkazgan, and the key Kazakh term for the three territorial groupings, often transliterated as the *zhuz*, is spelled herein in the preferred Kazakh manner: *juz*. This reflects the spoken sound of that initial consonant. Although there is a measure of regional variation, *J* is more accurate for English-speakers than the softer *Zh*.

This page shows a Kazakh police officer – not dissimilar to a Canadian 'Mountie' – on patrol on the Steppe.

Opposite Kazakh youngsters respond to a prying camera's eye.

CONTENTS

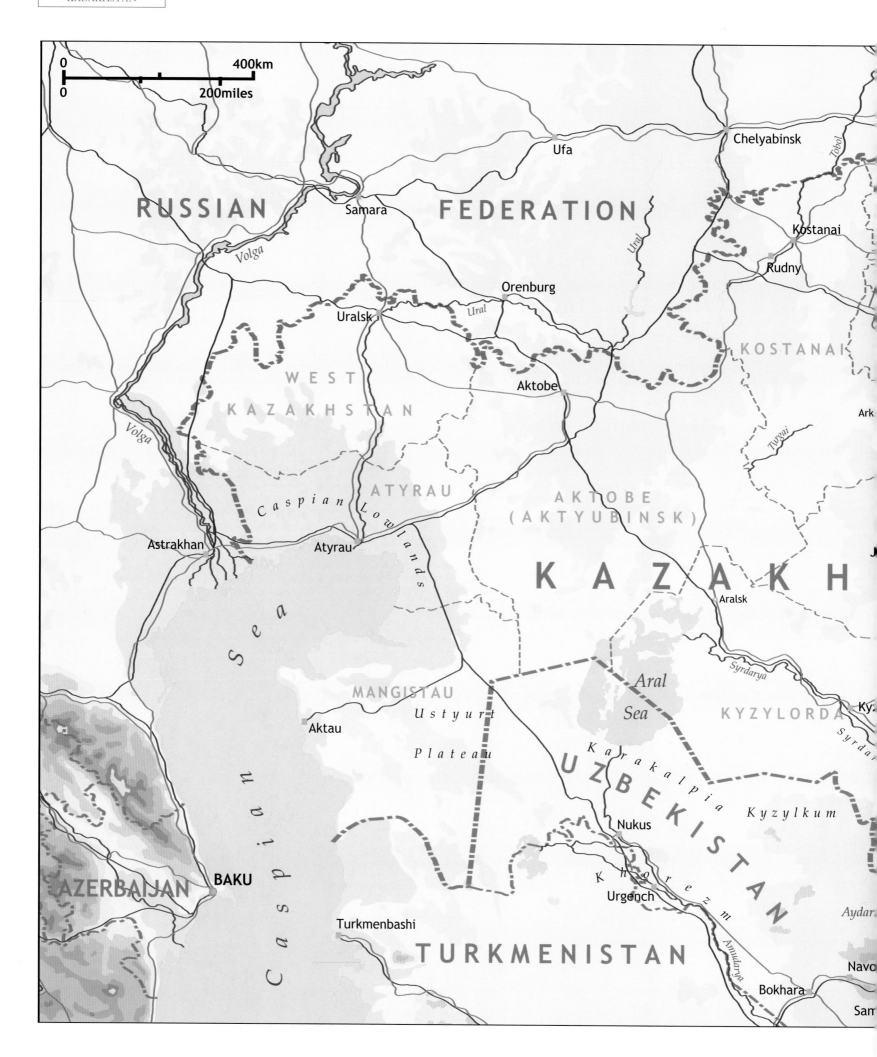

Foreword

Kazakhstan is a nation breaking in upon the consciousness of the world, as it masters the exploitation of its enormous hydrocarbon and mineral resources, and takes on its pivotal role on the map of Euro-Asia. For years its vast territory spanning from Europe to China has been a sleeping giant, a site of still largely undisturbed natural wealth and of a people of exceptional hardihood and resource. Pitched into independence in 1991 after a century and a half of colonisation by its successively Tsarist and Soviet Russian neighbour, Kazakhstan with its multi-ethnic population could lose no time in finding its feet in a rapacious and riven international community, and in establishing its own political moralities and stability internally.

This comprehensive work describes and celebrates Kazakhstan's coming of age, beginning with its place in the world.

Kazakhstan in the World

Above *The leaders of the countries which span half the globe meet in friendship:* **left to right** *Presidents Putin of Russia, Jiang Zemin of China (until 2003) and Nazarbayev of Kazakhstan.*

Opposite *This cauldron's handle was cast in bronze by Scythian craftsmen in the Kazakhstan of 500 BC, celebrating the stylized beauty of the Siberian stag.*

Few countries have been called upon to undergo and to cope with severer economic and social upheaval than the five former Soviet republics of Central Asia in the last decade of the twentieth century. This is a widespread opinion shared by Kazakh and outside commentators alike. In most respects those five were the most vulnerable republics of the whole former Soviet Union, and those that were confronted with the greatest reversal in their fortunes.

In its first ten years of independence after 1991, it was inevitable that Kazakhstan, by far the largest of the Central Asian republics, had to grapple with and to master entirely unprecedented problems and situations. The collapse of established markets, the massive shrinking of industry, the flight of Russian and German experts, the disappearance and break-up of agricultural collectives, the dissolution of its social services and pensions systems, the daunting problems of the dreadful Soviet environmental legacy: these were just some of the issues that Kazakhstan, as a newly independent nation, had to handle, and handle more or less alone. Kazakhstan experienced it all, and with no forewarning and no preparation. It was entirely understandable that some mistakes were made.

And yet Kazakhstan has weathered it all: not unscathed, it is true. Much remains to be done. Industry has still to get into its stride. Certain environmental problems have to be tackled head-on. Kazakhstan still needs to realise the fantastic agricultural potential which its vast land areas offer. Thousands more small businesses have to be created to give young people the realistic prospect of a job. Worn-out infrastructure left over from Soviet times still has to be restored. Unemployment is still higher than it ought to be in a country of such undoubted promise.

The Scythian (Sak) warrior is reproduced as a statue in ritual armour of cast or beaten gold, and rides upon a winged snow leopard, as a symbol of Kazakh heritage and authority. It is backed by the national flag's emblem of the sun, half-circled by the Steppe eagle in flight.

Far right, a guard-of-honour of Kazakhstan's élite Republican Guard in ceremonial uniform awaits the arrival of a foreign Head of State.

But then, much too has been achieved. Economic growth rates have attained double figures (13 per cent, for instance, in 2001). By dint of its own efforts Kazakhstan has become one of the world's leading oil and gas producers in the space of a mere decade. This has enabled it to establish a burgeoning National Fund of over two billion dollars which will mobilise surplus revenues to secure the welfare of future generations. In its first ten years, independent Kazakhstan was to attract more than 20 billion dollars' worth of foreign investment. This works out at more than five per çent of GDP, placing it well ahead of any other former Soviet republic. Kazakhstan was the first and so far only Commonwealth of Independent States (CIS) country to be accorded investment grade status by Moody's, the international credit rating agency. It has received Baa3 status, the same as Saudi Arabia and Bahrain. Kazakhstan is the first country in Central Asia to reform successfully its pensions

system, and unemployment has been falling consistently.

Kazakhstan's first years of independence could be termed a baptism of fire. And now, poised to exploit a truly formidable economic potential, Kazakhstan can be said well and truly to be coming of age.

People and Resources

Kazakhstan entered the third millennium with a population of 14.8 million, and rising. This approximates to Yemen (16 million), Côte d'Ivoire (14 million) and Syria (15 million). And yet Kazakhstan is a country vastly greater in area. With its 2.7 million square kilometres, it is the ninth largest country in the world, as large as Western Europe and over twice the combined area of its four Central Asian neighbours, Kyrgyzstan, Tajikistan, Turkmenistan and Uzbekistan. One single Kazakh province, Karagandy Oblast, with

little more than a million inhabitants, is larger in area than the Kingdom of Sweden and spans over 1,000 kilometres east to west.

The country's huge area combined with a small and scattered population makes it one of the world's least densely populated nations, with an average of about five persons per square kilometre. Only countries like Australia or Canada have similarly sparse populations.

In fact, between Independence in 1991 and the dawning of the new millennium, the number of people living in Kazakhstan actually fell by almost two million. And this is despite a healthy rate of growth in the ethnic Kazakh population who are young (with over half under the age of 30) and who traditionally – particularly in the south of the country – favour large families. The main reason for this unforeseen decline was an outflow, in the early years of Kazakh independence, of ethnic Russians, Ukrainians, Germans and others of European origin. Virtually all of those leaving the territory made for their ancestral homes in Europe from which their parents or ancestors had moved – or had been forcibly removed – during the twentieth century to Central Asia.

Since the recent turn of the century that outflow has dwindled: there are clear signs of the younger generation of ethnic Europeans preferring to take their chance in the independent Kazakhstan. They were born and bred in Kazakhstan, went to school in the country, had all their friends and acquaintances in the country, and many thousands had married Kazakhs and were raising families in an independent Kazakhstan. Word also got back that the streets of Yaroslavl or Berlin or Donetsk had not turned out to be paved with gold after all. The expectations of many 'returnees' of a new life of plenty in the West were dashed and many were to experience great difficulty in establishing themselves in a Europe which had changed beyond recognition in two or three generations. The manifest lack in Kazakhstan of any discrimination along racial lines in the general run of life, together with the unifying factors of the Russian language and Kazakhstan's obvious economic potential, was to make many young people think again about emigrating to the lands of their fathers in the West.

A less obvious reason for the fall in population was a temporary decline in the birth rate and an increase in the death rate. Experts attributed both to the fall in living standards associated with the unemployment and poverty resulting from the collapse of the command economy and the transition to the market economy in the early 1990s. Yet within ten years, that was to have altered. At the beginning of the new millennium, the economy was growing at over ten per cent a year; the trends were on the turn, and a growing and prosperous urban middle class was gaining the confidence to establish families. By the year 2002 it seemed that the outflow to Europe had been staunched. Those intending to move had already moved; birth and death rates were stabilising; the national population was set to rise.

With such a large country of such extensive natural resources, the interest of the Government of Kazakhstan is to increase the population. One way of doing this has been to encourage expatriate ethnic Kazakhs to return to their homeland. It has been estimated that as many as one million Kazakhs still live outside the country. These are termed Oralmans, many of whose parents or grandparents had fled the fearful privations of collectivisation of the 1930s. Within the first decade of independence over 180,000 Oralmans returned to settle in Kazakhstan. Some came from Russia, many from other CIS countries and from Mongolia; it was expected that up to half a million would emigrate to Kazakhstan from Uzbekistan in the first decade of the new century. Most Oralmans have retained Kazakh as a language of communication and most appear to have maintained the traditional Kazakh livelihood of livestock herding and pastoralism. The reintegration of the Oralman population is thus likely to increase the Kazakh component of the country's population.

The growth in the Kazakh population – supplemented by the Oralmans – in the first decade of Kazakhstan's independence, had made the country, at least from a demographic point of view, more 'Asian' in blood yet not necessarily so in outlook.

In a country with so few people and so much land, the balance between people and resources will always favour the country's inhabitants. Kazakhstan has supposedly the greatest array of exploitable minerals of any country in the world – virtually the entire periodic table. It is said to possess mineral deposits of more than 1,225 formulae, 70 of

*On the global scene, Kazakhstan plays a pivotal role as a bridge between China and Russia, whose leaders are pictured **right**, in 2003, with President Nazarbayev.*

*Pope John Paul II's visit to Kazakhstan in 2001, when he was greeted by the President (**right**), spoke of Kazakhstan's respect for religious freedoms, and for international accord.*

*To President George W. Bush of the United States, the trust of Kazakhstan's leader (seen **right**, together) is significant both politically and economically.*

*Nazarbayev entrusts the US amateur astronaut Tito (**opposite** on return to earth) to his Kazakh pilot, Musabayev.*

which have already been prospected and 60 actively exploited. These include iron, coal, oil, gas, lead, aluminium, copper, zinc, nickel, uranium, silver, gold, bismuth, cadmium and thallium. Perhaps even more important for the immediate welfare of the people of Kazakhstan is the country's supply of agricultural land. United Nations experts have estimated that the people of Kazakhstan are amongst the best endowed with farming land in the world. Although much of the country is mountain, Steppe and desert, at least 350,000 square kilometres, or one seventh of Kazakhstan, is classified as arable land. This amounts to about 2.5 hectares of arable land to every man, woman and child in the country. Such providence is superseded only by Australia, and is 25 times the amount of farming land available to the average Briton.

Fresh water, which is not plentiful, has to be husbanded by the people of Kazakhstan. Water comes not only in the form of three great inland seas, the Caspian Sea, the Aral Sea and Lake Balkhash. It also takes the form of the Syrdarya, Ili, Ishym, Irtysh, Turgai and Ural Rivers which provide drinking water and fresh fish to nearby populations. Notable efforts are being made to revive the moribund fisheries in the Aral and Caspian Seas (*see* Chapter 7, page 246).

Perhaps the greatest challenge thus confronting Kazakhstan's leaders in the first decade of the twenty-first century was the full mobilisation of the talents of its diverse peoples in the cause of exploiting the country's truly enormous land, water and mineral resources. Unlike most countries in the post-Rio, post-Johannesburg era, Kazakhstan is not confronted with the *impasse* of scarce resources: quite the opposite is true.

An Emerging Power

For Kazakhstan, the coming of Independence on 16 December 1991 was dramatic enough in Moscow yet relatively unspectacular at home, even for those who witnessed it on the ground in the capital (then Alma-Ata) or on some collective farm far out on the Steppes. Eventually ceremonies were held, flags unfurled, and troops in starched new uniforms paraded. It was to require more than a decade to take in the full significance of the events of 1991. Even today, well into the twenty-first century, there is frequently misapprehension about the status of Central Asia and many of the other former Soviet republics.

Yet there is little justification for confusion in the case of Kazakhstan. For this is a country rapidly emerging as a significant strategic, political and economic power. Because of its sheer size and position on the map of the world, Kazakhstan has a foot in many camps – with its neighbour China, its brothers and sisters in the four previously designated Central Asian republics to the south, the vastness of Siberia on its northern borders, the turbulent Middle East through its links across the Caspian to Iran and the Caucasus, and Europe and Mother Russia on its western border across the Volga.

That said, its infancy and early childhood as a free nation have not been easy. Kazakhstan's turbulent twentieth century history and the subsequent separation from Russia on the collapse of the Soviet Union had profound effects upon the economy and society. A largely nomadic nation of over five hundred years' standing with deep traditions, subjected to a forced marriage for over a century, has needed time to find its role and style in a fast changing world. It has needed to do three things, which are to find an appropriate stance for the twenty-first century in a world comity of democratic nations, to begin to realise the country's huge economic potential, and to tidy up after the Soviets.

Because of its location and its ethnic

composition, Kazakhstan has self-evident geopolitical significance. It is clearly neither exclusively of the East nor the West. It sees itself as a symbolic bridge between the two. The road bridge at Uralsk, taking traffic across the Ural River in western Kazakhstan, is said to link Europe with Asia, and to mark the continental border. The spanking new university in the capital Astana has consciously adopted the title: the 'Eurasian University'. This is designed to let the world know that a technologically-advanced university can and does exist in the East, but with growing links to Western business and investment.

Establishing truly democratic institutions in independent Kazakhstan has not been a straightforward task. Until the twentieth century Kazakhstan was a nomadic society with forms of government adapted to such a society. This gave priority to clan unity and gave rise to the emergence in the nineteenth century of a remarkable series of 'batyrs' or warrior leaders, such as Kenisary Kasymov (1801-1847), whose names are still revered amongst ordinary Kazakh folk. Their statues and portraits are increasingly in evidence on the streets of Kazakhstan's towns. It was they who fought during the nineteenth century for the cultural and economic integrity of the Kazakh nation. Eventually the might of Russian colonial authority prevailed. The Communists then imposed a system of Soviet conformity where loyalty to the Party was paramount, and where management by a hierarchical bureaucracy was the means of enforcing it. Such was none too promising a precedent for inculcating participatory democracy in the newly independent nation. People were accustomed to autocracy; they were obedient, not to say subservient; they were careful to respect the rule of law. Yet all at once, with the demise of the Soviet Union, they expected a greater say in their own affairs.

Nursultan Nazarbayev, born in 1940, first

President of the independent Republic, was better qualified than most for guiding Kazakhstan through its first decade of independence. He had worked in Karagandy first as a steel furnaceman and then qualified both as an engineer and as an economist. He was first and foremost a Kazakh, but his education had made a cosmopolitan of him, and it was this combination that Kazakhstan sorely needed. It needed an experienced Kazakh, well versed in the country's venerable culture, who could revive Kazakh identity and make respectable the use of the Kazakh language once again. But Kazakhstan also needed someone with a sound grasp of the country's great resource potential who could make the world aware of Kazakhstan as a new nation. Kazakhstan needed someone who could carve out a singular identity for the country and its people, so that it could also make its own mark on the world stage. The situation called forth the man.

By the first decade of the new century, Kazakhstan had the basic institutions of democracy in place and was experimenting with new forms of multi-party expression. In this it was encouraged, and at the same time closely monitored, by international agencies such as the International Helsinki Federation for Human Rights, the Organisation for Security and Co-operation in Europe (OSCE) and Transparency International (TI).

Kazakhstan has had to make an equal effort on the international scene. Until 1991 Kazakhstan was represented by Soviet embassies where any Central Asian diplomat, let alone a Kazakh one, was a rarity. By 2003 Kazakhstan had almost forty full-fledged embassies and numerous consulates, while over one hundred foreign countries maintained diplomatic relations with it. Because the country holds such a pivotal position between China, Russia, Europe and the Muslim world, Kazakhstan has also had to fashion various strategic regional alliances. The CIS, a largely

Kazakhstan's vast territory bridges Europe with China, with its internal Europe-Asia geographical meeting point marked by the canopy at Uralsk (opposite, top).

***Above,** Kazakhstan's Caspian oil terminal port of Atyrau serves the Caspian Sea's 'European' west coast ports.*

***Left, centre and opposite,** President Nazarbayev confers with Prime Minister Blair of Britain and President Chirac of France, and with the King of Spain, while Foreign Minister Kasymzhomart Tokaev partners UN Secretary-General Kofi Annan at an international forum.*

political organisation, which embraces the former Soviet republics, was actually established by the Alma-Ata Treaty of 1991. However, the most important alliance in Central Asian terms has been the Shanghai Co-operation Organisation (popularly known as the 'Shanghai Six'). It was originally established in 1996 by China, Russia, Kazakhstan, Kyrgyzstan and Tajikistan in order to address common border problems. However it has increasingly been viewed as a regional counterweight to growing American influence in Central Asia.

Despite the ambitions of some outsiders, religion has not become a contentious issue in the emerging Kazakhstan. The Kazakh people being of nomadic origin are not a dogmatically inclined folk and have little attachment to ecclesiastic structures and hierarchies. Mosques are only to be found in the largest cities, and then they are few in number. (The same is true of churches and synagogues.) The bogey of Muslim fundamentalism has little meaning in Kazakhstan, despite the country's venerable Islamic heritage and monuments and strong spiritual tradition in the south. A parallel fact is that ethnic conflict is an

unknown concept. The Kazakh element, now at last an overall majority, co-exists easily with the non-Muslim Russian element and other minorities.

Kazakhstan's emergence as a significant player on the world scene is likely to depend as much on the exploitation of its natural resources and environment as on its efforts in the fields of domestic governance and international diplomacy. For Kazakhstan's resource potentials are truly enormous. Even in Soviet times Kazakhstan was regarded as a treasure-house of land, minerals and nature. Now that the country no longer has to share these with the other republics, it has become a veritable land of plenty, at least in anticipation. Next-door neighbour China, with almost one hundred times as many people, has less than four times the land area of Kazakhstan, and only three times as much arable land. In terms of agricultural land, Kazakhstan, along with Australia, has the world's greatest potential. As we have noted, there are few minerals which Kazakhstan does not possess and

mine. It contains a quarter of the world's uranium, and a third of its chromium and manganese. In addition it exploits extensive resources of gold, silver, lead, zinc, copper, coal, bauxite and phosphorite. The new oil and gas fields emerging in Kazakhstan's sector of the Caspian Sea are the largest discovered in the world since the early 1970s and are now substantially larger than the North Sea reserves.

Kazakhstan, however, is likely to proceed in future with greater circumspection than it did in the first decade of independence. In that early phase, a wave of privatisation and poorly managed foreign investment meant that many national resources were lost to the Kazakh state, and that the jobs it had been hoped such moves would create did not materialise. Since then the Government has taken a much firmer line, seeking to give priority to Kazakhstani nationals, particularly in the petroleum sector.

Another challenge likely to confront the emerging Kazakhstan is the issue of

*A constitutional President, Nazarbayev (**opposite and right**) needs the trust and, indeed, votes of his people, as they need him as their spokesman and exemplar. As President, he is Commander-in-Chief of Kazakhstan's armed forces (**below**).*

the distribution of wealth. Under the pressures of private sector development, the egalitarian characteristics of the Soviet Union, with negligible unemployment and high standards of health and technical education, dissolved. The Government has been acutely aware of the redistribution problem. With the assistance of the World Bank and other Western donors it installed one of the first and most comprehensive post-Soviet national pensions systems. It has also implemented a comprehensive poverty reduction programme aimed at alleviating unemployment, strengthening the social services and reducing regional economic imbalances. It has to be added that, despite an inescapapably disruptive transition to independence, Kazakhstan still possesses one of the most literate and best-educated workforces in the world.

During the Soviet period, Kazakhstan was secluded, remote and sparsely populated. And so Kazakhstan was used for weapons testing, weapons research, rocket science and

polluting industry — in secret. The result was Kazakhstan's terrible environmental legacy.

Secrecy, Soviet style, was what allowed Kazakhstan to be used as a nuclear testing ground for more than forty years. Secrecy was what allowed the Aral Sea to be drained and Lake Balkhash to be polluted. Secrecy was what allowed 'closed' cities to be built (not marked on any map) to mine strategic minerals or test bacteriological weaponry. Secrecy was what allowed thousands upon thousands to be transported to a 'gulag archipelago' in the east of the country. One of Kazakhstan's most signal achievements since independence has thus been the complete dismantling of an ingrained culture of secrecy. One indication of this was President Nazarbayev's total renunciation of the country's nuclear stockpile. Promoting openness and eschewing secrecy augur well for participatory systems of government and for a fresh approach to the country's foremost challenges.

Chapter 2

Kazakhstan can lay claim to two natural borders, some three thousand kilometres apart – the majestic mountain ranges on the east and south-east determining, primarily, its boundary with China, and the broad waters of the Caspian Sea on the west. The forests and frosts of Siberia provide a far less distinct division to the north, as do the fertile valleys and deserts of the country's southern and south-western neighbours. Between, the vast Steppe of rolling grasses, the arid badlands; and the slow, snaking rivers... and the heavens above – the sun by day, and moon and stars by night, such as the Kazakh people of the Steppe perceived as the presiding genus of their universe.

The Land and the Skies

Such a massive sheet of water as Lake Balkhash is mostly fed by one great river, the Ili, whose upper waters are being claimed by China for irrigation.

Geography and Geology

The largest land-locked country in the world, Kazakhstan is impressive because of the great physical contrasts within its boundaries. In the south and east of the country, where it borders China, Mongolia and Kyrgyzstan, are mountains of truly Himalayan stature, decked out in eternal snow and rising to over 21,000 feet (7,010 metres). Dotted throughout the central plains of Kazakhstan are over 40,000 lakes. Most are remote, still and saline. Many are surprisingly large, often full of fish, and often attended upon by great flocks of the world's most northerly flamingoes. There are broad, sweeping rivers of continental dimensions, some flowing to the Caspian, and three joining the great Siberian rivers which meander thousands of kilometres north to the Arctic Ocean. There are the featureless prairie landscapes of northern Kazakhstan, horizon upon horizon. There are three of the world's largest inland seas: the Caspian, the Aral Sea and Lake Balkhash. All three have been a focus of human activity since earliest times. There are many varieties of forbidding badlands and deserts in the centre and the east of

Kazakhstan, which because of their inaccessibility are still known to few besides mineral prospectors and economic geologists. And everywhere in the country are the apparently endless rolling, grassy Steppes out of which the ancient Kazakh nation and the Eurasian culture of horsemanship emerged over five thousand years ago.

While these contrasts are striking, it is usually Kazakhstan's sheer physical size and extent that impresses the first-time visitor. While the highest point is almost 7,000 metres, the lowest point – the Karagiye Depression close to the Caspian Sea – is 132 metres below sea level. The country covers 2,717,000 square kilometres which makes it as big as the entire territory of western Europe. Its national boundaries with Russia, Mongolia, China, Kyrgyzstan, Uzbekistan, Turkmenistan and the Caspian Sea stretch over 12,000 kilometres. Kazakhstan is thus the ninth largest country in the world, surpassed in Asia only by China. It is often looked upon as a remote Asian country, somewhere 'beyond the Urals', and somewhere 'behind the Himalayas or the Hindu Kush'. In reality, a sizable portion of the country west of the Ural river lies on

European soil, and much of the west of Kazakhstan is closer to Europe's eastern metropolises than it is to its own eastern centres. Uralsk, provincial capital of West Kazakhstan Oblast, is closer to Helsinki in Finland than it is to Almaty, and is comfortably under two hours by plane from Moscow.

Kazakhstan is of course an Asian country too, and its stony deserts freezing in winter are much more akin to the wastes of neighbouring Mongolia and China than to anything in continental Europe. The great Ustyurt plateau is a remorseless limestone desert lying between the Caspian and Aral Seas. The Tien Shan Mountains of south-east Kazakhstan too are more reminiscent of the mountains of the Indian sub-continent than of the Alps or the Rockies and considerably higher into the bargain. Kazakhstan straddles the Eurasian divide and it is said that the sluggish Ural River, flowing from the mountains of the same name in northern Russia to the Caspian, forms the true border between Europe and Asia. Even for a landlocked country it has its coasts, having a shoreline of over 1,500 kilometres along the Caspian Sea.

Despite its physical diversity, which is

Tectonic and volcanic activity throughout the aeons have combined with erosion to give the face of Kazakhstan such dramatic formations as the fluted precipices of Baynaul (**far left**), the granite outcrops of the Jungar range's Zaeleeski ridge (**opposite, right**), the spectacular Red Canyon of the Charyn River (**above, and right**) and Mangistau's natural citadel (**below**) towering above the Caspian.

scarcely to be wondered at in a country so large, most of Kazakhstan is flat or rolling Steppe, pasture or desert. This gives the winds free play over vast spaces and has a major effect on the country's climate. Astana, Kazakhstan's burgeoning capital, is on the same latitude as Warsaw or London, but because it is thousands of kilometres from the sea in any direction, its climate is very much more extreme. In winter it can be swept by freezing blizzards – in the infamous *buran* – of the type familiar to inhabitants of the Canadian Mid-West. In summer it can be uncomfortably hot, and because of this, northern Kazakhstan, like many parts of Africa, can be plagued by swarms of locusts. This is the key to Kazakhstan's climate, its distance from any benign, maritime influences, and its generally flat terrain across which great weather systems can wander at will.

On the other hand, continental climates like Kazakhstan's are often remarkably stable, and much of the country can enjoy long periods of calm and pleasant weather. Unlike its counterparts in inland, continental America, Kazakhstan does not experience tornadoes or cyclones as it is probably too far from the sea. The south-west of Kazakhstan, apart from the mountains, is generally free from snow in winter and enjoys a sheltered central Asian climate similar to its neighbours across the border in Uzbekistan, where an early spring brings forth an abundance of fruit: mulberries, figs, apricots and walnuts. Much of the rest of the country is snow-bound in winter; the population is well used to it, and can operate as normal, and indeed find delight in what snow has to offer in sport and beauty. Because of Kazakhstan's distance from the sea and its

Rifting of the earth's crust made south-central Kazakhstan's Kyzyl (red) Amphitheatre (left) of the Charyn region. Yet the unforgiving aspect of the Chu-Ili piedmonts (right) conceal many a Bronze Age relic indicating well watered vales where man and his animals have always been able to sustain life.

topography, rainfall (or snowfall) is generally sparse in most of the country, ranging from 400 mm in the north to 150 mm in the south. This is just about enough to support agriculture or animal husbandry. But because of a lack of water, in much of the country the population has since antiquity resorted to irrigation or nomadic practices in order to survive. The cultivating capacity of much of the country is thus very limited. Average temperatures range from –20° C in winter to +26° C in summer. The growing period ranges from 190 days annually in the north to 290 days in the south.

The major topographical feature of Kazakhstan is the relatively recent massif of the Tien Shan mountains in the south-eastern corner of the country, which

straddles the border with Kyrgyzstan and, in turn, with China. Like the Himalayas, the Tien Shan range has been formed (and is still being formed) by a collision of tectonic plates to the south of India which continue to fold the mountains. It is estimated that the Tien Shan peaks are continuing to rise by no less than ten metres per century. Further north, and immediately to the east of the vast lake Balkhash, the frontier is formed by the Jungar range; and in the extreme north-east, at the convergence of the Russian and Chinese borders with Kazakhstan, by the remote but historically significant Altai mountains. These, with the Jungar, represent geographically a continuation of the Tien Shan chain. Most of the remaining 85 per cent of the country is flat, undulating Steppe or desert.

Mineralogically Kazakhstan is a veritable treasure-trove. Virtually all the elements in the periodic table of mineral elements are represented on or beneath the surface of the territory. It possesses large reserves of gold, silver, lead, zinc, copper, uranium, coal, iron ore, bauxite and phosphorite ores. In addition it has wolfram, molybdenum, barites, tungsten, beryllium, titanium and cadmium in commercial quantities. It has one third of the world's resources of chromium and manganese and a quarter of the world's uranium. Kazakhstan's huge oil and gas deposits beneath or in the region of the north-west Caspian Sea at Karachaganak, Tengiz, Kashagan, Novy-Uzen and the like, have attracted international attention and massive investment. Proven oil reserves in the Caspian are estimated to be three times those of the North Sea, and the Kashagan field in the north Caspian is the largest oil field discovered in the world since 1970. It is hardly surprising that the founder and first president of the Kazakhstan Academy of Sciences was a geologist by profession. He was Kanysh Imantaevich Satpaev, who was born in 1899. It was Satpaev's pioneering work in the field that laid the foundations for Kazakhstan's current mineral extraction and processing industry, to the incalculable benefit – in Satpaev's lifetime – the Soviet Union rather than, in the first place, the 'autonomous republic' of Kazakhstan of that era.

Forests

About 100 kilometres north-west of the Aral Sea, on the Almaty-Moscow railway line, lies the small town of Sexeuildi. There is almost nothing to distinguish it from

hundreds or even thousands of similar settlements in Kazakhstan... except in one minor respect. It has taken its name from Kazakhstan's most common tree, the saxaul. And little wonder: Sexeuildi lies at the centre of one of Central Asia's largest saxaul forests. Of course, a saxaul forest is not like other more familiar forests because white saxaul and black saxaul trees (*Haloxylon persicum* and *Haloxylon aphyllum*) are mainly bushy shrubs or small trees and rarely reach more than 30 feet in height. They are widely known as 'desert forest'. However they are a vital part of Kazakhstan's desert ecology.

The saxaul was more or less essential for traditional Kazakh nomadic life in three main ways. Firstly its root system is such that it binds sand and loose soil so that it stops sandstorms before they start and creates stable soil conditions for the formation of essential spring and autumn pastures. It makes Kazakhstan's deserts and semi-deserts liveable. Secondly it has unique water retention properties. Its thick, coarse,

spongy bark holds fresh water so that just by squeezing it the desert traveller can more than fill his water canteen. Thirdly the wood itself has a high calorific value so that saxaul serves as readily available fuel to nomadic herders.

The natural vegetation of Kazakhstan is largely treeless Steppe and desert so that the country has a lower forest coverage than most countries. In fact less than five per cent of the area of Kazakhstan is forested and more than half of this is the low, sparse, saxaul 'desert forest'. Despite this Kazakhstan can nonetheless claim to shelter some of the most important genetic tree

*The birch glades of Borovoye, near Kokshetau, burst with leaf in the spring (**left**), while the forests of the Jungar Mountains (seen **above** and **opposite**) hunch against the onset of winter.*

***Overleaf**, the vigil of a Kazakh herder of sheep in the upper Chilik region is the immemorial role of the oceanic Steppe.*

resources in the world. The Zailijskij Mountains (or 'Alatau' in the vernacular) behind Almaty are thought to be the place in the world where the apple tree evolved, and it is still here where the widest range of wild apple species grow. Alma-Ata itself takes its name from the Kazakh word for apple. Kazakhstan's fruit forests (which also include apricots and walnuts) in the foothills of the Tien Shan mountains are some of the most extensive in Central Asia. They represent unique biodiversity and genetic resources and perform important functions in controlling drainage, reducing climatic extremes and in binding the soil. Because of they constitute part of the original genetic pool of today's fruit trees, they have been included in Kazakhstan's *Red Book of Endangered Species*. Foreign and local NGOs

as well as the United Nations have come to the assistance of the Government in developing schemes for conserving the wild apple species of Kazakhstan.

Much of Kazakhstan's original forest has been cleared to make way for large-scale agriculture, especially in northern Kazakhstan on the borders with Russia. Large areas have also been ravaged by fire, and the Government has introduced very firm measures to reduce forest fire risks. Forests are particularly exposed to fire danger in early spring and autumn.

Of course the forests with which most tourists in Kazakhstan are familiar are those around Almaty. These are the cedar, larch and fir forests, a short bus ride out of the city on the mountain slopes of the Tien Shan. These never fail to impress the first-time

visitor. However, Kazakhstan also contains extensive stands of pine and birch from the Siberian *taiga* in the northern oblasts of north Kazakhstan, Akmolinsk and Pavlodar. A feature of southern Kazakhstan's forest is the so-called 'Tougai' forests which grow in sheltered valleys of the southern mountains. These include willows, poplars and other low-growing species. They are of value in soil protection and soil conservation and provide important habitats for animals and birds.

The Steppe

The Steppes of Central Asia is some of the Russian composer Borodin's most spell-binding and evocative music. It immediately conjures up images of caravans slowly wending across vast and empty grasslands. Nonetheless, despite its exotic origins, the word 'Steppe' has been in use in the English language for three centuries. It derives from the Russian *stepi* which denotes a dry, cold, largely treeless grassland. Steppe landscapes are widespread in Asia, America and parts of South America (Argentina). They usually form, far from the sea, in the lee of high mountains which cut off rainfall. They represent a transitional zone between desert and forest, where annual precipitation is between 250 mm and 750 mm a year. Because of their distance from the sea, winters can be very cold and snowy. And in the case of Kazakhstan they are. Summers are hot, with frequent droughts and natural fires. It has been estimated that over 40 per cent of Kazakhstan's physical area or 1,100,000 km² consist of Steppe and that much of this has been affected by human activity. The original chestnut coloured Steppe soils are fertile but also very sensitive, and there appears to have been large-scale degradation of Steppe soils especially in northern Kazakhstan because of mass ploughing between 1954 and 1960

and isolated instances of over-grazing. It is estimated that now two thirds of the Steppe of Kazakhstan is subject to erosion.

Kazakhstan is the country of the Steppe *par excellence*, and it is estimated that over half the country is Steppe of one type or another. It is not always easy to distinguish Steppe from wetter pasture or drier desert in Kazakhstan, although it is not difficult to recognise Steppe when you see it. The Steppe is the essence of Kazakhstan, its nature, its people and its culture.

There is nothing more evocative of Kazakhstan than to sit in the Steppe, on a mid-May afternoon far from motor-roads, listening to the larksong soaring in the winds, watching the waving wild tulips and experiencing the billowing cumulus clouds as they scud across the empty heavens. The Steppe is the sound of the wind, the sun, the herby scent of the saxaul (*Artemesia*) plant, and the view of distant Kazakh grave sites atop a rise.

Left, above For some 8000 years, every Steppe-dweller's mastery of the horse has ensured the survival of man. Right, the formidable Tien Shan mountains provide Kazakhstan its south-western frontier with China, opposite, above, the outcrops of Kentau interrupt the central plateau of South Kazakhstan; and at Butakovka, in the Jungar range, autumn leaves and berries paint the landscape.

The Kazakhs, more than any other Central Asian nation, are a people of the Steppes and most of their culture has emerged from it. In fact, human culture first emerged on the Steppes of Kazakhstan some 4,000 years ago, and well before the

first millennium BC Steppe people had begun to breed and herd domesticated animals. The Steppe was too dry for conventional cropland agriculture so that the Kazakhs practised animal husbandry, moving with their herds of horses, cows, sheep and goats in search of pastures and water. The Kazakhs therefore became nomads or *transhumants* (taking their animals alternately to the mountains and the plains). At Akkol in Jambyl Oblast in the south of Kazakhstan one can still come across nomadic collectives which move their animals on a seasonal basis in response to the availability of pasture and water. And from nomadism developed a whole life-style which has come to shape today's Kazakh identity and sense of

nationhood. It therefore may come as a surprise to visitors to Astana Museum to view the immensely beautiful and complex gold ornamentation fashioned by these Steppe peoples. These ornaments required a sophistication and a skill in their manufacture which are not easily associated with a culture which spent so much of its waking hours on horseback.

As a physical environment the Steppe has not a great deal to offer, and it can only really serve mankind when used for nomadic herding as the Kazakhs have done. The saxaul desert forests of the Steppe have done much to make the Kazakh Steppe habitable by providing much needed fuelwood, by providing emergency supplies of drinking water (from squeezing the bark) and by creating sheltered pastures both in winter and in summer. Because it is open, offering little shelter, it is the habitat for relatively few animals. Nonetheless, the Corsac fox (*Vulpes corsac*), the Saiga antelope (*Saiga tatarica*) and the Saker falcon (*Saker cherrug*) have all established themselves in the Kazakh Steppe. Falconry is therefore a sport of the Steppes. The Steppe wolf is common all over Kazakhstan, and in Kyzylorda Oblast is widely regarded as a pest because of its depredations on herds of Bactrian camels in hard winters. Another curiosity of the Kazakh Steppe are the world's most northerly flamingoes which make brief but spectacular seasonal visits to Lake Tengiz, about 200 kms south-west of Astana.

Mountains

At first glance, Kazakhstan with its sweeping plains and Steppes must seem one of the least mountainous countries in Asia. A visitor can board a flight in Astana, fly

The summits of Ordjonikidze dominate the Jungars' challenging skyline.

more than 2,000 kilometres west to Uralsk, and emerge in the same seemingly featureless plain left more than three hours earlier. And yet Kazakhstan contains some of the most spectacular mountain ranges in the world. From Almaty itself part of the reality is revealed. For the city, snuggling into its plain, is located against a spectacularly jagged skyline of the snow-capped Jungar Mountains, peaking at 4370 metres, a northern outlier of the Tien Shan massif. When there is no mist to mask the view from downtown Almaty, Talgar mountain – higher than Mont Blanc – is clearly visible.

The Tien Shan range extends into China and Kyrgyzstan yet covers 1,500 sq. km. in south-eastern Kazakhstan. The highest point in Kazakhstan is the summit of Khan Tengri (6995m), the all-but inaccessible frontier point with Kyrgyzstan and China. The soaring peak bears a mystic significance for the Kazakh race as a symbol of the union of heaven and earth, of eternity and time, of the realm of the spirit and earthly materiality. Because of their relatively northerly location and their height the Tien Shan contain hundreds of glaciers, the largest of which – Inylchek – is over 50 km long.

Notwithstanding its location on a gently sloping plain, Almaty can consider itself as a mountain town because of the proximity of the mountains. Only twenty minutes from downtown lies the vast Medeo Speed Skating Ring which, because of its altitude at 1,600 metres, produced world speed skating records throughout the 1970s and 1980s. Another twenty minutes further into the mountains takes the visitor to Shimbulak, at 2,200 metres, Kazakhstan's main downhill ski resort. From here chair-lifts carry the skier to over 3,000 metres, and the summer rambler to a fine network of footpaths which gives access to neighbouring Kyrgyzstan's beautiful Lake Issyk Kul.

Mountains comprise and dominate all of

Kazakhstan's eastern borders – with Kyrgyzstan, China, Mongolia and Russia. East of Lake Balkhash the Jungar Range bars the route to China. Further north and close to Mongolia lie the Altai Mountains or Golden Mountains, perhaps the geographic site of the mythic golden fleece. They have always been difficult to visit because of their remoteness from centres of civilization beyond. Latterly, access has been restricted on both sides because of the sensitivity of the border with China and mutual concerns over smuggling and illegal immigration. The Altai are characterized

by Alpine tundra, Siberian birch and great cedar forests. Mount Belukha (4,506 metres) is the highest point, on the border with federal Russia's Altayskaya. Because they are untouched and unspoiled, the Altai Mountains are home to flourishing pristine wildlife, notably lynxes, bears, snow leopards and golden eagles as well as the more ubiquitous marmot. The human population is similarly unspoiled, for it is here in the Altai Mountains that the traditional horse-based nomadic Kazakh life-style has survived. It is here too that the nomadic hunters and shepherds who

The high Tien Shan, least known of the great ranges of Asia, makes its own marvels of ice and snow, as in the storm-swept rowan (left), Mount Tengri's sacred pinnacle (top centre), its tallest peak at 4,951 metres, and its rumpled Inilchek glacier (below left and centre).

straddle the Russian/Kazakh border sing the traditional Khoomi overtone *melisma* in which the singer produces two or more distinct pitches simultaneously.

Two further ranges warrant attention. The Karatau uplands, running north-east to south-west in today's South Kazakhstan Oblast, and the Chu-Ili hills straddling the Jambyl and Almaty borderland, are negligible in height compared with the eastern ranges. Yet for defensive potential and dependability of water, both have played their historic part in Kazakh civilization.

Kazakhstan has traditionally been a country of the people of the Steppe. Here the great Sak (Scythian), Hun, Turkish and ultimately Kazakh traditions evolved. Yet those traditions have always depended on the interplay of plain and mountainland, and on well-watered upland summer pasturage.

Rivers

Largely arid, Kazakhstan can yet claim over 7,000 rivers more than 10 km long in the country. Many run out into sand or a salt marsh. Yet southern Kazakhstan is graced with the sweeping splendour of the Jaxartes as it was known in classical times and to the army of Alexander the Great or, in today's nomenclature, the

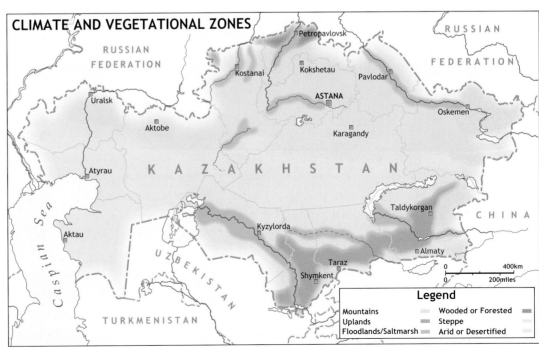

CLIMATE AND VEGETATIONAL ZONES

land formerly grazed by the Kazakhs' fellow-Turkic neighbours, the Uighurs.

Further north, one of Siberia's largest river systems, the Irtysh, rises in the Altai mountains close to the border of Mongolia and China flowing west to feed East Kazakhstan's vast Lake Zaisan and provide for the city of Semey. Thereafter it flows no less than 3,000 kilometres north to the Arctic Ocean. It is joined on its way by the Ishym River upon which Kazakhstan's new capital, Astana, has been built.

Syrdarya.

It rises in the Tien Shan, a couple of hundred kilometres south of Almaty in today's Kyrgyzstan and flows over 2,000 kilometres through Uzbekistan and Kazakhstan to spill via a great inland delta into the northern Aral Sea. The waters of the river have been grievously raided to irrigate cotton plantations of what is today's independent Uzbekistan, an industry established over half a century ago under the totalitarian rule of Moscow and now largely decayed; yet, however valuelessly, the water is still diverted. What remains of the river feeds the delta that still serves as a habitat for rare migratory birds, a region protected by Kazakhstan.

Part of Kazakhstan's western border is formed by the mighty Volga as it pours into the Caspian near Astrakhan. The Ural River too, traditionally accepted – in its southerly course in Kazakhstan – as the boundary between Asia and Europe, and rising in Russia's Ural mountains far to the north, empties itself into Kazakhstan's sector of the great Caspian Sea. It is famed for its magnificent specimens of sturgeon, one of Kazakhstan's greatest culinary delicacies.

On the opposite perimeter of the country, where – north-east of Almaty – China and Kazakhstan share a frontier, the once great Ili River feeds another inland sea, namely Lake Balkhash, the world's third largest inland stretch of water with no outlet. Here too is a story of Kazakhstan being deprived of its rightful – and vital – waters by diversion for the purposes of irrigation by a neighbour, in this case China, engaged in a policy of settling Han Chinese on newly cultivated

Lakes and Inland Seas

Three bodies of water in Kazakhstan, that is the Caspian Sea, the Aral Sea and Lake Balkhash, are so large that they are instantly identifiable on a globe of the world. However an assiduous United Nations hydrologist has calculated that there are more than 3,000 lakes in Kazakhstan measuring more than 1 sq km. Many, such as Lake Tengiz in Akmolinsk Oblast which is more than 2,000 sq. km. and Kambyz in Kyzyl Orda, are large and very shallow (less than six metres deep), but the vast majority are small, with varying degrees of salinity, about 30 parts per million. This often means they are unsuitable for watering cattle or human beings, but good for fish – and fishing.

The Caspian Sea which Kazakhstan shares with Russia, Turkmenistan, Iran and Azerbaijan, is the world's largest inland sea, measuring 370,000 sq. km. (about the same size as Germany). The Sea is fed by over 130 rivers and streams, all of which enter on the north and west coasts of the Sea. Only the Ural River enters from Kazakhstan. Periodic variations in the Sea levels have puzzled hydrologists. Between 1933 and 1941 water levels fell by almost two metres, whilst between 1978 and 1994 water levels rose by more than two metres, causing extensive coastal flooding. Levels are expected to continue to rise because of changes in global climate and tectonic activity.

The only thing most people know about the Aral Sea is that it has been progressively dried out. The Aral is in fact a fairly recent phenomenon, having come into being in the

last 10,000 years, that is, since the last Ice Age. Excessive irrigation upstream – mostly in Uzbekistan – began as early as the 1930s to reduce the area and volume of the Sea. By 1994 the volume of the Aral Sea was one third of its 1960 volume, and salinity had increased threefold in the same period, engendering the relentless desertification of the region and further hardship for the Aral's indigenous population. Similarly threatened is Lake Balkhash, which every airline passenger heading from Almaty to Astana crosses high above. At the time of writing, Balkhash is the sixteenth largest inland body of water in the world and is more than 600 kilometres long and 40 kilometres wide. It is a shallow lake divided by a sandbar into a western half which is freshwater and an eastern half which is saline. Much of the region's climate is dependent on its great area of surface water, providing moisture and rainfall. But its days are numbered, and current estimates by global egologists are that open water comprising Balkhash will have been reduced by half by 2015, given the fact that some 89 per cent of the feed waters of the upper Ili river are being diverted for agriculture in China's Sinkiang Province.

Freshwater Resources

Despite the fact that the country has so much surface water in the form of lakes, this water is seldom of direct benefit to the inhabitants. Water for human activities must come from the country's rivers rather than its seas and lakes.

Kazakhstan is far from the open sea. Most of it is low-lying. These two facts have an important bearing on the country's river resources. Far from the sea, Kazakhstan receives relatively limited precipitation. Over half the country receives less than 400 mm of rain or snow a year and this is classified as subject to desertification. Some particularly arid areas receive less than 50 mm (two inches a year). Most of Kazakhstan is less than 500 metres above sea level. However it is bounded by some of the world's highest mountains. This means that most of Kazakhstan's rivers rise outside the country and flow through it.

It also means that the country has little control over the waters it receives. The country's main rivers, the Syrdarya, the Ural, the Ili, the Chu and the Irtysh, all rise

*Expeditions tackling the demanding ascents of the Tien Shan (**top left**) are rewarded by the breathtaking beauty of the mountainscape, and the high valleys of the Ibis tributaries (**centre** and **below**). The lake, **right**, lies above Almaty.*

*Literally thousands of freshwater lakes are scattered across Kazakhstan's vast landscape, like Lake Primal, **left**, near the Kyrgyzstan border, but few are more beautiful than Borovoye, **opposite** and **below***

and about 20 cubic kilometres is actually consumed. Five per cent of annual consumption is estimated to come from underground sources. About one quarter of the consumption is lost in transmission. Agriculture, irrigation and livestock watering account for almost two thirds of Kazakhstan's consumption, and industry accounts for another fifth. Less than five per cent of water consumption in Kazakhstan actually goes to household and

in other countries. In fact over half the river water in Kazakhstan rises outside the country. A notable exception is the Turqai, which both rises and finishes in Kazakhstan, while sustaining a significant population along its course. Collecting its waters among the downs of central and eastern Kostanai Oblast and eastern Karagandy, it meanders southwards for some 400 km to lose itself in the salty depression of Ghalkarteniz in Aktynbinsk. A similarly ignominious fate awaits the Shirderti in western Pavlodor flowing northwards, the Nura flowing north and then westwards in Karagandy and Akmola.

Because of the seasonal distribution of rain and snow and the seasonal flow of rivers there are many geographical and seasonal water deficits in Kazakhstan. Spring and early summer are the seasons of

plentiful water because of the melting of the snows in the high peaks, while high summer and autumn can be seasons of dearth. Generally speaking the south of the country has more adequate water resources, mainly because its proximity to the Tien Shan mountains.

Rivers, and to a very much lesser extent, underground water thus provide the people of Kazakhstan with their renewable sources of water. Of course the country does possess huge resources in the form of lakes and glaciers, but these are rarely used for water supplies either because they are too salty or because they are too remote.

Rivers flowing in Kazakhstan are estimated to produce about 100 cubic kilometres of freshwater (100 billion cubic metres) annually. Of this about 45 cubic kilometres has been available for off-take,

drinking water purposes.

The relationship between production of water and its consumption in Kazakhstan needs considerable study to understand its complicated working. It seems as if water consumption in the country fell considerably in the first decade since Independence. Most of this decline can be attributed to decreases in demand owing to reduced economic activity. However, decreases in supply also arise because of factors often outside Kazakhstan's control. These factors can also play an important role in how much water the country uses. Water consumption fell by over 30 per cent between 1991 and 2001 from 28 cubic kilometres to 20 cubic kilometres. This was principally because of reduction in activity by the main consumer, agriculture. However, comparable reductions were also experienced in industrial and domestic consumption. The main reason was the decline in economic activity, and thereby the demand. The extent of irrigated farming in southern Kazakhstan, for example, was greatly reduced: because of a distinct decline in the market for sub-tropical fruit products. But there were other reasons too for this reduction. They were a lack of new investment, because of the outdated equipment and because of a lack of capital. Yet another reason for reductions in consumption may have been

the curtailing of the grossly inefficient use of water which had characterised much economic activity in the Soviet period. In a situation of acute shortage people could simply no longer afford to waste water as they had done for decades. In Soviet times if you wasted water there was always more to come. After Independence this was no longer the case. In the towns and villages throughout the country, domestic water consumption often plummeted for two main reasons. Firstly, failures in the electricity supply did not allow the authorities to pump water – the water simply did not flow. Secondly, lack of funds meant that it was impossible to maintain leaking pipelines.

Changes in supply often had a dramatic impact on consumption. It has been postulated, with some justice, that the next major wars are likely to be fought between countries over water rights. Water shortages increasingly cause tensions between nations. Disputes between countries on the use of water from the Nile (Egypt, Sudan and Ethiopia), from the Mekong (Thailand, Laos, Cambodia), from the Jordan (Israel, Palestine, Jordan), from

the Tigris and Euphrates (Turkey, Iraq), from the Colorado (USA, Mexico) and from many other major rivers are becoming all too familiar. And the examples are very numerous. As populations grow and consumption rises, the water available to everyone is that much less. Those living upstream tend to retain more for their own use to the inevitable detriment of those living downstream. Perhaps the most extreme example of this in Kazakhstan is the Syrdarya River. In 1960 it was estimated that 55 cubic kilometres of water flowed from the Syrdarya river into the Aral Sea in Kazakhstan every year. But between 1960 and 1980 its flow was diverted upstream for hydropower, irrigation and livestock watering purposes. By 1985 the flow reaching the Aral Sea from the Syrdarya had been reduced to about five cubic kilometres a year. In other words 90 per cent of the flow disappeared, and what did reach the Aral Sea was now highly polluted with pesticides and other agricultural chemicals. Two thirds (or 1,400 kilometres) of the river's length was in Kazakhstan. Yet upstream users in

Uzbekistan, Tajikistan and Kyrgyzstan had simply taken over the flow, with little or no consultation or thought for their downstream neighbours. In this extreme case Kazakhstan lost not only a river but an entire Sea. Lake Balkhash, as we shall see, is likewise threatened.

The Aral Sea is shared almost equally by Uzbekistan and Kazakhstan. It was formed by inflows from the Syrdarya (the classical Jaxartes) entering the north from Kazakhstan and by the Amudarya (the classical Oxus) entering the Sea from the south. Because of excessive irrigation upstream, and diversion for hydropower, the area and volume of the Sea began to be reduced as early as 1930. By 1994 the volume of the Sea was one third of its 1960 volume.

The area was reduced by half from 68,000 square kilometres (about the same size as Ireland) to 35,000 square kilometres, and salinity had increased threefold in the same period from 10 parts per million to 30 parts per million. The changes, of course, had a dramatic impact on life in the region. The traditional fishing life of the Aral died, and with it a prosperous fish processing industry. Increased salinity also had a profound effect upon the ecology of the Sea (*see* 'New Hope for the Aral' on page 248), and allowed the introduction of new fish species. There has also been some talk of re-

introducing the indigenous Aral sturgeon (*see below* in this section, 'Wildlife').

There has been much speculation as to whether the Aral can ever be restored to its former glory. The consensus is that it cannot. However all hope has not yet gone. A reduction in the areas occupied by irrigated agriculture upstream on the Syrdarya has already led to an increase in the flows entering the Aral. Even more encouraging news has been brought by the dam which was constructed between the smaller Northern Sea and the rest of the Sea. The purpose of this dam has been to refill gradually the Northern Sea from the increasing flow of the Syrdarya river. Over

the years this may allow the Northern Sea to be restocked with fish, and even to affect the micro-climate of the region. Although partially financed by the World Bank, the Kokaral Dam, as it is known, was conceived and planned by local people eager to do something themselves to restore their environment and their livelihood. The World Bank project also includes rehabilitation of the Chardara Dam and improving hydraulic control on the Syrdarya river.

At the same time it is also important to realise that the drying out of the Aral Sea was a result of conscious and deliberate water management and planning. Regional

*Kazakhstan is said to have 7,000 rivers, which number among them (reading from the top picture on the left) the Tien Shan Mountains' torrent of Gorelbnik, the Chilik (flowing into Lake Kapshagay), and the Charyn, fast-flowing in its gorge (**far left**) and serene and broad, **left**; and Kulsay (**right**), and the north-east's formidable Irtysh (**above, right**).*

*Near to Koktal, the Ili river is majestically spanned (**above**), while (**left**) the Irtysh is pictured where it is joined by its tributary, the Oskeml.*

Kyrgyzstan which regulated water for both irrigation and hydropower purposes.

What they sacrificed was a fishing industry and a lively shipping trade across the Aral Sea. They may also have caused climate change and an increase in desertification. How far the drying up of the Aral Sea has been responsible for climate change has been a subject of considerable professional dispute for many years. In defence of the planners, it must also be recalled that when the decision to empty the Aral Sea was taken, the five Central Asian republics were all within the same Union, and the philosophy was to allow individual regions to suffer for the benefit of the whole.

Some attempts have since been made to foster regional co-operation on restoring the Aral Sea. It is perhaps too early to say how successful such attempts have been. The International Fund for Saving the Aral Sea (IFAS) was established in 1992 and has worked to co-ordinate international aid programmes for the Sea.

As the case of the Syrdarya River and the Aral Sea shows, Kazakhstan's water resources are particularly vulnerable to the whims and decisions of other countries. Because it shares all its major rivers with other countries, none of which rise in Kazakhstan, the country is obliged to negotiate the flow in its rivers or the amount of water available for its agricultural, industrial and domestic consumption. The reality is that Kazakhstan's water supplies are very much at the mercy of its neighbours in Central Asia, China and Russia.

International problems on water-sharing are also well exemplified by the case of the Irtysh, Ili and Chu rivers in eastern and southern Kazakhstan. The Irtysh River rises in the Altai Mountains in China, flows west into Kazakhstan and then travels north into Russia where it eventually joins the River Ob, which

continues thousands of kilometres to the north and the Arctic Ocean. China hoped to boost its national oil production and to replace its depleted oilfields close to Beijing with potential oil reserves in Xinjiang Province on its border with Kazakhstan. This required the development of new communities in China's relatively empty far west. A policy was already under way for the agricultural settlement of Han Chinese on relatively arid land requiring irrigation. All of this would require the extraction of huge amounts of fresh water. China has planned to extract about one cubic kilometre (over five per cent of Kazakhstan's total surface water supply) from the Ili and Irtysh. This will seriously impact on north-eastern and eastern Kazakhstan, wholly dependent on water from these rivers. China, Russia and Kazakhstan have been holding high level meetings for several years on how to share the water of the Irtysh. Any significant curtailment of the water could have serious economic impacts for Kazakhstan.

The problems in the Ili-Balkhash Basin represent another type of threat. The issue here is not purely one of exploitable water; it is a matter of climate. Hydrological forecasts point to a fate for Balkhash similar to that of the Aral by 2015 – the lake divided, half of it gone, and consequent regional desertification. The river basin covers over 400,000 square kilometres of which 85 per cent is in Kazakhstan and 15 per cent is in China. Over three million people live in the Basin, including over one million in Almaty. The Ili River rises in China and most of the water it contains is generated in the Chinese mountains. Diversion of water for irrigation in the Chinese part of the catchment has already seriously reduced the flows in the Ili in Kazakhstan and, specifically, the levels of Lake Balkhash into which it flows. Between 1961 and 1999 the area of Lake Balkhash fell from 21,400 sq. km to 17,100 sq. km The water flowing into Balkhash from the Ili

water planners carefully weighed up the consequences of diverting the water in the two rivers. They estimated that the diminution of the Aral Sea to today's levels was worth it. It was planned to increase the area of irrigated agriculture along the Syrdarya river from two million hectares in 1960 to six million hectares by 1999. This would permit increases in the production of thousands of tons of cotton and other semi-tropical agricultural products which the Soviet Union would otherwise have to import. It also allowed them to generate hydropower to serve the Tajik and Kyrgyz republics from the huge Toktugul Dam in

reduced from 19 cubic kilometres to 12 cubic kilometres a year. This affected not only the area of the lake but also the volume, the shoreline, the Ili delta and the overall ecology. The delta has always had an important function in regulating the flow of the Ili. It too was reduced in size from 3,000 sq.km to 1,800 sq.km. This has already affected fish stocks and hunting for muskrats. High level discussions between

sturgeon and its caviar, Kazakhstan's prized gastronomic delicacy. Much of the 1,000 kilometres of Kazakhstan through which it flows is sparsely populated, before it reaches its mouth in the Caspian Sea. Demand for water is thus low so that there are also fewer conflicts with upstream users in Russia.

The Caspian Sea is the world's largest closed inland body of water and Kazakhstan shares it with Turkmenistan, Iran,

by dam construction. Periodic variations in the Sea levels have puzzled hydrologists. Between 1933 and 1941 water levels fell by almost two metres whilst between 1978 and 1994 water levels rose by more than two metres, causing extensive coastal flooding. This has meant the flooding of oil wells, refineries and other installations near Atyrau.

As the Caspian is one of the largest and

the Governments of China and Kazakhstan Governments have been going on for a number of years in order to develop a water resources management plan which can satisfy the needs of both countries, yet so far fruitlessly from the Kazakh point of view.

The Ural River in western Kazakhstan, as its name implies, rises in the Ural Mountains in northern Russia. In Kazakhstan the Ural is perhaps most renowned for its magnificent specimens of

Azerbaijan and Russia. It measures 370,000 sq. km (about the same size as Germany). Its mean water depth is 208 metres but this varies widely over the Sea. The Sea is fed by over 130 rivers and streams all of which enter on the north and west coasts of the Sea. Only the Ural River enters from Kazakhstan. It has been estimated that 80 per cent of the Caspian's inflow is provided by the Volga which enters the sea on Kazakhstan's western border. Some of the flow may have been diverted in recent years

most promising oil producing regions in the world, there has been considerable concern over the potential environmental impact, and particularly by oil pollution on water quality, fish (notably sturgeons) and the Caspian seal. Almost all the oil production and exploration is carried out by Western companies well used to the stringent requirements of operating in the North Sea or the Gulf of Mexico, and they have avoided major spills to date. In addition the Government of Kazakhstan has adopted an aggressive attitude to oil companies that pollute and has imposed punitive fines on companies that have failed to observe environmental legislation (the Chevron-Texaco consortium was heavily fined in August 2001 for ecological damage although the penalty was reduced by a factor of ten on judicial appeal a year later. Vigilance among the oil majors is in fact exemplary). Of greater concern to the

trackless stony desert south of Lake Balkhash is one of the Earth's true empty quarters. At the same time it is not easy to draw a distinct line in Kazakhstan between desert, semi-desert and dry Steppeland, or between the different types of desert. Geographers have now formally classified as much as 1,240,000 square kilometres or 44 per cent of the country as being within 'desert ecological systems'.

much of this falls as snow. Most precipitation occurs in winter and spring. Mean temperatures range from –15°C in January to +26°C in July. Kazakhstan's deserts have also been divided into four different soil types by the National Geographical Society. These are clay deserts characterised by a brief flowering period in spring before being dried out by the summer sun and the salt flats, which contain

authorities is trans-boundary pollution brought down the Volga from industrial zones from southern Russia, or from oil pollution transported from the Azerbaijani production fields.

Deserts

Flying the 1,250 kilometres between Kazakhstan's two major cities, Almaty and Astana, one can gain an impression that much of the country is desert. The

In fact, Kazakhstan contains three main deserts. The Kyzyl Kum (the Red Sands) desert lies to the south-east of the Aral Sea between the Syrdarya and Amudarya rivers and is shared with Uzbekistan. The Ustyurt desert occupies the area between the Aral Sea and the Caspian Sea. The Betpak Dala desert is located in the area between the Aral Sea and Lake Balkhash.

A primary feature of all Kazakhstan's deserts is their low precipitation which rarely exceeds 200 mm a year. In the northern part of the country of course,

*On the great rivers like the Ili (**far left** and **above**) and the Syrdaria (**centre**) there depends not only the entire system of life along their valleys and estuaries, but the fate of the inland seas – Balkhash and Aral – that they flow into.*

salt-tolerant plants and salt lakes. There are stony deserts, most of which are covered in gravel, and sandy deserts which are found mainly in southern Kazakhstan. Each of these desert categories has its own particular physical and ecological characteristics. One peculiar feature of the Betpak Dala desert between Almaty and Lake Balkhash are the so-called 'singing sands' which are giant *barkhans* of up to 150 metres in height which can produce quite a musical squeak when trodden upon.

The Kyzyl Kum desert of southern Kazakhstan tends to be sandy rather than stony, and this has influenced the ecology. It is characterised by white (*Haloxylon persicum*) and black saxaul (*Haloxylon aphyllum*) bushes and trees, also known as 'desert forest'. In spring after rain the desert floor is often covered with wild tulips, giant brome, sagebrush, bindweed and wild stocks. Sandy acacia (*Ammodendron conollyi*) grows on the sand dunes themselves. It is said that in recent years saxaul trees have been over-exploited for fuelwood and that they have been replaced by desert moss which has little if any nutritional value.

Many of the mammals of Kazakhstan's deserts are endemic. These include species of jerboa, dormice and the Pallas cat. Kazakhstan's endemic cheetah is now extinct in the country itself. Other common desert mammals include species of hedgehog, hares and small rodents like gerbils and jerboas. Numerous mammalian species like honey badgers, sand lynxes, sand cats, polecats and gazelles are threatened with extinction.

The special nature of deserts encourages the evolution of endemic species and many of the reptiles of Kazakhstan's deserts are indeed unique to the region. They include toads, lizards (including the giant grey monitor lizard), gekkoes and various species of snake, including the now rare Central Asian cobra (*Naja naja oxiana*).

The desert lark (*Ammomanes deserti*) is one of the most enduring symbols of the deserts of Kazakhstan. Other common Steppe and desert birds are wheatears, desert ravens, desert shrikes and desert warblers. Some of the rarer (and larger) species of bird, for example the houbara bustard (*Chlamydotis undulata*), the Asian desert sparrow (*Passer zarudnyi*), the golden eagle (*Aquila chrysaetus*), the short-toed eagle (*Circaetus gallicus*), the Steppe eagle, (*Aquila rapax*), the Egyptian vulture (*Neophron percnopterus*), and the saker falcon (*Falco cherrug*) have become endangered through injudicious hunting.

How far the nature of deserts in Kazakhstan are a result of climatic conditions and how far they result from human activity (nomadic pastoralism) is uncertain. However it seems most probable the climatic factors are more important and that the pastoralist lifestyle of the Kazakhs was in fact a direct response to climatic conditions. Recent research has postulated that large areas of the desert rangelands in Kazakhstan were degraded by over-grazing in the Soviet period. But in certain areas the degree of degradation has been exaggerated. The economic and institutional changes which Independence brought to Kazakhstan at the beginning of the 1990s does seem to have had a number of impacts on Kazakhstan's deserts. After Independence it became more difficult for local authorities to manage the animal and

vegetation resources in the deserts because of lack of transport and facilities. Poaching and illegal hunting increased and took several years to control. It also seems clear that the livestock population of Kazakhstan fell sharply after Independence for many reasons and that it will take many years to recover. This has meant that large areas of marginal and threatened desert lands have been unutilised for many years. Pastures and grazing areas have been left fallow and so recovered their previous productivity. This augurs well for the future productivity and wellbeing of the desertlands of Kazakhstan.

Wildlife

Because of its physical extent and contrasting habitats, Kazakhstan possesses a highly varied wildlife. Much has come under threat, and for many different reasons. Some is highly spectacular, others less so. However, generally speaking, because Kazakhstan is one of the least densely populated large countries in the world, wildlife has been able to survive undisturbed longer here than in many other countries in the world.

The distribution of Kazakhstan's wildlife is, of course, determined by the spread of its habitat. The alpine fastnesses of the Tien Shan

and the Altai Mountains shelter one distinct animal community, the Steppes and deserts of western and central Kazakhstan, a very different one. The great rivers and inland seas of Kazakhstan provide a continuing refuge for yet another.

Perhaps the most famous, even fabled, of Kazakhstan's wild animals is the Snow Leopard (*Uncia uncia*). It is known as *Irbis* in both Kazakh and Mongol. The snow leopard is portrayed in some of the very earliest Scythian gold jewellery and this probably came from contact with the animal over 2,000 years ago in the Altai Mountains. As they are amongst the

*West of the gravely depleted Aral Sea, the Ustyurt plateau (**left**) is a region of spectacular and virtually waterless badlands, which nonetheless support a variety of natural life, and where the indigenous domesticated Bactrian camel (**above**) can find its forage.*

world's shyest and stealthiest mammals, living in some of the world's most inaccessible terrain, they are almost never seen. Its alleged propensity for killing domestic animals, sheep and goats has often made it feared amongst rural people. However its unapproachability has invested the beast with an almost mythic quality which has attracted the imaginative immemorially. The American writer Peter Mathiessen immortalised the animal with his book, *The Snow Leopard*, of 1973, which gives an account of his travels in Nepal with

Far to the east, the shallow waters of Lake Balkhash, seen in winter and summer in the top two pictures, are under a comparable threat.

*The Aral Sea – or what is left of it – (seen **left and below**) has come to represent in the global imagination perhaps the most notorious ecological scandal arising from man's presumption that he can remake creation. The theft of the waters of the Syrdaria to irrigate the now largely abandoned cotton plantations of Uzbekistan led to half the sea's disappearance – the stranding of its steamers and the destruction of its fisheries.*

naturalist George Schaller in search of the animal. Adventure travel companies catering to wealthy and sophisticated tourists offer expensive expeditions to the Himalayas and to Kazakhstan in the expectation of catching a glimpse of the animal. So the myth of the inaccessibility and remoteness of the snow leopard's territory grows. The International Snow Leopard Trust has estimated that there are between 3,500 and 7,000 snow leopards living in the wild, of which about 120 live on Kazakhstan's territory. But this cannot be more than informed speculation. In Kazakhstan they inhabit about 70,000 square kilometres in the Tien Shan and Altai Mountains. They are usually found at elevations between 3,000 and 4,500 metres in the Altai Mountains where there is often a permanent or semi-permanent snow cover.

The snow leopard has long, thick greyish-coloured fur covered with blackish rosettes and spots. It can weigh as much as a grown man, say 70 kilograms. Its tail is long and can be up to a metre long. It is used by the animal for keeping balance in difficult, rocky terrain high on cliffs. Many of the stories associated with the snow leopard are probably apocryphal. However, it is reputed to possess immense powers of mobility and to be able to leap at least fifty feet in one spring.

Serious attempts are now being made to conserve the animal's habitat and the threat of poaching appears to have diminished. Nonetheless stories do still emerge of illegal snow leopard skins being sold in Far Eastern markets and the appetite of Chinese dealers in animal-derived medicine is relentless.

Another important large mammal from the mountains of Kazakhstan is the so-called Isabelline bear, or Tien Shan brown bear (*Ursus arctos isabellinus*). It has also been known in some parts as the 'red bear' because of the russet hue of its skin. This has also been hunted for its pelt and has become increasingly rare. However some tour operators now offer trips to the Western Tien Shan nature reserve of Aksu Jabagly to view these rare animals, and such business stimulates the motive for its preservation.

In addition to the spectacular leopard and red bear, a diverse range of large mammals inhabit the Altai and the Tien Shan. They include the ibex, the Siberian stag, the lynx and the wolverine. The Tien Shan ibex is the largest mountain ibex in the world and lives at altitudes of above 4,000 metres. It has been estimated that there are 15,000 such animals in the Altai. The Maral stag which is a species of elk is also found in the high Altai mountains, and has been caught by the camera of Alexei Senin in the picture on page 52-3.

Our knowledge and understanding of the original wildlife of the Altai and Tien Shan Mountains are due in some part to the expeditions to China and Kazakhstan of the nineteenth century Russian geographer and naturalist, Nikolai Przhevalsky (1839-1888). Outside Russia he is known for the rare Przhevalsky's Horse of Mongolia which took his name and which is seen by some as similar to the ancestral horse first caught and domesticated by man in the Kazakh Steppe some five thousand years ago.

On the Steppes of Kazakhstan some of the most important wildlife are the five species and sub-species of wild sheep, similar to the better known Marco Polo sheep. All of these are registered as endangered species in the IUCN *Red Book*. The best known of these is the Kazakhstan Argali (*Ovis Ammon collium*) of which there are estimated still to be 10,000 individual animals. They are found only in a small area of low hills close to the city of Karagandy. A very limited and controlled programme of hunting of these wild sheep has been initiated. As the hunting fees are in the region of several thousand dollars per animal, these funds are used for the conservation of the wild stock. The moufflon and the Transcaspian Urial are other rare wild sheep which occur on the steppes and lower hills of Kazakhstan.

The Serektas desert lies some 200 km west of Almaty.

Four small sand deserts, like the Taukum south of Balkhash dot the southern Kazakhstani landscape.

These waterless canyons are a feature of the Mangistau region.

The recent fate of the saiga antelope (*saiga tatarica*) in Siberia, Central Asia generally and the Steppes of Kazakhstan has been a sad one, and a man-made one. It has been thoroughly documented by the British magazine, *New Scientist*. The saiga antelope has been an important source of protein for the peoples of Central Asia for centuries and was hunted as such with little impact on its numbers. However, zoologists estimate that in the decade after 1993 the population of saiga antelopes on the plains of Russia and Kazakhstan

passive victim. At the beginning of the 1990s it had been discovered that the African rhinocero had become dangerously depleted because of the use of its horn as an ingredient in Chinese medicine. At the same time it came to be supposed that the horn of the saiga antelope had roughly the same medical effect. To reduce the pressure on the demand for rhino horn, conservationists then began to urge the substitution of rhino horn by saiga horn. At that point the saiga antelope was by no means an endangered species and no one

transport in the deserts. The under-manned, underfunded Oblast authorities were no match for the poachers whose work was undisturbed hundreds of miles from centres of population.

With the aid of international conservation agencies, Kazakhstan is now struggling to put things to rights. All hunting in the Betpak-Dala Desert was forbidden from 1998 and all hunting of saiga antelope was banned throughout Kazakhstan in 2000. But controlling illegal hunting is no easy task and it is not yet known whether saiga antelope

'crashed' from over one million individuals to a mere 30,000. The reason for this was that the huge numbers of male animals were slaughtered for their horns. In large areas this left only females, upsetting totally the gender ratio and therefore the antelopes' fragile system of reproduction. The population collapsed. One of the worst hit areas was the hostile and parched Betpak-Dala Desert in the southern part of Karagandy Oblast at its border with Jambyl Oblast. The reasons for this ecological disaster had little to do with Kazakhstan itself which was largely a

visualised the forthcoming danger until it was too late. What appears to have happened was that demand for the horn in China exploded whilst Rhino horn became increasingly difficult to obtain. At the same time, impoverished hunters and unemployed in Russia and Kazakhstan, desperate for new sources of income, saw in the saiga antelope quick rewards. Saiga antelope horn could fetch per kilogram in China a sum equivalent to a month's wages. Illegal hunting flourished and hunters slaughtered the saiga with high-powered rifles, using cars and motor-bikes for

stocks can recover.

The musk deer (*Moschus mosvhiferus*) or *kabarga* in Kazakh, which lives in the foothills of the Altai Mountains, is also threatened with a similar fate to the saiga, because of the demand for its musk as a basis for perfumes. Its forest habitat, especially across the border in Siberia has been threatened by over-logging, but the main threat is from poachers.

Not all Steppe animals have suffered the same fate as the saiga antelope or the musk deer, which have been victims of a very special circumstance and changes in the markets for traditional Chinese medicines. The Kazakh wolf (*Canis lupus lupis*) or Eurasian wolf as it is more commonly known continues to thrive on the Steppes of Kazakhstan. And it lives in a symbiotic relationship with antelopes, gazelles and other grass-eating prey on the Kazakh Steppes. Given the continuing urbanisation and industrialisation of Eastern Europe and Russia it is thought that the Eurasian wolf is finding refuge in the remoter, less disturbed reaches of Central Asia, so that the wolf population

as the desert lynx or the sand cat. Probably no more than 200 of these survive in Kazakhstan, most in Mangistau Oblast on the Caspian. Found in most of Africa and Asia, the caracal reaches the northernmost limits of its distribution in Kazakhstan.

The main other Steppe/desert-dwelling animals are the gazelles and antelopes. The Mongolian and Persian gazelles and the goitred antelopes have all reduced in numbers because of poaching. One animal which in 1936 became extinct in Kazakhstan, the Asiatic Wild Ass (*Equus*

attributed to oil pollution, but it was subsequently found that the seals had died of a virus related to canine distemper.

Some of the most typical desert creatures in Kazakhstan are the reptiles. Being cold-blooded they are easily capable of enduring the severe conditions of hot summers and extremely cold winters. There are three species of venomous snakes, namely two adders and a moccasin species related to the American rattlesnake. Records show, however, that no one has died from snake-bite in Kazakhstan in twenty years. There

Integral to the life cycle of the Steppes are the predators and the scavengers, not least those of the canine family – the Tien Shan fox (far left), wolves illustrated (left) feeding on the carcass of a saiga, and (right) on a mudbank. Wolves are prevalent; jackals are widespread in the south of the country.

of Kazakhstan is actually on the increase. This is the impression one gets in casual conversation with the ordinary rural dweller. Experts report that Kazakhstan has at least 60,000 wolves and that each year they despatch three times that number of cattle, sheep and goats. Certainly the wolf is not popular with local inhabitants of the Steppe, and wolf-hunting is a common pastime, although it is controlled by the local authorities.

Another important but much rarer predator of the Kazakh Steppes and deserts is the caracal (*Caracal caracal*), also known

hemionus) or kulan, has been successfully re-introduced from Turkmenistan and now there are over 100 individuals. A group are illustrated overleaf.

The only marine mammal occurring in Kazakhstan is the Caspian seal (*Phoca caspia*). It is the sole mammal native to the Caspian. It was estimated that there were about 1.2 million seals in the Sea at the beginning of the twentieth century but that by the beginning of the present century only 400,000 remained. The main cause was probably hunting. There were also large-scale die-offs in 2000. At first this was

are also several non-venomous species. Perhaps just as formidable as a snake is the rare Transcaspian Desert Monitor Lizard (*Varanus griseus*), which is one of the largest monitor lizards in the world and its sometimes aggressive when cornered. Geckoes and tortoises are also common in desert areas of Kazakhstan.

Freshwater fish are not often regarded as important wildlife. Because of their considerable economic significance to the country, however, sturgeons in the Syrdarya and Ural Rivers and in the Caspian Sea are some of the best-known

creatures in Kazakhstan. Yet they too suffered from over-exploitation and from uncontrolled harvesting, as had been the case with the saiga antelope. Two important sub-species of sturgeon, the Aral Sturgeon (*Acipenser nudiventris*) and the Syrdaria shovelnose sturgeon (*Pseudoscaphirynchus fedtschenkoi*) are thought to have become extinct in recent years. However, stories have circulated that specimens of the Aral sturgeon exist in captivity and may be re-introduced to the wild. Because of pollution and overfishing,

sturgeon, landings in the Caspian Sea, largely in Kazakhstan, Azerbaijan, Iran and Russia, fell from 30,000 tonnes in 1985 to 5,000 tonnes in 1995. In 1990 Kazakhstan landed almost 2,000 tonnes of sturgeon whilst in 2000 its landings had fallen to 300 tonnes. Kazakhstan produced about 25 tonnes of caviar which amounted to ten per cent of the total Caspian production. A scientific survey undertaken in 2002 of the entire Caspian sturgeon fisheries showed that poaching exceeded official landings by 15 times and that the fishery was in danger

of being wiped out. Belated attempts have now been made to revive the industry and to conserve the basic resource, that is the sturgeon, and a total moratorium on fishing has been declared. At the beginning of the twenty-first century, wildlife conservation became very much a live issue in Kazakhstan. With the coming of Independence and a complete transformation in the system of government, many local government organisations and wildlife conservation agencies in

*Among the Steppe's smaller creatures commonly found (**left to right**) are Menzbier's marmot, skink, jerboa, viper, and Steppe vole.*

Kazakhstan seemed to lose their power to control events. With the ensuing economic difficulties their priorities necessarily shifted. Speculators and get-rich-quick merchants saw their chance and took it, and exploited the country's wildlife for what it was worth. Wildlife in Kazakhstan had been victim of external pressures rather than of forces from within the country. The government of Kazakhstan has done much to recover lost ground and is now actively seeking to rectify matters and to restore its rich and unique heritage. The re-introduction of the Asiatic Wild Ass is a profound testament to this effort.

Wildlife conservation is a national priority.

Opposite, above, a re-introduced herd of Dziggetai – the Asiatic wild Ass – roam the Mangyshlak Peninsula and the Betpak-Dala desert in Almaty Oblast's Altyn Emel National Park.

Above, a fine specimen of an Asian Boar pauses in its search for roots.

Overleaf, the rare maral *antelope is found only in Kazakhstan.*

Birds

It is hardly surprising that Kazakhstan's flag should feature a bird. The golden eagle, on a cerulean blue background, symbolises more than anything else the soaring, uplifting spirit of the Kazakh Steppe.

The range of birds in Kazakhstan is possibly not one of the world's most extensive. Birdlife International (one of the world's major authorities) lists a total of 376 bird species for Kazakhstan, of which 16 are 'globally threatened'. Continental Europe, on the other hand, is estimated to contain 730 species, or almost twice as many. However, most ornithologists consider the avifauna of Kazakhstan as one of Asia's most diverse and fascinating, and the country is becoming an increasingly popular destination for ornithological tourism. This is because the country's enormous physical diversity provides a seemingly endless range of habitats and breeding places for birds. It can offer alpine peaks, montane pastures, many different types of forest, extensive Steppe, desert and

For the snow leopard (**right**), a Kazakh national symbol, a natural quarry is the Siberian mountain goat (**left**), or, indeed, the moufflon (**below**). But the saiga – a victim of relentless poaching in the Ural region (**far right**) lives well beyond the snow leopard's habitat.

Illegal trading in wild animal 'medicinal' body parts, across Kazakhstan's eastern border, remains a serious threat to the country's wildlife.

semi-desert plains and hills, great inland seas and some of Asia's most productive and interesting wetlands. In addition Kazakhstan provides resting places and refuge to numerous migratory species.

Kazakhstan harbours many rare species including the greater flamingo (*Phoenicopterus ruber*) which is the world's most northerly breeding flamingo, the imperial eagle (*Aquila heliaca*), the Saker falcon (*Falco cherrug*), the Houbara bustard

(*Chlamydotis undulata*), the white-headed duck (*Oxyura leucocephala*), the red-breasted goose (*Branta ruficollis*), the sociable lapwing (*Vanellus gregarius*), the Dalmatian pelican (*Pelecanus crispus*) and many others.

Of particular interest to ornithologists is the wide range of bird habitats in Kazakhstan which, because they are so remote and so far from urban and industrial complexes, can give shelter to

species whose habitats have been invaded and over-run elsewhere in Europe and China. One such habitat is Lake Tengiz and the Korgaljinski Lakes, a whole group of large brackish and salt lakes. These lie on the borders between Akmolinsk and Karagandy Oblasts, about 200 kms south-west of Astana. The entire region is dry Steppe and virtually uninhabited with few if any access roads. Almost 300 bird species have been recorded at Lake Tengiz. In the late spring as many as 50,000 pairs of great flamingoes migrate to Lake Tengiz from the Caspian Sea, where they have spent the winter. And the rarely-visited islands in the lakes provide a sheltered habitat for 500 nesting pairs of Dalmatian pelicans, whose range extends as far west as Greece. This spectacular bird, which can sometimes be seen flying in formation across the Steppe, is globally threatened because of the drying up of wetlands and the use of its usual delta habitats for industrial purposes. Their numbers in the Volga delta have been much reduced.

Another such area is Naurzum Reserve,

in a very typical feather-grass Steppe interspersed with brackish lakes and pine and birch forest. This is in the south of Kostanai Oblast, also in Northern Kazakhstan, and is one of the best birding areas in the country. There are over 20 species of birds of prey at Naurzum with most of the species of Kazakhstan eagles and falcons, including Golden Eagles, Steppe Eagles and Imperial Eagles. In the lake areas most of the waterbird species in Kazakhstan are known to breed. Migratory geese, swans, ducks and cranes also pass through the wetlands of the Naurzum Reserve. As many as 160,000 geese were observed there at the Naurzum Reserve on one October night. Finally the area is particularly well known for its species of Steppe larks, a delightful feature of the Steppes of northern Kazakhstan.

The Tien Shan Mountains north and east of Almaty, close to the border with China, are also an attractive area for bird-watching. The very spectacular 200-metre deep Charyn Canyon in particular, 200 kilometres east of Almaty, is well known

for its raptors such as various species of eagle and kestrel, vultures and the Lammergeier.

It has been estimated that over ten million migrating birds from Northern Europe and Siberia use the north coasts of the Caspian Sea (most of which are inside Kazakhstan) for resting and feeding stops each year. These are classified as wetland areas of international importance. The Volga delta (just outside Kazakhstan) is of particular significance. Of course the whole territory is inevitably under threat from onshore and offshore oil spillages. The authorities and the oil companies alike

Migrants from Africa visit Kazakh lakes, such as the pelican (opposite, top and above) or the Nile swan (far left). But the flamingoes, (above, right) astonishingly winter on the unfrozen waters of the southern Caspian – as do the oyster-catcher (centre, right) and the swamp owl, (Asio flammeus) (right).

are keeping a watchful eye on the situation.

Traditionally, because the country is rich in birds of prey, many have been used in Kazakhstan for hunting, and falconry is rooted in antiquity. Kazakhs have used sparrowhawks, falcons, peregrines and even golden eagles in hunting. These were – and are – used for hunting birds, but also mammals, that is rabbits, deer and foxes. The so-called *berkutchi* or eagle hunter will train his eagle over several years, and it is said the birds could bring down even young wolves, although this is probably a rarity. Hunting with a golden eagle is invariably the profession of an old and highly experienced hunter. The Kazakh Saker falcon is still highly prized in falconry. Unfortunately there is said to have been a trade in the export of Saker falcons to the Middle East, threatening to wipe out Kazakhstan's stock of native birds. The government has been taking stringent measures to preserve these rare birds. At the same time wealthy tourists have been coming from the Middle East to hunt in the Kazakh Steppe using indigenous falcons. The Saker falcon is about 18 inches high and is a formidable hunter. It is said to be able to dive on its prey at 200 mph. There are thought to be less than 1,000 nesting pairs in Kazakhstan and part of their problem is that their traditional prey, ground squirrels, have recently disappeared from the Steppes.

Kazakh and foreign ornithologists have

been making determined efforts to safeguard Kazakhstan's rich avifauna. They have established the Chopak Ornithological Station in the western Tien Shan mountains between Taraz and Shymkent, close to the Aksu-Jabagly Nature Reserve in southern Kazakhstan. It lies about 600 kilometres south-west of Almaty. Its purpose is to study bird migration and to ring birds for future

identification. The station also serves as an important base for visiting foreign ornithologists who are making up a growing proportion of Kazakhstan's tourists.

Flowers of the Tien Shan

Yellow and blue irises, wands of creamy white desert candles and pure bright red, orange and yellow tulips make for a kaleidoscopic show on the spring-green Steppes that stretch northward from the Tien Shan's snowy heights. Travellers in

There's rare *Tulipa zenaida*, pale lemon-yellow *Tulipa altaica*, glossy vermilion *Tulipa albertii* and elegant yellow and white *Tulipa kaufmanniana* – the waterlily tulip.

In spring the architectural stacked leaves of various juno irises are a magical sight – yellow *orchioides and kuschakewiczii* and blue *willmottiana and subdecolorata*. By

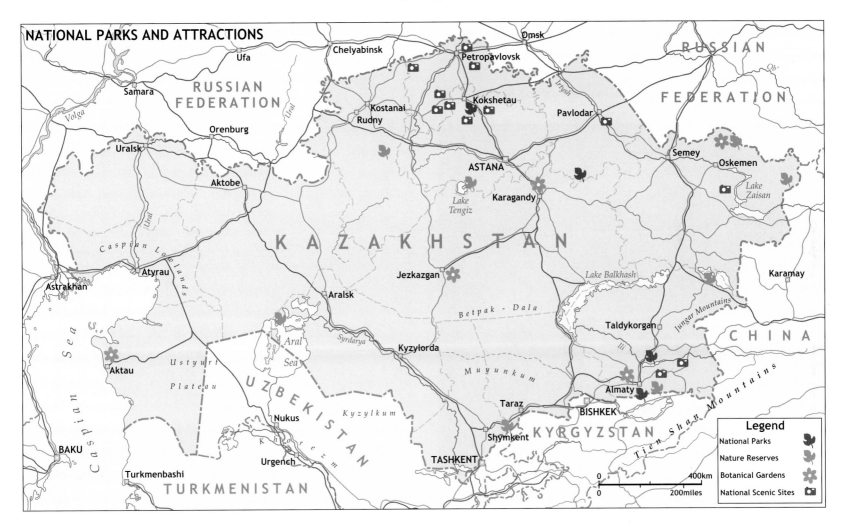

NATIONAL PARKS AND ATTRACTIONS

Legend

National Parks

Nature Reserves

Botanical Gardens

National Scenic Sites

0   400km

0   200miles

*While the map **above** shows the existing National Parks and Nature Reserves and Botanical Gardens of Kazakhstan, the Republic has in hand a substantially expanded programme of further protection of its natural heritage.*

*A newly-hatched griffon (**far left**) inspects its world on the shore of Lake Balkhash, while a vulture (**left**) feasts on the carcass of a saiga.*

Opposite, an osprey guards its eyrie.

April and early May along Kazakhstan's main highway are regularly greeted with such sights. Yellow grass turns out to be little yellow gageas – tiny members of the lily family. It is the tulips that grab the attention. Kazakhstan is home to about 30 of the world's 80-odd species of tulip including the magnificent Greig's tulips whose genes are scattered throughout the garden tulip world, and which species, when introduced to the Dutch some three hundred years ago, spurred the great tulip craze that is hardly less in vogue today.

snow are lovely white starred *Crocus alatavicus* and the blue, purple and yellow iris *Iridodyctium kolpakovskianum* – as unpronounceable as it is beautiful. Pretty pink *Rhinopetalums* and butterscotch and green *Korolkovias* are to western eyes yet more wonderful *fritillarias*. As summer swings into gear the Steppes produce magnificent shows of desert candles. *Eremurus regelii* has two metre tall wands of flowers and *Eremurus lactiflora* glowing white 'foxtail' heads. Further north in the unpopulated wildernesses of Kazakhstan's

The Steppes can blaze with poppies (as, **left**) or delight with clusters of cuckoo-flowers and campions among Kaindy's hills (**below.**)

The exquisite Tulipa greigii.

Once the reputed source of Scythia's famous gold, today the Altai mountains (**right**) are treasured for their unique wildflowers.

Altai Mountains, June sees hillsides coloured red with a million peonies and above them sheets of vibrant blue *Aquilegia glandulosa*. Here are saxifrages and louseworts growing in 'mountain tundra' – species that one can find in the Arctic – and back down in the Tien Shan are yet more varieties of saxifrages and *pyrethrums* clinging to rock faces high above Almaty as July burns the lowlands brown. *Paraquilegia anemonoides* is now a mass of pretty pale blue or cream forming perfect clumps up to half a metre across, the anemone-like flowers hiding delicate aquilegia-like foliage. Brilliant red *Primula minkwitiae* and pink *Primula turkestanica* adorn alpine meadows turned brilliant blue by *Dracocephalum grandiflora*. There is no finer sight in the clear dry summer air of these peaceful mountains than slopes of swaying alliums changing colour as one species replaces another – it is quite possible to put half a dozen species of chives on your plate without moving a hundred metres here. Late summer in the highest parts of the mountains sees some of the more bizarre and unusual species flower, and perhaps the strangest of all is the thistle *Schmalhausenia*

nidulans whose odd shape and covering of long pale hairs makes it look as if it has been transported from the Bolivian Altoplano or even outer space!

The steep sides and sharp peaks of the Tien Shan attest to the youth of these mountains. They and their plants are still evolving. However, just to the north lie the much older Karatau Mountains which have been isolated by seas, Steppes and deserts for millions of years. As a consequence, many ancient forms of plantlife have survived, sheltered in the steep ravines. This area holds a high percentage of plants found nowhere else on the planet, from the tiny primitive purple-leaved *Raphidophytom regelii* to trees such as the *Fraxinus potamophila* and *Populus karatavica*, the latter of special significance as only the one tree has been found.

The Kazakh Steppes and mountains have something to offer everyone interested in plants, from specialists who seek original crop plants (of which many are to be found here) to those of us who seek a magnificent spectacle – the spring tulips and the summer mountain meadows are as fine as anywhere in the world.

The Paeonia anomala *flourishes in the high Altai, on Kazakhstan's north-eastern perimeter, also pictured* **below**.

The Paraguilegia anemonides *(***right***) draws botanists worldwide to the Tien Shan mountains.*

The Tulipa greigii *red, in delicate glory.*

Chapter 3

When there is an antiquity to a way of life and a mode of coping with a challenging environment, there will be a wisdom buried amid the people which will never dissolve. Just this will have been shown to be true of the Kazakhs as they settle into independent nationhood after long vassalage; indeed the same will also be true of those many and various others who by choice or habitude have accepted Kazakhstan as their homeland and a locus of national loyalty. For if there is a truth common to all inhabitants of Kazakhstan, this same truth is common to the inhabitants *and* the place: its terrain, its winters, its summers, what is demanded of men and what it rewards them.

Habitat and Ways of Living

*Proud new blocks of offices and apartments
grace Astana's waterfront on the Ishym river.*

Astana

Astana is a city of Civil Servants. Most are young, well motivated and Kazakh. They are the high-achievers and the cream of the country's universities. They have come from all over Kazakhstan for one purpose: to get on... Naturally they work long hours. Often twelve hours or more a day. In sleek new Government offices. Often at weekends. They came to work, and work they do. So Saturday night is often the only time they can relax. In winter they hold parties where they exchange experiences with their new neighbours or colleagues, eat the traditional Kazakh sheep dish, *Bishparmak*, and sing the mournful songs of the Kazakh Steppe. In spring and summer it has become habitual for thousands to promenade along the newly-constructed corniche on the Ishym River. There the city authorities put on free 'Sound and Light' shows with the latest dazzling Western effects and music. By this token, the young Kazakh movers and shakers who will certainly shape the future of the country realise that by moving to Astana they have finally arrived.

The *Washington Times* has called Astana the first 'post-Soviet city' and thought it looked more like San Antonio. Much of its architecture has a distinctly Eastern feel about it which can put the first-time visitor in mind of Bahrain or Kuwait. The manic tempo of construction, however, is more reminiscent of contemporary Shanghai than anywhere else in the former Soviet Union.

The decision to relocate Kazakhstan's

*Astana rejoices in its winter, making sculptures out of its ice (**left**), and (**far right**) magic castles in its plazas, which fire the imagination. Even the Chief Prosecutor's golden headquarters (**right**) can look inviting, rising above the snowscape.*

*Summer brings the young people of Astana to the water of their river (**far left**) and beside the fountains of Parliament's square (**right**). The biggest emporium of the city elegantly dominates the riverscape.*

administrative capital from Almaty (Alma-Ata) was taken in 1994 and was met with scepticism. It meant moving the capital from the temperate south-east of the country, 1,250 kms north-eastwards to an insignificant agricultural processing town on the Steppe, characterised by an extreme continental climate, not unlike central Canada. The reasons, however, for moving were sound. Almaty was essentially a Soviet or Russian city with which the new Kazakh majority found it difficult to identify. Tucked into a corner

of the country, Almaty is simply thousands of kilometres away from most of the country's population --- Astana is much more readily accessible to the north and west of the country. And Almaty was prone to earthquakes.

A Japanese architect Kisho Kurokawa was thus commissioned to prepare a city master plan, threading a new so-called 'eco-city' around the River Ishym. Already Astana is filled with imposing modernistic Government offices, a national library, a national sports stadium, a national museum; and a spanking new international

airport started construction in 2003. Astana is designed to create an enduring symbol of the new Kazakhstan and the new Kazakh majority. Nonetheless the city designers have left a space for the venerable wooden Orthodox church from 1854 which still serves the sizeable Russian population.

Before 1994 Astana (then known as Tselinograd, and founded as Akmola) was a provincial trading centre of 100,000 souls, serving the collective wheat farms of the Virgin Lands. By 2010 it will have been totally transformed. It is expected to house

over one million people, with its own bustling diplomatic quarter, its cosmopolitan restaurants and elegant residences.

Almaty

Almaty is a city where all four seasons of the year are wonderful and clearly distinct. Spring is a time when apple, pear and cherry blossoms are blowing on the streets, when the air is full of lilac scent and flower

tinted ranks of trees – maples, oaks, elms, birches and poplars – form quiet, picturesque carpets underfoot. In the winter the trees are often spectacularly festooned with snow. It has a population of one and a half million and for a century has been the country's largest city.

The city is situated at a height of 700 to 900 meters above sea level, beneath the foothills of the Alatau section of the Tien Shan mountain range. Almaty citizens instinctively give directions in terms of 'up' and 'down' and continue to do this even

findings indicate that Almaty territory was a settlement since the sixth century BC. It served as a staging post on the trade route from China to Europe and the Middle East during the eighth and ninth centuries.

Like many other cities in Kazakhstan, Almaty was established as a Russian fortress. This was in 1854, with the name of Verny 'loyal'. In 1921 it was renamed Alma-Ata ('father of the apple') by the regional political leader the Jandosov. From 1929 Alma-Ata was the capital of Kazakhstan, up to the designation of

beds are filled with tulips. (It is not widely known that the ancestry of Holland's famous tulip belongs to Almaty's nearby mountains.) Almaty is the greenest city in the world. Virtually every street is tree-lined. City authorities take scrupulous care of street verdure. A ditch network helps to keep the streets clean and tidy after heavy rains. In the autumn, leaves from the

after they move to other cities. This is because Almaty is on the tilt: south Almaty mounts towards the snow-capped range; the north tilts down towards the great Kapchagay saline lake, some fifty kilometres north of the city.

Thanks to its very suitable geographic position this land was always a site for settlements: the records and archeological

Almaty's founding fathers graced the city with parks, like that surrounding St Nicholas' cathedral (left), broad tree-lined streets (above) and geometric gardens as that which fronts the City Hall (opposite).

Astana as capital in 1995. Almaty is a Kazakh version of the name, bestowed in 1993.

Being situated in a zone of high seismic activity, the city experienced catastrophic earthquakes in 1887 and 1910, and mudflows caused by the melting mountain snow in 1921, 1973 and 1977. To protect the city from the mudflows, a big dam was built in the Medeo gorge. This, however, interfered with the circulation of the city's atmosphere, which as a result of industrialisation can become a dense smog.

cheap and posh cars.

The temperature varies dramatically not only between winter and summer (from minus 20 to plus 40), and between day and night (10-15 degrees), but also between the highest and lowest parts of the city's environs. During the cold season you can enjoy skating wearing a T-shirt at Medeo stadium, or late in the spring you can go alpine skiing in Chimbulak, twelve kilometres from the city centre.

Despite the capital's transference to Akmola/Astana, Almaty retains its

sophisticated business city of Kazakhstan, redistributing its revenue to other regions.

Oblasts

Because of the country's great physical extent, the average size of each of Kazakhstan's 14 administrative regions (oblasts) is almost 200,000 sq. km (five times bigger than Switzerland). Within the country's 14 oblasts are two city-administrations (Almaty and Astana), 84

Nevertheless, Almaty is without any doubt the most charming city of Kazakhstan with luxury supermarkets, shops of every variety, hotels, casinos, smart restaurants and cosy cafés, shaded parks, straight and wide streets built on a grid system, marvellous fountains and statuary, friendly people of diverse origins, roller-skating children, light-hearted students, multi-language bazaars,

significance as the financial, scientific and cultural centre of the country. Almaty is home to the National Academy of Sciences, museums, libraries, universities, national and international headquarters, the National Opera, drama theatres, the circus, the main sport stadia, trade centres, cinemas, the grand mosques and principal cathedrals. It is the wealthiest and most

towns, 159 *rayons* (or districts) and 7,936 *auls* (or rural hamlets).

Akmola Oblast is the region surrounding the new capital of Astana. It was established in the mid-nineteenth century by Russian traders opening up commerce in Siberia. It was also the centre of the 'Virgin Lands' movement of the 1950s. It contains important nature and

wildlife reserves around Lake Tengiz. And as in almost all other oblasts, Akmola has important mineral resources in the form of gold, bauxite, copper and coal. The Oblast contains about 900,000 people of whom the majority are Russians, Germans and Ukrainians, most of whose families moved here in the 1950s and 1960s.

North Kazakhstan is the smallest Oblast in Kazakhstan (44,000 sq. km) and is wedged in against the Russian border. The Oblast is largely wooded Steppe with birch predominating. It has extensive wildlife and is renowned for its hunting potential. However, it also has extensive agricultural production, mainly grain but also livestock. Its population is above 600,000, of whom most are of Russian origin because of its proximity to Russia.

Pavlodar Oblast in the north-east with the capital at Pavlodar (founded in 1861) lies on the Irtysh river. The population comprises many Russians, Ukrainians and Germans. Coal, aluminium, hydropower, steel and chemicals are its industries. The Bogatyr open-cast coal mine is one of the world's largest. Pavlodar played a key role in the 'Virgin Lands' campaign of 1950-60.

Karagandy Oblast is the largest Oblast in Kazakhstan stretching 500 kilometres from north to south and 1,000 kilometres east to west, making it larger than Sweden or Germany. Most of the Oblast is undulating tableland, Steppe, semi-desert and desert. The majority of it is unsuitable for agriculture or human settlement. Most activities are concentrated around Karagandy City, Jezkazgan and Lake Balkhash where much of the mineral processing activity takes place. Karagandy City and its surrounding satellite towns make up over half of the Oblast population of about 1,400,000.

Karagandy City was, until the beginning

Industrialisation in the region of Almaty is nowadays kept at arm's length from the city itself, nestling beneath the piedmonts of the Tien Shan mountains.

of the twenty-first century, Kazakhstan's second city after Almaty. However Astana, the new capital, was by then already gaining ground fast, with Karagandy's population falling, and Astana's increasing rapidly. Karagandy, with a population of 437,000 in 1999, had lost 130,000 in the previous two decades with those of non-Kazakh origin returning to Europe. The city was established in 1856 as a coal-mining town, gaining city status in 1934. It was the centre of a conurbation of over fifty settlements established in the 1920s to exploit a huge field of bituminous coal. The plain of Karagandy is studded to this day with colliery workings. Over seventy per cent of the population was of European origin – Russian, German and Ukrainian engineers, technicians and workers attracted by the job opportunities provided by the city's iron, coal and metallurgical industry. Thousands more were also descendants of European prisoners deported to the gulag complex outside Karagandy during the 1930s and 1940s. One of Karagandy's most striking buildings is the city theatre, constructed during the Second World War by Japanese prisoners-of-war, with a neo-classical façade featuring seven statues (*see* page 229). Neighbouring Temirtau is one of Asia's most productive steel-making centres, exporting its product worldwide. Some 400km to the south-west, Jezkazgan is a copper mining and light industrial centre.

East Kazakhstan Oblast is mostly mountainous, since it contains part of the Altai mountains bordering Russia and China. It is also the site of numerous nature reserves and two large lakes (Markakol and

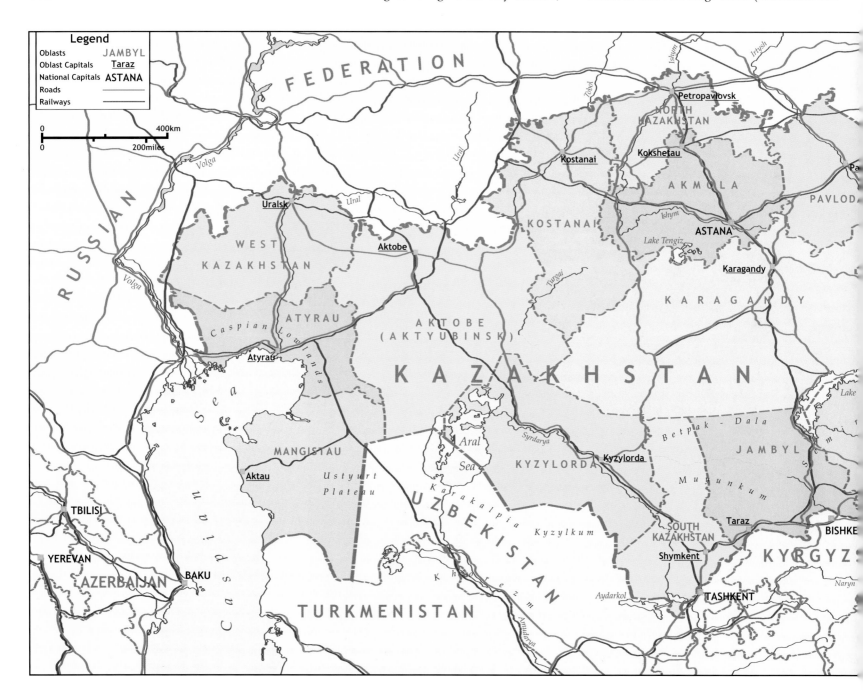

Zaisan). The valley of the river Irtysh (which eventually joins the Ob) is the main lowland area in the Oblast. Because of the variations in altitude the vegetational range is very great, from feather-grass Steppe below 500 meters to alpine forest and pastures at over 3,000 meters. Over seventy percent of Kazakhstan's forests are to be found in East Kazakhstan. The main resource of the Oblast is its minerals, which include lead, zinc, copper, silver, gold and rare earths, all processed locally, mostly in Semey (formerly Semipalatinsk).

Oskemen (formerly Ust-Kamenogorsk),

by virtue of its minerals houses Kazakhstan's National Mint, established by the National Bank of Kazakhstan in 1992. The mint produces not only coins but also official plaques, medals, plates and table silver. The mountains around Oskemen are rich in uranium, tantal, berillium, zinc, titanium, magnium, gold and silver. The industrial giants of non-ferrous metallurgy (Titanium-Magnium Combinat and Kazzinc) and atomic fuel sell their production in the world market, including five per cent of the global production of zinc. In the north-east of the Oblast, at the headwaters of the river Ilba, which feeds the Irtysh, in the Altai piedmonts, a goldmine was established in the eighteenth century by the English entrepreneur Ridder, whose name was given to the local mining town (known as Leninogorsk in the Soviet period).

Southern Kazakhstan – Kyzylorda, Jambyl, South Kazakhstan and Almaty Oblasts – is predominantly Kazakh. Over ninety per cent of the 600,000 inhabitants of Kyzylorda Oblast are Kazakh and speak Kazakh as their first language. The ancient cities of Turkestan and Taraz are regarded as the cradle of the Kazakh civilisation.

Almaty Oblast consists of the Tien Shan mountains and its foothills and plains to the west, and the deserts sloping down towards Lake Balkhash. It also contains the city of Almaty, discussed elsewhere. The Oblast is therefore highly varied in climate, ecology and vegetation. The Ili is the largest river in the Oblast and forms an extensive delta as it approaches Lake Balkhash. Kapchagay Lake, almost 2,000 square kilometres, is the largest lake apart from Balkhash. The Oblast engages in wide agriculture with grain production, livestock rearing and fruit – not least the apple, which bequeathed its administration capital its earlier name of Alma-Ata, 'father of the apple'. Industry consists of engineering, metal processing and wood working. The population of the Oblast (apart from Almaty, with its 1.5 million) is just under one million.

Jambyl Oblast has varied topography. In the north it consists of the Muyunkum desert. This gives way to arid plains and to the Karatau range of hills. Along the border with Kyrgyzstan are outliers of the western Tien Shan mountains, rising to over 4,000 metres.

The Oblast contains about a million people. It is one of the oldest settled areas of Kazakhstan. Phosphorite and coal are mined; livestock is reared and crops grown on a large scale because of the temperate climate. The Oblast is named after the great nineteenth-and-twentieth century Kazakh poet Zhambyl (Jambyl) Zhabayev.

Taraz City in Jambyl Oblast is one of the oldest cities in the country, first mentioned in Chinese sources in the first century BC. It celebrated its 2000th anniversary in 2002. It was at a key point on the northern Great Silk Road linking China with the West. It still contains remains of a glorious culture from the eleventh and twelve centuries in the form of numerous monuments and ancient buildings. Today the town had all the elements of a modern city, including public saunas.

South Kazakhstan Oblast is the most populous Oblast in Kazakhstan with almost two million people. This is because of the favourable climate and environment. It is surrounded by deserts, but much of the Oblast consists of Steppe. It is also fed by the rivers Syrdarya and Chu which provide irrigated agriculture. Otherwise, the vegetation is varied on account of the large range of altitude. South Kazakhstan contains southern outliers of the Tien Shan mountains. This Oblast produces cotton, a major industry. Further agriculture consists of cereals, melons and other fruit crops grown along the Syrdarya Valley. The main city, Shymkent, with a population of 400,000, contains a major oil refinery and also processes lead-zinc. It trades regionally with neighbouring Uzbekistan.

Kyzylorda Oblast is one of the largest

oblasts in the country but is sparsely populated with about 600,000 inhabitants. It is largely Steppe and desert and contains what remains of the Aral Sea. The Syrdarya River which feeds the Sea is the main river and the lifeline of the Oblast. Intensive irrigated agriculture has been practised for many centuries along the river and in its delta on the Aral Sea. The Oblast also contains the Baikonur Cosmodrome and rocket-launching range. Oil production is becoming increasingly important with new reserves being developed in the Kyzylkum desert.

Kyzylorda City is the chief town. It was established as a fortress and town in 1853 by the invading Russian forces. Today Kyzylorda constitutes the Kazakh heartland and over ninety per cent of the regional population are Kazakhs and speak Kazakh. In Kazakh the name means 'red capital' and between 1925 and 1927 Kyzylorda was capital of the then Soviet Kazakhstan. The town, with a population of 150,000, lies adjacent to the sluggish Syrdarya (the classical Jaxartes) as it wends across a treeless plain to the Aral Sea, about 300 kilometres north-west. The irrigated plains around the city produce excellent rice and melons. Most of the architecture is of an unprepossessing Soviet style, although there are still traces of the old wooden Tsarist town close to the river, and a wonderfully ornate railway station. A contemporary note is struck by the gleaming new offices of Hurricane, a Canadian oil company which has been producing oil from the Kumkol field, three hours into the desert north of the town. The United Nations Development Programme has offices in the town to monitor and manage the UN projects in the area, one of the poorest in the country.

Aktobe Oblast is more or less in the centre of the country, and is almost 300,000 sq. km, yet with fewer than 800,000 people. It is mainly high plateau with extensive semi-desert. The climate is relatively extreme and the agricultural potential is limited, although cereals and livestock-rearing are important in favoured areas. Aktobe's main assets are its minerals and its metallurgical industries, with chrome-nickel predominating.

Kostanai Oblast in the north-west, with its eponymous capital on the Tobol river, is rich in economic minerals such as magnetite, iron ore (exploited at Rudny and Lisakovsk), bauxite, coal, asbestos and gypsum. In Kazakhstan terms it is a small Oblast with 114,000 sq. km and 224,000 people. It is rightly considered to be one of the largest granaries of the country. The greater part of its arable lands are taken by the main food crop – wheat.

Atyrau Oblast forms the western border with Russia which is actually the Volga basin. It is made up of the Caspian lowlands and the Ustyurt desert. The climate is extremely dry, despite its

Separated by the length of Kazakhstan, two contrasting townships thrive on the water's edge – one (left), near the petroleum capital of Atyrau, on the Caspian, and the fishing community of Oktarrskie on a peninsula jutting into the beautiful Lake Zaisan, which feeds the Irtysh river in East Kazakhstan Oblast.

proximity to the Caspian, and most of the Oblast is semi-desert or desert. The sea provided the traditional occupation, now overtaken by oil and gas production and processing. With a population of under 500,000, Atyrau is the richest Oblast in Kazakhstan. The oil industry accounts for some thirty per cent of Kazakhstan's revenue, and oil for half of its exports.

Atyrau city is Kazakhstan's main port on the Caspian Sea. Atyrau was founded as a Russian military outpost, and before 1992 was known as Guriev after the Russian merchant who built the first stone structures there. The first oil refinery was built in 1911, supplied with oil from the Emba field. In 1913, the then well-known Swedish company Nobel (founders of the prizes) opened the second oil field, Makat. The first oil was transported in skin-bags on camel caravans. Today Atyrau city serves as a transshipment point for petroleum and gas from Emba and the newly developed Tengiz

oil field, by ship and railway and as a pipeline juncture linking also the Karachagak project (to the north) and the Kashagan project (offshore, to the south) with the now swiftly expanding pipeline network. (*See also* Chapter 7.)

Mangistau Oblast has a varied topography, consisting of the Mangistau Mountains, the Ustyurt Desert and the Karagiye Depression. However, most of the Oblast is desert because of the lack of precipitation. Nomadic pastoralism is practised but the Oblast is too dry for arable farming. Traditionally the area was important for fishing and fish processing, but now oil and gas production has become predominant. The main town of Aktau was established as a completely new city in 1963, and expanded fast. The population of Mangistau is 350,000.

West Kazakhstan Oblast is in the northwest of the country, surrounded by Russia on two sides. It is largely flat. The main

feature is the Ural River. It is one of the most important grain-producing areas. It contains the Karachaganak gas field (*see* Chapter 7) bringing new wealth. A third of the Oblast's 660,000 live in the main city, Uralsk, the Kazakh city closest to Europe and also the country's oldest. It was first established in 1613 by Cossack adventurers fleeing the Russian Tsar. Even before that, in 1591 work had started on Uralsk Old Cathedral (still open for worship). The boundary between Europe and Asia runs along the Ural River which divides the city – so that one half of the city lies in Europe, and one half in Asia.

Uralsk's greatest resource is its proximity to the Karachaganak oil and gas field which is being developed 150 kilometres to the east at Aksai. Uralsk is the closest airport and serves as an administrative centre for the Karachaganak Integrated Organisation (KIO), a consortium of British, Italian and Kazakh oil interests.

The Kazakh Pattern of Life

A contemporary Kazakh writer (Shakhimardam Kusaoinov) has referred to the identifiable concentric circles of the Kazakh social pattern as 'birthmarks on the face', which makes each face 'un-repeatable'. The circles are commonly described in the Kazakh language, in order of enlargement, as *ru*, *taipa*, and *juz*, which may be translated approximately as the circle of clan kinship, the circle of tribal

Age is accorded honour in the Kazakh family, as suggested in the three-generation family snaps reproduced (left) and (right). It is incumbent on Kazakhs to have some knowledge of their ancestry up to seven generations.

allegiance, and the circle of tribal union. There is of course the further circle of ultimate consanguinity, of Kazakh-hood.

A palaeoanthropologist may trace down the millennia the expansion of the smaller units of *ru* into the nomadic *taipa*; and in turn into the broad genetic union of *juz*, which was to result in the triune structure of the modern state comprised of the Great Juz (Uly Juz), the Middle Juz (Orda Juz) and the Junior Juz (Kishi Juz). The territory of the Great Juz is southern and south-eastern Kazakhstan; the Middle Juz, central, northern and north-eastern Kazakhstan;

and the Junior Juz, western Kazakhstan. Evolution of the tripartite structure can be readily explained by the varied formulae of nomadic life and transhumance in the varied geographic and climatic zones of Kazakhstan's vast territory. The divisions into Juzes has benefited the defence of a people across their collective homeland. This lightly partitioned unity is the key to the ethnic confidence of the Kazakhs. The Juzes have a unifying function and have nothing to do with ethnic divisions within Kazakh ethnicity.

Certainly, in the course of history, hostile forces have sought to distort these foundations of Kazakh society, and wilfully to exploit such distortion with – usually – the intention to 'divide and rule'. They have attempted to characterise this or that *ru*, or *tiapa* or *juz*, with this or that disparaging characteristic of, say, exclusivity and self-serving brotherhood.

The truth has always been that the achieve-ments of the Kazakh people have never derived from inward-looking affiliations but the inter-action of the component parts inspired by a strong sense of purpose, diligence, and respect for professional skills. All these qualities are leavened by broader national characteristics of humour, fortitude, and an instinctive comradeship, circumscribed by the common language and the common heritage. The *juz* structure, no less than the national, has been likened to a vessel without which identity would be sunk into the ocean of universal humanity. But the uniqueness of Kazakh-hood is not the aim, so much as the starting point, for national confidence.

Here is a young diplomat, educated in Russia, speaking of his Kazakh allegiance: 'I am a representative of the Lesser Juz. I am aware of three sub-divisions within the *juz* and how each of those three breaks down into smaller groupings, and I have grown up to be aware of the last seven generations of my family. My wife, however, comes from the Middle Juz. We met and liked one another. My first question to her when we met was as to which *juz* she sprung from. When I learned she was from the Middle

Juz, I was relieved. If she were from my own *juz*, I would then have to have enquired as to which *taipa*, and if it had been the same as mine I would then have had to ask her about her *ru*, and if she and I had been related, we might well never have got married.'

A Kazakh proverb runs, 'All Kazakhs are birds of one nest'. But each person's knowledge of their own ancestry, the *jeti ata*, seven ancestors, serves as a kind of network in the generality of society. Each child grows up with an awareness of a ring of kinship deriving from seven generations. Rings overlap and intersect

The moment of the plighting of the troth comes when the bride is unveiled – bet ashar ('opening of the face'), when family and friends toss their 'confetti' of flowers, sweets or coins.

A typical Kazakh marriage of this early twenty-first century will comprise a signing by the couple at a Registrar's office, in the presence of family witnesses and, most commonly, a representative of the mosque to accord his blessing, and then a celebration by family and friends for the bride, dressed in white, and the groom to eat and drink and sing traditional songs to the accompaniment of the dombra.

To hang a knotted or woven rug above the bedhead is a practice derived from the days when the home was a yurt. Nowadays it will more probably be a modest flat in a modern block, and daily family fare will be bought at the supermarket.

a branch of a genealogical tree – which of course became linked with other neighbouring trees and branches.

A young women becoming betrothed to a young man who had no relatives within her seven-generation span of kinship brought into her new family a new characteristic, a new lilt of speech, a new argot, new songs and legends, perhaps new norms of upright conduct of a different region, which in turn opened the way to greater and always meaningful bonding.

There is a superstition among Kazakhs that a woman's hand, offering food, must be in some manner decorated. A guest, being offered food, will always throw a sharp glance, checking upon those decorations which, if they were not present, would be thought as of making the hand in some way impure, without the inner constraints and disciplines of an ancestral allegiance.

However true it is that, over the last century and a half, there have been national endeavours to diminish – even eliminate – the role of awareness of the inner kinships, the Kazakh people have instinctively – and valuably – clung to their sense of genealogy, and have honoured ancestry and their own elders among any given *ru*.

with other rings. Containing such a sense of kinship, this union of relatives becomes a factor within society that knits it and strengthens the entire fabric of the *ethnos*. Knowledge of the seven-generation ancestry governed relations among people of such kin, and in the past it had influence on the routes of the nomadic grazing groups. It grew to be a mechanism of not only psychological adaptation within society but also to some degree physical, on the ground, across the huge pasturelands. It was strengthened and in a measure inspired by a verbal tradition which carried (and carries) from one generation to the next tales of heroic deeds of the *batyrs* (warriors), of truces, betrayals and the like. Every man felt himself to be

*Astana's ice sculptures (**left and right**) bring wit and adornment to the capital in the winter months. **Above, left**, street vendors in Almaty offer birch twigs to stimulate the long wintered physique in the sauna, while a snowfall beautifies the city's trees. In central Karagandy (**middle picture**), the florists' pyramidal cabins defy the icy buran winds.*

The Family

Thus, Kazakhstan has instinctively built a society upon the sense of family, the nuclear family and the broader, extending family, where a sense of warmth and solidarity is paramount.

It is illustrated at the family dining table – *dastarkhan* – carrying a tradition called *batas* (willing good) by which the right to lead the conversation at table is accorded to the eldest one present. In the traditional household there was a complex system of family regulations and everyday constraints, called *tyiym sozder* – of which present day Kazakhs are still aware: that they should 'not spill milk', 'not spit into the fire', 'not prop the head in the hands' ... and many another.

Kazakhs, in common with many other people, have been familiar with the manner of life of the patriarchal family, but in their case a patriarchy which was governed and coloured by the circumstances of the nomadic way of life. After the father died, the widow would be married off within the family; likewise, no single woman was left excluded. Such practices ensured there was always a new pair of hands to play its part within the family and household structure, and none was left to the mercy of fate.

Since the nineteenth century Kazakh society has been underpinned by the 'nuclear' family because even the relatively narrower family structure has continued to preserve the most ancient tradition in the field of marriage relationships.

One such tradition has been the coining of a nickname by, say, a daughter-in-law for a mother-in-law or father-in-law – a sobriquet characterising an aspect of the personality, like *momyn aga* (silent brother) or *erke bala* (little imp). These verbal intimacies are nonetheless strictly curtailed lest they result in any incestuous deviation within a family.

The traditional forms of marriage in Kazakh society certainly persisted right up to the imposition of Marxist ideology in the early 1920s. Up to that period,

*In a park in Shymkent, youngsters (**below**) launch a snowball assault, while (**top right**) a leather-worker plies her craft, and Father Frost brightens a Karagonda sidewalk.*

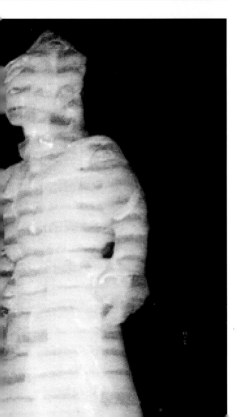

marriages were commonly arranged by the families concerned – even the betrothal of babies not yet born. Even today, advertisements are sometimes taken out in Kazakh newspapers providing a prospectus of suitable candidates, male or female, for a traditional pattern of wooing – *bsik kuda* – leading to marriage.

The recall of the old *taipa* traditions is known as *sybaga*. The *sybaga* requires, for example, the prosperous wing of any family to share the meat and milk of its herd of cattle in rich times with other less successful parts of the kinship's structure. *Sybaga* is evoked by presenting to the most respected and honoured of guests the best of what can be provided at table. The rules of how such a ritual dish is served strictly apply right down to the present day. For the most respected of guests, the head of the slaughtered sheep is traditionally prepared, marking the respect in which the guest is held; and the liver and the fat of the tail of the animal is offered to the in-laws (brothers-, sisters-, mothers- and fathers-in-law); friends are offered the rump of the animal; girls allocated the hearts and the fat

for their presumed goodness and blessedness; the children – for their sprightliness – the kidneys.

By ancient tradition, Kazakhs have presumed the spirits of the dead to be visiting their surviving relatives each day for the period of forty days after death. For that reason, Kazakh families are still disinclined to switch the lights off, or to go visiting, during the period, and they keep their dining tables draped with tablecloths and laden with votive food, not least the little pastry balls called *bursak*. By the same token of sound and ancient tradition the relationships of the husband's family (*ata jurt*) and the wife's family (*nagashy jurt*) are strictly governed.

Family and religion

Ancient forms of primal religion survive as belief or half-belief in spirits of good and evil, in Zyn (an equivalent of Satan), the black eye and the wicked tongue, which can subtly harm another's life. To elude such bad influences, Kazakhs may still employ ancient techniques by which evil spirits are deceived with the vertebra of a

sheep cleansed by immolation in honour of a newborn child – such bones being hung at the door and symbolising that the baby's neck will soon become strong and it will hold up its head.

In past times, nomadic Kazakhs

Direct from the farm or orchard or the abattoir to the customer in the open market is the familiar pattern of providing the family fare throughout a country whose farmers grow a great range of produce, illustrated on these pages – squashes, apricots, sweetcorn, rare vegetables of every kind – and produce plentiful meat.

such amulets. And there survive, too, the cult holy men and many a ritual concerning the grave or gravestone, and the drinking of water from the holy spring – all widely practised in today's Kazakhstan, reflecting beliefs of ancient times.

Likewise from antiquity, in Kazakh society there persists the presumed equality of man and woman. In traditional Kazakhstan, the women rode alongside the men on their horses, and were never veiled in the manner which has spread throughout much of the Muslim world. Certain words in the Koran, which the Kazakh nomads held to, are often repeated; 'To mother, to mother, to mother and then to father' – which implies that the child is everywhere called upon to place the mother first.

The Modern Family

The contemporary world – the consumer society, the market economy, urbanisation – inevitably presents a challenge to the ancient and invaluable norms. Adults of today find the need to work to inculcate in their children respect for the elders of the

customarily wore amulets (*tumar*), which often contained a tiny sample of their own soil. With the spread of Islam, habits changed and Kazakhs came to seal in such amulets a verse from the Koran. People even today – not excluding young men of business – wear

family, and to align national traditions with universal human values that strengthen the national unity of the country and provide the struts of a civil society. President Nazarbayev has stressed the value of the contiguity of other peoples whose home is Kazakhstan alongside the ethnic Kazakhs. The requirement to sustain such successful interaction provides some of the muscle for national solidarity.

While Russian remains the country's *lingua franca*, the status of the Kazakh language is constantly growing, and with a respect for the Kazakh language and culture by members of the other Kazakhstani ethnicities – Russians, Germans, Uighurs, Jews, for example – as evidenced in the work of Gerold Belger, Nadezhda Lushnikova, Moisey Kopylenko, and Victor Frelich. The Kazakhs themselves, with growing enthusiasm, are recapturing awareness and knowledge of their own history and culture and the role of other ethnic groups within the host community.

In independent Kazakhstan, ethnic and

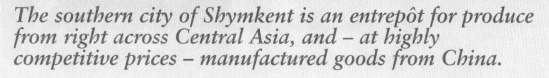

The southern city of Shymkent is an entrepôt for produce from right across Central Asia, and – at highly competitive prices – manufactured goods from China.

religious traditions are kept alive in ordinary families. Typically every Russian family takes it as a duty to baptise a newborn baby in church. Children of various nationalities attend their Sunday schools, where they recapture the language and traditions of their own ancestral people.

In the process of globalisation, the lure of the computer, the satellite antennae, the ubiquitous English language, the mobile telephone and all the rest of it, is as prevalent in Kazakhstan as anywhere else in the world. By and large the roots are holding. At the weekends, families seek the nearest mountains. The people flock to their theatres. On Sundays, grown-up offspring attend upon their parents, and the younger generation looks after the older. Respect for the sagacity of age is maintained as an immutable law of contemporary Kazakhstan.

The Industrial Habitat

The twentieth century changed Kazakhstan radically. It changed it from what was essentially a mediaeval society of nomadic herdsmen at the beginning, to a post-industrial one at the end. In 1897 when Kazakhstan's first census was held, only 300,000 people or seven per cent of the total population lived in urban areas. A mere 40,000 of these were Kazakhs. One hundred and two years later in 1999, almost 8,400,000 people or 56 per cent of the population lived in urban areas. These included 3,620,000 Kazakhs. At the end of the nineteenth century with so few people in urban areas, the traditional rural Kazakh culture could be said to have been intact, little changed from its beginnings in the sixteenth century. The largest and oldest city in the country then was Uralsk or Orel with 37,000 people, established by the Cossacks in 1613. At the beginning of the twenty-first century the country had experienced a further twenty years of Tsarist colonial government, three quarters of a century of Soviet rule and ten years as an independent state. Russians and others were still in the majority in urban areas, but half of the country's Kazakh population had moved into the towns, and its bustling futuristic new capital in the heart of the country.

The twentieth century saw Kazakhstan becoming a country of industrial towns. Many of these were so-called company towns or 'monogorods', that is, planned communities based on one or a small number of mineral resources and industries. There are at least sixty of these towns spread throughout the country, usually located close to a mine or a processing plant. Most were planned and built by the central Soviet authorities in Moscow. The mine was sunk, the processing plants were established, power and water was mobilised, workers' flats were constructed and the workers moved in. These towns were self-contained units and little was provided in the way of shopping facilities or entertainment. It is still difficult to find shops, cinemas, restaurants or hotels in any of these towns. Good examples of such towns are Janatas in Jambyl Oblast in southern Kazakhstan which was founded on the basis of the mining and exports of phosphorites, and Rudny in Kostanai Oblast in northern Kazakhstan which is based on iron ore extraction. In many cases towns were sited close to the mineral resource but often far from water or electricity and water often had to be brought by pipeline a hundred kilometres or more. Aralsk on the Aral Sea receives its freshwater by pipelines from an underground well field 150 kilometres away.

Two factors were important in shaping

A Hansel-and-Gretel lampoon (above) makes a party go. Below a Russian Kazakhstani Chauvin wears his campaign medals with pride.

The Inter-ethnic Mix

While the host community is confident in its Kazakh-ness, the country rejoices in its reputation for inter-ethnic harmony. Outstandingly the largest non-Kazakh element is Russian, which today is stabilizing at some 30 per cent of the population, significant contributors to the Republic's economy and skills. Russians are illustrated here in the pictures partying with Kazakh friends, and displaying medals earned in wars fought alongside Kazakhs. Many are loyal to their ancestral Orthodox Christianity, beautifully maintaining their churches and cathedrals.

For the older Russians, the cathedrals and churches are a gathering point.

Next in number and significance is the German community, seen here at a German cultural gathering (below, left) and serenading a visitor (below).

the urban industrial scene in Kazakhstan after independence. These were privatisation and the inevitable industrial restructuring which came with the collapse of the Soviet Union. Industrial cities in Kazakhstan based on mining and manufacturing were not spared the economic and structural difficulties encountered in the rest of the former Soviet Union, in the first decade of independence. Huge mining and industrial combines which had once provided local communities with an entire range of daily necessities like wages, pensions, health facilities, education, vocational training, vacations, transport and housing, were swiftly privatised. New owners sought to maximise returns on investment. Many surplus workers lost not only their jobs but also a whole range of privileges which they had enjoyed through their entire working life. When the coal and iron complex at Temirtau in Karagandy Oblast was privatised and bought by the British-Indian combine, Ispat Karmet, the new owners found they were responsible for the welfare of thousands of people

and, amongst other things, for the operations of a complex inter-urban tramway system.

The collapse of the Soviet Union also meant extensive industrial restructuring, loss of markets and loss of sources of raw materials with the inevitable loss of production and jobs. The results were often painful. Skilled workers were laid off. In many cases these were Russians, Germans or Ukrainians whose families had moved to Kazakhstan in the previous years. Many saw little to look forward to in an independent Kazakhstan and preferred to up sticks and move back to Europe to try to carve out a new life there. Behind them they left a flat which they were often not able to sell and a so-called 'dacha', in fact a wooden cottage on an allotment outside the city. Most cities in Kazakhstan now have their forlorn share of empty flats and abandoned 'dachas'.

Nonetheless the downsizing and privatisation of Kazakhstan's heavy industry was not all bad news. The consumer market economy has mushroomed so that every industrial city

in Kazakhstan now has its own private market place where small traders sell everything from Caspian caviar to fake Rolex watches. Women travel regularly to nearby China to purchase cheap, mass-produced clothes, textiles and other consumer goods for sale in local markets. Instead of remaining passive and unproductive in a grossly over-manned industrial complex, thousands of people have had to take their fate into their own hands, and start their own businesses, however small they may be. Perceptive observers have also noted that more and more former industrial employees with innovative skills are starting small production and processing industries,

Kazakhstan's booming Western economy is fuelled by the extraction, processing and export of oil and gas. The working community takes a break – at the Caspian's Tengiz oil field (top picture), at the refinery site of Uralsk (pictures below) and in the workers canteen, (centre, left).

using their technical and vocational skills to great effect. To support and promote this sort of development many so-called 'Business Incubators' have been set up throughout the country, often with donor assistance. These have made a lot of difference to potential businessmen who, until now, have spent their entire working lives as employees in a large firm, and must now brave the vagaries of the private market.

Although Kazakhstan has been producing petroleum for over a century, the oil and gas settlements in western Kazakhstan are still frequently characterised by provisional/temporary buildings and 'Portakabin' architecture. Aksai in West Kazakhstan Oblast is typical and is a more or less temporary town to house over 12,000 workers who moved here to participate in the development of the Karachaganak oil and condensate field. Periodic fluctuations in the level of the Caspian Sea have often given rise to flooding in the oil field regions and made construction problematic.

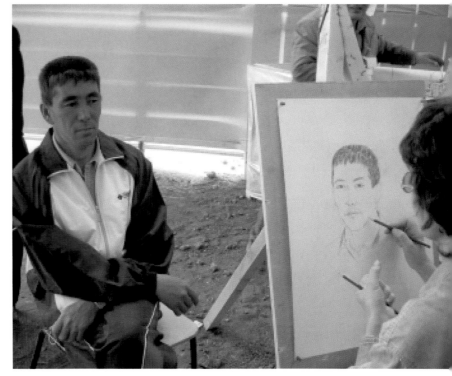

The Rural Scene

With Kazakhstan being the ninth biggest landmass in the world, large enough to contain France, Spain, Scandinavia, Germany, Finland, Italy and Great Britain combined but home to a mere 14,800,000 people, it is no surprise that agriculture plays a central role in the life of the nation and provides one third of the Republic's Gross National Product. The massive availability of land stands witness for the huge potential of this segment of Kazakh economy. Its 21 million hectares of cultivatable soil give almost 1.5 hectares for every man, woman and child in the land. Beyond all that are vast regions of dryish rolling Steppe, suitable for the rearing and grazing of cattle and sheep. Yet although 40 per cent of Kazakhstan's population lives in the country, only 9.4 per cent work on the land.

Agricultural commodities exported from Kazakhstan include grain, cotton, wool, meat and livestock, raw material for leather manufacture, and deer antler velvet (for pharmaceutical purposes). Climatic conditions for Kazakh agriculture are akin to Canada's. There is no winter pasture – for months on end. A cultivator must seize his moment to sow and reap. The Republic lies in the zone of 'risky' agriculture, demanding bigger investment than the countries with good soil and climatic potential. Nevertheless, Kazakhstan – in common with other countries of the former USSR – was always significantly behind the leading countries of Europe and North America in investment in the agricultural economic sector. But since the end of the century the corner has been turned and progress is afoot.

The critical state of Kazakhstan's agriculture became apparent in the 1980s. Poor equipment, soil exhaustion, overgrazing, erosion, outdated techniques of irrigation, and irrational use of water resources, all contributed to falling output. The situation became worse with the collapse of the Soviet Union. The breakdown of the cooperative links and markets in the rest of what had been the Soviet empire, exposure to erratic world commodity prices, rising energy costs, and disorderly privatisation between 1990 and 1995, led to the halving of food production, within a short span of years. By the start of 1998 the indebtedness of country dwellers to the state exchequer and to other creditors had reached an astronomical sum – a figure comparable to one year's gross output of all agriculture nationally.

The Soviet era finished abruptly for Kazakh agriculture. With the dissolution of the 'kolkhoz' farm – collective – and the 'sovkhoz' – State farm – investment vanished and market structures crumpled. Many decades of Soviet management had conditioned farmers either individually or in the group with little capacity to think for themselves, to innovate, to adapt swiftly to the mercurial market of the free economy and the requirement of reaching that market. For many sovkhoz farm workers the right to own land comprised no more than receiving and thus passing across their new land certificates as often as not by the former state directors who now came to run restructured, private enterprises. And for vast, remote ranges of the Steppe, which farmers cannot exploit profitably and which without livestock is virtually worthless, the explosion of private ownership has still to be taken up.

When, by 1999, the process of virtually total release from State-controlled economy was complete, more than 80,000 units of supposedly productive economy – farms, peasant organisations, cooperatives, associations and joint-stock companies – had appeared, to replace 2,528 kolkhozes and sovkhozes. The government hope was for a proliferation of family farms – a logical and worthy expectation which in the field of

animal husbandry is coming true.

All the new units were based on the principle of private property, yet for the most part are neo-collectives. Profitability has been slow to come.

Such wholesale privatisation of the land created an urgent requirement for a new infrastructure and entrepreneurial marketing and support such as is today emerging: dairy distributors, for example, providing bulk milk storage tanks to villages, or specialists proving winter fodder like maize silage, Agropyron, lucerne, barley grain and wheat meal.

Meanwhile there were hard times for the farming community. Kolkhoz and sovkhoz debts were inherited and often onerous. Local facilities such as kindergartens and community centres struggled to survive. Power cuts became common, and schools had to manage with erratic heating. Local roads were left unrepaired. Regular wages faltered as the turnover of money in the countryside sharply fell away between each harvest. Pensions no longer came through dependably. People kept going mainly thanks to the fact that they had their kitchen gardens and handful of animals – principally, cows or horses or chickens – and a space to enclose them, and a source of winter fodder. Too much mutton

coming onto the market (farmers selling their sheep to meet their debts) reduced the price sharply, and flocks across the country diminished by two-thirds in the first decade after independence. With worldwide over-production, wool became unsaleable at a profit. Country folk who lived near the towns could sell their meat, fruit and vegetables in the urban markets readily enough; the life of those who lived in villages in the depths of the country was to prove significantly tougher, being sustained largely by barter. There were those villagers who continued live in or close to their own patch of land who, a full decade after independence, had never so much as laid eyes on the national currency – the *tenge*. Those more isolated have migrated to the nearest central village.

As for Kazakhstan's remaining herdsmen – apart from that small but important remnant in the country's dry south-west who have held on to the nomadic way of life – the migratory patterns of the Soviet period have come to be spontaneously curtailed. The flocks of any one shepherd, commonly between 50 and 150 sheep, are no longer moved four times annually (between, say, desert, Steppe, hills and valley), but twice. Yet by 2003 the size of the flocks was again on the increase; and the larger the flock the

greater the incentive to migrate.

Gradually, the rural scene is improving and the agricultural economy is finding its feet again, after a decade in which both the acreage of arable land had dropped by 60 per cent, and the number of livestock had fallen by an even greater proportion. The cost of replacing engine-driven equipment became prohibitive for most farmers, and with cheap imports from more efficiently farmed regions with easier conditions, the market value of local produce plummeted. The State undertook to aid the financing of rural enterprises and to act as the marketing board for a substantial proportion of Kazakh-grown wheat.

Today it is providing seed, petrol, diesel and lubricants, breeding cattle, pesticides and fertilizers. Foreign investment has been brought in to support irrigation and the processing of foodstuffs. At the end of the 1990s, under the decree of the President, 400-dollar micro-credits were allocated for the development of small business in rural areas. Larger credits became available from the banks although, in practice, there have been few candidates for such credits. The ratification of property rights can prove a laborious and often expensive process. Moreover, the notion of offering a 'business plan' comes strangely to the minds of a rural workforce

Rural life is finding its feet after the end of state-patronage and collectivisation so cruelly enforced two generations earlier.

Self sufficiency is the name of the game, but winters can bring some hardship.

To be a herdsman will always remain the prime occupation of the Steppe   and sheep the prime domestic animal reared, for its meat and its wool.

long accustomed to Soviet presumptions of guaranteed employment and a virtually total absence of personal initiative.

In his annual Message to the Nation, of 2002, President Nursultan Nazarbayev declared a three-year period for the revival of the *aul* – the village – through the Agricultural Programme of the Republic of Kazakhstan, as ratified by Parliament for 2003-2005. A priority for this programme was to overcome accumulated organisational failure under the challenge of the free market. The Programme will not entail State subsidising and non-returnable financing of all that is needed. Rather, the emphasis today is one of self-help and sustained family commitment, with the new landowners or yeoman farmers receiving assistance with credit, with guidance, and the marketing of their produce.

The key tasks are being tackled stage by stage: reducing the tax burden, legalising property rights, simplifying access to credit sources, streamlining administrative procedures, protecting the farmers against bureaucratic high-handedness and the arbitrariness of inspection bodies – the last two of which are obvious incentives for petty corruption.

Regional centres of support for small and medium businesses are being established to help with market research and the mechanisms of selling, with the moving of goods from the farm gates to the market or the factory, and to the improvement of professional skills. A whole raft of measures on the legalisation of property rights is now in hand.

Coupled with these reforms is the facilitating of middle-sized and large-scale processing and packaging business serving a market for home grown produce, both of meat and crops. The Government is to supervise the quality of produce, put in

The immemorial skills of the Kazakh in taming and training not the peregrine but the eagle as a means of protecting his lambs have survived the grievous ructions of the twentieth century to be practised in earnest to the present day. Wolves are wily predators, which eagles can be employed to harry; but the raiding fox is a genuine prey for a falconer-directed eagle.

A good *hunter* protects *his lambs.*

order the veterinary system and sanitary inspection, and strive to raise average skills, technology and produce to international standards. Government is further committed to the expansion of foreign markets and to sustain a policy of under-writing external loans for agricultural enterprises. The role of the NGOs (non-governmental organisations), engaged in research, is increasingly to bear upon government policy, especially where financial aid is involved. Yet the reform and effectiveness of agriculture is now in the hands of the local rural elite learning to handle a free-market economy, which, given time, will prevail and surely succeed. While

the majority of farmers – mostly pastoralists – are still orientated to subsistence, keeping themselves and their families nourished by their animals and what they can earn from them, a new group of richer farmers is progressively increasing their number of animals, buying modern equipment, exploiting good pasture, and marketing on a planned commercial strategy.

Tengrism

Down the centuries, from ancient times, a remarkable range of influences came to bear on the people of the huge territory

The steppe is wide as a sea
It's decorated with flowers.
It lays beneath people's feet;
So, be fertile, be people's joy.
We call you our Mother.

From the Kazakh of S. Seifullin

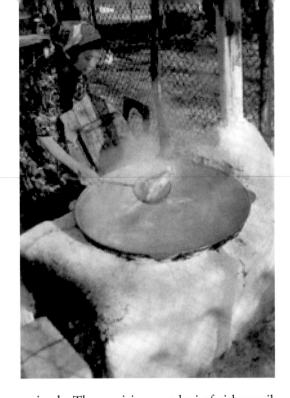

The nomadic heritage is a source of Kazakh pride, and the yurt is a symbol of that heritage. Yet in real life, the yurt encampment (or aul) retains an essential function in the seasonal pasturage of animals, in which an extended family will be engaged.

comprising today's Kazakhstan. Among these influences may be named Buddhism, Zoroastrianism, shamanism, Judaism, Nestorian Christianity and Islam. The catalyst was the Steppe itself – the boundless reach of land and the fathomless bowl of sky. This vastness and emptiness brought into being one of the most significant systems of belief on Earth, a profound combination of monotheism and polytheism that has come to be known as Tengrism. The concept of Tengrism – the religion named after the supreme deity Tengri ('The Sky') evolved out of a primal heathen pantheism into a coherent and lively faith in the 'unity of all things' that continued to live alongside Islam and Christianity up to the fifteenth century, and may be said to be present in the Kazakh soul even today.

The word 'Tengri' was extracted from the ancient runic inscriptions found in Kazakhstan, and interpreted by the Danish scholar, Vilhelm Thomsen, in 1893. The Turkic origin of this word is no longer in doubt. The idea of Tengri in all its beauty appeared at the time of the Turks in the most ancient manifestation and finally took form as a pagan – country-dwellers' – religion at the time of the Huns' early state (third century BC). The cult of the Substance (or 'being') of

Heavens (*Kuk Tengre*) – according to the investigator of Tengrism, Kutluay Erdogan – as well as the cult of the Substance ('being') of Earth (*Jir Tenre*), was characteristic of the Turkic tribes inhabiting all regions of ancient Asia. For these nomads, roaming the Steppe, moving their herds from one pasture to the next, the heavens, the mountains, the hills, the rivers, the trees and the creatures were all holy manifestations of a single Whole worthy of adoration.

Arising from contacts with Indian, Tibetan and Chinese cultures, the Tengrist cult was penetrated at its root by the ideas of Buddhism with its characteristic hierarchy of spirits, often represented on the ground by

animals. These spirits were loci of either evil or good; to avoid the disfavour of the forces of evil, men were to win the favour of the forces of good. Various sacrificial rituals (not excluding human) were performed by shamans at elaborate ceremonies, seeking salvation from the spirits of sickness and poverty, and admission in the afterlife to one of seventeen levels of the Tengri's Heavens. These shamans (or *kams*) vividly described their journey to the Heavens during the rituals. After sprinkling the sacred hearth with *kumys* (fermented horse's milk), the shaman would fall to the ground in ecstatic shaking and would start narrating – often rhythmically, to collective chanting – something allegorical, to be interpreted by the gathering and seized upon as revelation.

The rituals customarily were executed at the summits of hills or in the mountains, or on river banks, or amid sacred beech or juniper groves.

The mountains played a very special part in the formulation of Tengrism. Drawing upon numerous sources, the twentieth century Turkish scholar Abdulkadir Bnan has highlighted the role of the stone cairns (*uba*), such as still survive in the Altai mountains and southern Urals. They were built by the ancients as votive structures for the spirits of the mountains. The highest peak of the Tien Shan inevitably took the name of the deity, Mount Tengri. Rising against a background of the endless spaces of the Steppe, the soaring and virtually unscaleable mountains naturally presented themselves as a physical bridge between

Rarely photographed, shamanistic practises endure in modern Kazakhstan while, elsewhere in the world, the spiritual principles of shamanism are being re-explored and exercised: the induced possession of a trained shaman by the divine force, for the purpose of guidance and healing. The burial of the dead even in the Islamic tradition will (in some regions of the country) provide a heaven-pointing canopy for the separated s lingering presence.

Earth and Heavens. Words whose root implied 'height' soon became synonymous with the 'divine'. This led to the ultimate narrowing of the idea of 'height' to the concept of the One god Tengri – a proclamation, in effect, of monotheism.

In the sixth century, Tengrism resisted an assault by Christianity; in the seventh it survived the endeavour of Judaism to penetrate the territories of Tengrist adherence. By the birth of Islam in the seventh century and its militant sweep across Asia in the ensuing generations, Tengrism was subtly enhanced and refined with all the attributes of a millennium-old religion: temples, priests, prophets, a verbal tradition, and written canons. For several centuries yet, it was to prove an effective competitor with other, more codified and dogmatic

In the seasonal migration of flocks the horse (as in the **top** picture) may sometimes be supplanted by the 4 x 4 motor vehicle (**middle left**). Yet the preparation and provision of fermented mare's milk, the deliciously smoky kumys, is essential to country life and festivities (as **above**), and among those from the countryside who, trying their luck in the big cities, make a colourful splash of shanty yurts as at Alma Ata (**below**

religions. Only in the fifteenth century was it overwhelmed by Islam. Yet it is still evident in prayer in certain mosques and among certain communities by the transposition of Allah as the name of God with Tengri, and in the prevailing attitude among Kazakhs of reverence for the singleness of creation.

Traditional Kazakh attire may have given way to China-manufactured trousers, pull-overs and frocks, but the migrational life and devoted husbandry of surviving Kazakh peasantry persist in various regions of the Steppe, based as ever upon the yurt.

The Herding Life Today

These days, the seasonal migration of livestock persists (or has been resumed) among only a small proportion of the herding community – perhaps not more than four or five per cent. For most herders, the ancient nomadic patterns have become either too difficult or unnecessary. The number of animals privately owned can be frequently too low to justify the costs of moving, which today involves motor transport. Families can no longer turn to the services formerly provided by the State farms, nor do they wish to move away from villages with their facilities like electric power, water supply, schools and access to television. Then again, the loss in the number of animals being grazed (especially sheep) in the years following privatisation has been such that more accessible pastures are only lightly grazed, so that there is no need to move

animals far away for richer forage.

Even so, since the late 1990s some pastoralists have resumed the practice of moving their animals by season, when the costs of moving are outweighed by the benefits. This is especially so in the drier zones. Desert dwellers have few alternatives to raising livestock, since crop agriculture is not possible except for small, irrigated vegetable plots. Desert, wisely grazed, provides year-round forage for the indigenous breeds of livestock such as the Karakul and Ebilbayski sheep, camels and local Kazakh goats. Elsewhere, in the semi-Steppe and mountains rural dwellers often have alternative income from jobs in nearby towns or from crop cultivation; livestock plays a secondary role.

Pastoralists nowadays vary greatly in material resources and in the number of animals in the flock. A modern type of large-scale pastoralist rancher has appeared.

These farmers own anything from one hundred sheep to several thousand, together with large trucks and winter barns, and they rely on hired herders. It is these new pastoralists who are most likely to have resumed the practice of seasonally moving animals to distant grazing areas. They are evolving improved strains of livestock, they market their animals efficiently and invest in modern technology. They refer to a grazing outpost as a 'fazenda', a term borrowed from the Spanish-style ranches seen on popular television programmes produced in Hollywood. Yet despite the higher incomes from selling animals to meat markets, recent research in Kazakhstan has shown

*The idealized yurt of ancient times, pictured **right**, is today preserved in the Folk Museum.*

resource for Kazakhstan as a supplier of meat, wool and diary products.

The pastoralists of Kazakhstan are themselves a key resource for the future of the livestock industry. They possess irreplaceable knowledge and skills for managing livestock in a challenging environment. They can supply high-quality livestock commodities already in demand domestically, and with a comparative advantage internationally. They can serve as guardians of the biodiversity of the land.

The nomadic culture, both material and ideological, has somehow out-lived the Soviet era. Kazakhs, both urban and rural, cherish

that larger flocks are still less profitable per head of animal than small flocks. Overall, the smallest flock owners – illustrated on these pages – are gaining more income per head of each animal than larger owners, in that the animals provide not only something to sell in the markets but meat,

milk and wool for the household. For smaller owners, animals provide a larder and an emergency source of cash income.

After the initial period of the shock of the privatisation of land, and a fall of between a quarter and a third of the number of sheep, cattle and horses grazing the Steppe, by the late 1990s marketing systems had spontaneously developed to meet the cities' demand for meat. A proportion of newly-privatised livestock owners and an emerging group of traders were swift to respond to commercial incentive. Marketing is now firmly in the hands of private entrepreneurs. Yet a majority of pastoralists, especially in remote areas, still find it hard to profit from the meat markets. Private flocks are too small to provide enough animals, and it is expensive to reach the markets.

The upside of the fall in stock has been the regeneration of traditional rangelands, and these are fast becoming a new latent

their nomadic roots and value the nomadic idioms of the past that encompass the clan system and the yurt, fermented horse milk (*kumys*), hunting with eagles, and many cultural artefacts – such as now frequently reappear in modern formats such as advertising. Among city dwellers, knowledge of the practicalities of animal husbandry in a harsh environment may be sketchy, but the notion of a nomadic past remains pervasive. Rural Kazakhs from livestock backgrounds are proud of their heritage and many wish to continue shepherding.

Today, pastoralists are reorganising themselves in various new institutional forms to manage their livestock, either centred around the extended family or relying upon hired herders. Together with the introduction of open markets, all this is altering the goals and methods of livestock production. Yet, to be a herder is still to be the truest Kazakh.

Chapter 4

What shall be the 'history' of a country born half a generation ago? It shall be the story of a swathe of the surface of the globe – a certain swathe of Central Asia – and that race of man thereby nurtured into a singleness of identity, belonging there, inheriting all that had preceded them, formed for the place and by the place – its terrain and climate, its raiders and predators – which served to make folk of shared experience, custom, conduct, language, faith, talents, consanguinity and expectation. For all its newness as a national unity, Kazakhstan is vastly and most anciently endowed in heritage, and emphatically itself, unique, recognisable, and singularly rich in human and natural resources.

Heritage and History
to the Present Day

*The southern city of Taraz, site of the Aisha-Bibi and Babaji
Katun mausolea, flourished as a centre of trade and Muslim
scholarship under Timur in the fourteenth century. It is here
visualised by a twentieth century model-maker, re-created on
the basis of surviving buildings and archaeological research.*

Prehistory

Palaeolithic man was present on the territory of today's Kazakhstan from as early as the end of the penultimate period of major glaciation until the beginning of the last Ice Age, some 200,000 years ago. The Acheulean flints of *homo erectus* have been excavated at sites in the regions of the Ili and Syrdarya rivers, Lake Balkhash and the Aral Sea. However, descendants of these early

and the Caspian Seas. While the still cold climate during the post-glacial mesolithic period restricted the pace of man's achievement, the temperate neolithic period saw dramatic colonisation by the hunter-gatherers. Refined stone flake-tools are found in abundance on the Kazakh plains.

Then, some ten thousand years ago, came man's first mastery of the horse – in this very region of Steppe and hill; and soon thereafter the skill of smelting copper

and tin for bronze. These so-called Andronovo people were also capable potters. The entire region from the Jungarian Gate and Chu-Ili valleys to the hill country of Karatau, is rich in ceramic evidence of the Bronze Age tribes undertaking their seasonal migrations, and tilling the land, shifting from one oasis to the next as the soil was exhausted.

Bronze Age man's rudimentary means of survival is depicted in petroglyphic

hunter-gatherers would have been driven south at the onset of the last Ice Age. Only when the final ice caps melted, around fifteen or sixteen thousand years ago, did man return. The resultant tectonic rise of the Karatau range of low mountains paralleled the revival of man's presence in southern Kazakhstan. Evidence from his stone culture documents the transition from the palaeolithic to mesolithic and subsequent neolithic periods. By DNA, we can trace the genetic inheritance of the Kazakh of the present day from the peoples of those far-off times.

Flints reveal palaeolithic man living on the terraced slopes of the Karatau and along the Mangyshlak isthmus between the Aral

*A chronicle of petroglyphs across the Steppes, pecked into the metallic patina of the rocks, give modern man a running commentary of life in prehistoric times, notably as to what beasts were hunted, what domesticated, and what revered – the categories sometimes overlapping. **Left**, a dwelling site of three millennia ago has been uncovered in eastern Kazakhstan. A henge of rocks (**opposite**) erected as sacred stelea tell of a prehistoric shrine overlooking the Ili River at Beshatyr.*

engravings of wild and domestic animals – bulls, goats, horses, dogs and (later) camels, and of the predators: wolves and leopards. Ceramics depict symbolically elemental components of human life: man, woman, the sexual urge, birth. One petroglyph found near the archaeo-logically rich site of Tamgaly, in southern Kazakhstan, portrays, astonishingly, the image of the saddled elephant, evidence of apparently settled man's contact with merchants of the earliest 'Silk Road' between China and India more than three millennia ago.

The Saks, or Scythians

Knowledge of the Saks, who dominated the first millennium BC in what is today's Kazakhstan, and indeed the entire Steppe west of the Caspian to the Sea of Azov and the Black Sea, comes primarily from Greek

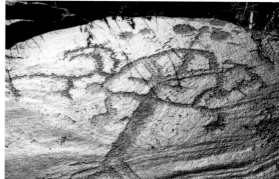

The rocks reveal ancient preoccupations, including (left) the life-giving sun's rays; and (above) with 'time's wingèd chariot' – the cartwheel chronometer, mystically linked with annually-serrated ibex horns. The stone mortar (below), found in the river at Banyajerek, was for the extraction of smeltable ore.

sources. Herodotus' *Histories* records his personal observations and earlier Persian writings on the Saks. Cuneiform rock inscriptions of the Persian and Median rulers tell of Emperor Darius' ferocious campaigns against a people whose presence as mounted warriors was felt from the Mediterranean and the Black Sea across northern Iran and the illimitable spaces of central Asia. These were a people distinguishable by their pointed headdress. They were referred to in Greek literature as Scythians, by the Chinese as Saijuns, Shizhuns or Shimo. The term Scythian has remained in the parlance of the western world. Modern scholarship prefers the Persian name 'Saks', or 'Saka'.

Indeed, it is Iranian Zoroastrian accounts of the Persia-Sak wars that tell us of the

Below: seeking help by sympathetic magic, a prehistoric hunter pricked out the image of a wild ox. Perhaps a later artist thought to have it assaulted by an outsize wolf. At **left,** *a halo-headed avatar is conjured.* **Bottom pictures** *show the skill of Bronze Age Andronovo potters.*

Tomiris, enticed Cyrus into an ambush. Cyrus himself and a reputed 200,000 men – according to the contemporary Persian account – were slaughtered. Not a single Persian survived to bring the news to the Persian capital. Queen Tomiris dropped the severed head of Cyrus into a leather bag

Saks' victory over the Median Emperor, Cyrus II, who had conquered the entire Persian region but was thus withheld from Central Asia.

Herodotus' account of the Persian emperor Cyrus II's battle with the Saks reveals their formidable strength. After Cyrus had destroyed Babylon in 539 BC and was preparing to conquer Egypt, he annihilated the entire Sak force together with the Sak heir. Nine years later, in a manoeuvre of vengeance, the Sak Queen

*Sak pendants (**above**) of gold and onyx.*

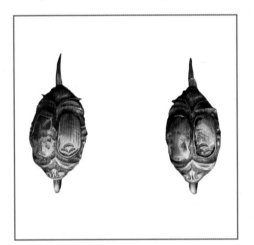

*Brooches (**left above**) and earrings of Sak design.*

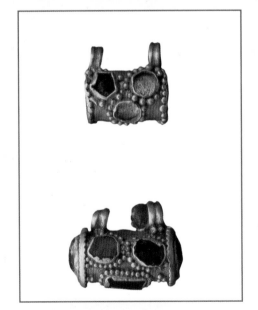

Pendant and earrings from a Sak kurgan.

The 1960s' unearthing at a 'Kurgan' burial mound of a Sak warrior's full ceremonial armour of cast and beaten gold, at Issyk near the border with Kyrgyzstan, allowed archaeologists to reconstruct the amazing regalia of the so-called 'Golden Man'. It is the work of an advanced civilisation, which honoured gold and worked it in an array of imaginative designs – pendants, brooches, finger-rings, earrings, *hirz* adornments for the forehead or the hair. They also fashioned mail armour, belts, scabbards and hafts of refined gold, and votive objects. The culture appears to have spanned the entire Steppe, from the Altai to the Black Sea. Yet its fountainhead was the region of today's eastern Kazakhstan.

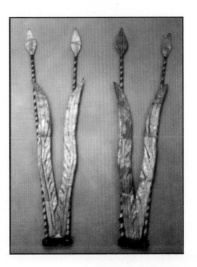

Above, an exquisite half motif adorns a clasp; and a sacred bird tops a ceremonial mace of wrought gold.

*Fully caparisoned, the Scythian chieftain stands (**left**) or is seated (**right**) in all his splendour.*

A Siberian goat atop a peak.

The snow leopard in its mountain habitat

A decorative frieze of many animals.

A stylized horse, rolling on its back.

Dazzling creative confidence is evidenced by the extraordinary range of gold artefacts produced by the Sak (Scythian) craftsmen. The origin of the gold is thought to be alluvial, possibly from the streams of the Altai mountains, with the gold particles 'panned' by a fleece weighted in the stream bed.

filled with the blood of his own army, declaring, 'Be satiated now with the blood you thirsted for and of which you could never have enough.'

Some clues as to the Saks' governance have reached us. The monarchy's authority was certainly sacred. Kings had important priestly functions. Women – by virtue of the strong exogamous rules which enlarged the societal networks – were highly respected. A woman was thus as rightful an heir to the monarchy as a man. There was no dominance of a military aristocracy. All were mobilised in time of war and all were armed with the new iron weaponry. All fought on horseback. There was an equality of rights among all warriors, who exclusively were eligible to join the regular people's council, which met to discuss day-to-day issues no less than external threats.

The Sak tribes combined three pastoral

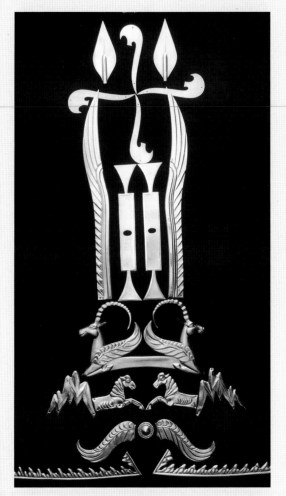

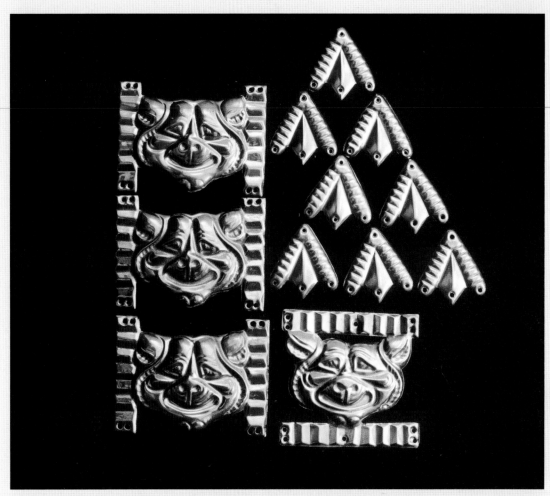

Clasps, buckles and adornments of Sak attire.

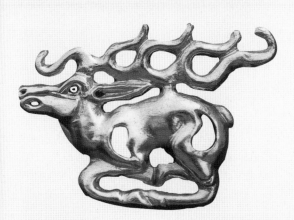

*A dramatically stylized version of a deer (**above**) and a snow leopard (**above right**).*

techniques: nomadic, semi-nomadic and settled. The rearing of sheep predominated, while the horse was treasured both as the means of mobility and as portage and as a source of meat and milk – as, in more arid regions, the camel was likewise. Nomadic herding was dependant on the horse. Yet where there was a reliable source of water, there was also settlement, subsistence agriculture and the development of irrigation, most likely derived from Persian techniques. Yet nomadism predominates. The nomadic herdsmen lived in yurts – transportable tents made of thick felt – or in houses of adobe and wood. Apart from their traditional headgear, Saks traditionally wore tight kaftans with belts and pantaloons, and heeless shoes.

A primordial cult of the Saks was honour of ancestry – the implicit link with an 'eternal' in which the living were

Nomadism and Civilisation

'In the beginning God created the heavens and the earth.' So does Holy Scripture declare the foundational dualism of reality, a dualism to which man is inured. Life and death, day and night, heat and cold, summer and winter, cohabit in the mind organically. Culture and civilisation long sustained a comparable dualism – and most literally so in that region of Euro-Asia comprising today's Kazakhstan – in the nomadic and settled modes of existence. It was, always, a dualism dramatised in that same first book of the Bible, Genesis, which narrates the symbolic murder of Abel, herdsman, by his brother Cain, cultivator. The settler killed the nomad, on the grounds that the Creator himself recognised wandering herdsman as closer to Him than the settled cultivator.

For many centuries the nomadic tribes of central Asia were surrounded and even interspersed by settled communities. Only now are we learning something of the cultures of those peoples, and we still know almost nothing of the historical happenings, least of the nomadic tribes whose role in the past it is sometimes more convenient to overlook – as indeed is their role down to the present day. We should however remember the very foundational inventions that emerged among those supposedly primitive wandering peoples: the calendar, metallurgy, the art of writing, chemistry, domestication of the horse, development of the boot and the saddle and the bridle; the list could go on and on. Those of the settled communities have had no right to presume a lesser sophistication among their nomadic fellows.

*A warrior of the Usuns, who displaced the Saks
(researched and drawn by Alexander Podushkin)*

involved. Bodies were embalmed or mummified and were transported to central burial chambers (*Kurgans*), as large as 100 metres across and ten metres high. Horses were buried alongside the warriors or dignitaries that rode them.

The Sak also adhered to a cult of sun and fire, as attested by early Persian – that is, sun-honouring Zoroastrian – chroniclers. In 1969 there occurred an archaeological discovery of unprecedented significance. This was of the full panoply of 'the Golden Man': a figure caparisoned from head to foot in no less than 4,000 cast platelets of gold, somewhat like the scales of an armadillo, and evidently *(continued on page 108)*

We will do well to remember that while settled civilisations were still pagan, it was the nomadic tribes which wrestled out a meaning to life and nature in loyalty to an almighty, single and invisible god, and aspired to come closer to him and to be his servant to the last breath through structures of discipline and perception such as may be said to prevail to this day.

From time immemorial, nomadic tribes, or hordes, have been roaming the boundless Steppe of Central Asia. The groups ramified according to ancient tradition; the eldest son of the leader of the tribe, born of his senior wife, would stay with the tribe to become the legal heir to his father while the younger sons, or those born to other wives and concubines, would frequently comprise a cadre which would become the core of a new tribe, a new ethno-political unit. According to oral tradition, just such a division is cited as the origin of the juzes indentifiable in Kazakh society down to the present day. (See page 122 *et seq.*)

The pastoralists ranged, of course, relentlessly and widely, forever moving on for the sake of richer grazing for their horses and their sheep. Migrations were often seasonal. At times they covered many hundreds of square miles. In the course of such journeys, Kazakh nomads wove for themselves an imperishable and precious intimacy with their land and its natural treasures. They could extract gold with unprecedented ease. In summer, during the tribes' seasonal migration, a fleece would be weighted on a riverbed to collect particles of alluvial gold. Upon the tribes' return, the fleece would be sheared, burned, and a gold ingot the size of a horse's hoof would result. The *tay tayak* (the horse's hoof) was a unit of gold for a long period: a measure of golden metal rather than money, since gold was not fabricated as currency. Usage of gold was essentially spiritual – as emblems of priestly office, of prizes for physical prowess in ritual sport, or as adornment of the sacral ceremony of marriage. Kazakhstan's inherited treasure of Scythian gold artefacts tell the tale. The ore meant for the Kazakhs' ancestors the highest spiritual revelation, the reward of a hazardous and intricate procedure, of which word leaked into the mythology of classical Greece in the story of Jason's ultimately ill-fated journey to the region of Colchis east of the Black Sea – that territory which arguably lay across Scythian culture's most westerly frontier. The nomad's fleece was mythic and mystic authority.

The 'black legend' of nomadic tribal warriors appears and spreads throughout Europe in the Dark Ages. The word 'horde', whose Turkic root meant the nomadic kraal, became synonymous with the mobile tribal army of the Steppe, and hence a greatly feared, barbarous collectivity that the Mongolian warlord, Genghis Khan, came to exemplify. Yet

The communal burial sites, or kurgans *(as **opposite**) containing many individual wooden chambers of the pre-literate nomadic inhabitants of Central Asia were venerated and maintained in use for several centuries. **Below**, the role of the artist in capturing the essence of an animal was surely sacred.*

etymologists know 'horde' also as a phonetic variant of the word 'order', sharing a definition as an 'elite spiritual and military organisation', and rooted in the Sanskrit *rta*, which combination of sounds implied the order and harmony of creation for all humanity.

To those reared in the tradition that sees Europe as the fountainhead of civilisation, this juxtaposition of the word 'horde' and 'order' would seem to baulk the historical reality of Mongolian expansionism in the early thirteenth century. Let us bear in mind earlier facts. The nomadic Turkic peoples (who were the first to be subdued and to some extent absorbed by Genghis) wanted to enjoy trade with the farmers and artisans of surrounding settled – and in particular, Chinese – peoples. The Chinese empire deemed such proposals as the height of impudence, and to its own detriment spurned any such participation; instead it sought to round up the nomad 'hordes' like wild beasts. Despite their unquestioned military mastery, the nomads were withheld from responding equivalently to such hostility by their reverence for the Oneness of God and His creation. This sustaining constant of the pre-Islamic (and for the most part pre-Christian) religious ideal under the nomadic ancestry of central Asia has been encapsulated by the nineteenth-century Russian sage, Vladimir Soloviev: 'The national ethos is not what a people thinks about itself but what God thinks about a people.'

The submission of the nomads was not to be permanent. As we have seen, the nomadic spirit and urban culture were not always compatible. Genghis Khan in his *Yassa* – his 'manifesto' – awakened the Turko-Mongolian people of his forging of a global mission. Genghis's aim was the unification of nomadic tribes and the building of a nomadic empire. He confronted the Chinese empire and other settled powers to the south-west and west of his Central Asian territory, and he prevailed. He himself, his generals and descendants were successful against the Chinese, Russians, Germans, Arabs and Persians – against, indeed, Islam and Christendom alike. In an astonishingly short time he radically changed the ethno-political map of the late mediaeval world: his empire stretched from the eastern reaches of China and the Korean peninsula to the territory of modern Poland, and from territory bordering today's Saudi Arabia almost to Finland. The Central Asian 'nomadic' empire controlled all these territories. Genghis Khan had instructed his descendants to take the Silk Road under their control from sea to sea. It was nearly achieved.

Today we can only speculate how and why that expansion came to a halt. And the world knows that the more self-regarding, more refined civilisation becomes, the weaker it grows. From our own point in history we can survey the decline and mighty falls of the ancient Egyptians, the Greeks, the Romans and the Byzantines. The list is long. What happened to Genghis's empire? Behold, great numbers had become Nestorian Christians; and, under Timur's dominance and inspiration, Muslim.

attached to a garment of fabric or leather. This discovery riveted the attention of the world of archaeology. It seemed to imply the deification of man, and unquestionably points to the sacral use of metal gold. (*See also* 'Nomadism and Civilisation', *pages 106-107*) The buried figure lay next to a gold-tipped spear and held a whip with a gold-bound haft. A treasury of gold artefacts have come down to us, objects used as personal adornment, most probably in ritual situations, as armament and armour, as vessels (as for food or liquid), and seemingly as free-standing animal figures. The animal figures – wild, domestic, and mythological, lovingly configured – powerfully suggest a sense of the divine unity of creation.

Yet the pictorial is not the only remnant of the Saks' contribution to the story of man. Today we can trace the languages spoken by this people on the Kazakh plains to east-Iranian or Turkic origins. Ancient runes indicate the high levels of social interaction between the peoples along the southern and south-western frontier of this extensive empire. Diplomatic contacts with the Saks were taken seriously by the Persians, and by Alexander the Great, who confronted them on the Syrdarya in 328 BC. But at least on its southern reaches, the Sak realm appears to have weakened by the third century BC.

One Sak ruler, Khaomavarga, became a subject of the Persian emperor. Meanwhile, by the end of that third century BC, Sak political authority elsewhere stood aside from Persia to develop complex tribal unions in the nomadic regions of Central Asia, such as are evident from the ensuing period.

The Usuns

At the end of the third century BC, a new political amalgamation was emerging, headed by a people known as the Usuns. In 160 BC, the Usuns, of possible Turkic origin from the East, appeared in the Jeti-Su – that is the land of the Seven Rivers – and defeated the Sak army. The Usuns were quick to spread their authority and were the first on Kazakh territory to establish a hierarchy of clan leaders. Such leaders reported to the Great Beg, or Gunmo, whose office was hereditary.

The territory of the Usun union stretched from Lake Balkhash in the north to Lake Issyk-Kul in the south and from the Tien Shan Mountains in the east to the Talas river (now close to present-day Taraz). Their capital was sited on the shores of Lake Issyk-Kul, at Chiguchen (the City of the Red Vale). We know from Chinese sources – as researched by Kazakh historian, Nygmet Mynzhan – that the population of the Usuns reached 630,000 at its zenith, in approximately the fourth century AD.

Ancient Chinese Emperors were apparently on good terms with the Great Beg. They sustained ambassadorial links with the ruler until the weakening of the Usun realm at the end of the third century, as a new invasion force was looming east of the mountains that border the great central Asian steppe.

The Huns

These were the Huns. They had been present in parts of the Steppe from as early as the third century BC. Their reputation was barbarous and warlike. Now, in the fifth century AD, under the Attila ('little father') from east of the Tien Shan, they were to assert their power. With Attila to lead them they swept across central Asia

*The Sak funerary dish **on the left** depicts two wolves devouring a goat – exemplifying the life cycle.*

*The inscribed stone (**pictured right**) carries lettering of the Sogdian script, spontaneously developing in the region of southern Kazakhstan, the earliest written form of the Kazakh language.*

leaving a trail of devastation, eventually to make an equally dramatic impact on Europe and the faltering civilisation of Rome.

The very first mention (in Chinese records) of people named Hun dates from 822 BC. They emerged from the plateau north of Tibet. Chinese sources claim that, at the turn of the third century BC, the Huns brought pressure to bear eastwards on Han territory, obliging the Chinese emperors to build the Great Wall.

In 209 BC, the Hun leader Mode pronounced himself Sengir ('the highest') and energetically started to build a Hun state, uniting twenty-four tribes. The wars between China and the Huns, exhausting and seemingly endless, persisted until 188 BC. Mode was at the height of his power. As a result, the Chinese dynasty, under the Han, was in a state of vassalage to the Hun Empire. China dutifully paid an annual tribute to its aggressive neighbour. After 59 BC a series of savage conflicts resulted – twelve years later – in the division of the Hun dynasty into two. The northern part reverted to the full authority of the (Han) Chinese empire, while the southern remained independent – and Hunnic.

The Huns' Sengir was further entitled 'the one born of Heaven and Earth, and placed on the earth by the sun and the moon'. His was absolute power. He was

Above, *a Hunnic warrior of the sixth to eighth centuries AD (drawn by Kaliola Akhmetjan).*

Right, *an elegant jar of the period, built on a potter's wheel.*

responsible for the military, for diplomacy, and was himself an object of worship. Succession to the throne was determined by the Sengir's choice, yet most often was passed to the eldest son. Blood relations of the Sengir sustained or comprised the elite of the Hun regime. The bureaucracy was complex. The legal system evolved a 'Code of Laws' by which evasion of military duty warranted a death penalty. The Huns also pioneered a feudal land system. They introduced taxes and spread literacy, using an orthography of their own devising.

By the beginning of the first millennium AD, the Huns had reached the land between the Volga, the Don and the Aral Sea, having evidently spread north of the territory dominated by Saks and Usuns. There was intermarriage and the absorption of dominated peoples, including Alans and Kangars. By 375 AD they had crossed the Don and broken the defences of the Eastern Goths. All this had initiated a surge of migration in Western Asia and Eastern Europe. It was only when Attila had gained power (by killing his older brother, his father's heir) that the Huns formalised their authority throughout much of the Steppe.

Attila's death in 453 AD led to the unravelling of the Hunnic empire.

The Huns' own style of nomadism engendered a re-design of the yurt. A framework of iron tubes, circulating warm air and placed inside the felt of the walls of the yurt, provided a heating system. The Huns used leather for clothing and also wove cloth of cotton and wool, while buying Chinese silk for the nobility's formal attire.

By the later fifth century AD, the Huns had been eliminated – or, at least, their power was gone.

Upon this fragmentation of a once formidable empire, the Huns were apparently pushed south across the Syrdarya by the western Turks (a branch of the so-called Kök – or 'Blue' Turks) who, in 559 AD, allied with the Sassanids of Persia.

Thus were the Huns ousted, plunging the Steppes of Kazakhstan into another era: the early mediaeval years of competing Turkic-speaking groups among which may be discerned what scholars define as the Proto-Kipchak dialect, a significant linguistic ingredient of the Kazakh tongue of today.

The Turks Emerge

Kazakhstan's early medieval history is far from easy to piece together. Turkic regional groups competed for dominance. Religious rivalry further confused this pattern of events.

Turkic tribes entered Kazakh territory in the sixth century, subsequent to the Huns' great sweep across the Steppe, transforming nomadic pastoralism into feudal society. These tribes too came from the east – from beyond the Altai range.

This early society, the Turkic Kaganate (a term meaning both a people and

*The early Turks (imaged, **opposite**, in mail armour, by the artist Kaliola Akhmetjan) accorded honour to their forbears by the erection of stelae as gravestones, stylised yet facially distinct (**as left**). Oil lamps with wicks of moss were in common use. The plates, **far right**, of glazed porcelain, found in southern Kazakhstan, date from the eleventh century.*

***Right**, an elaborately decorated stoneware flask of the period.*

territory, governed by a leader known as the 'Kagan'), lived under permanent hostility from the eastern tribes immediately beyond the mountains, competing for control of the Eurasian Steppes and the trade route – the Great Silk Road – bringing Chinese silk to the Mediterranean, and a host of other goods (semi-precious stones, furs, metalcraft, and horses) along the way, a route which amid varying fortunes had already operated for one millenium and would continue for another.

In 552, the Turkic Altaic tribe ruled a confederation which included the Mongols. Extending their empire by their mastery of the horse, they eventually dominated the Steppe as far as the Aral Sea and ultimately to the Black Sea. Under the Ashina clan, the tribe maintained a military and political grip on this vast territory by keeping their headquarters on the Steppe: a nomadic headquarters. They ruled by guaranteeing the regional freedom of their subjects.

They lived a life governed by spiritual convictions, honouring in structured yet probably varying forms of worship the infinite space of the sky and its heavenly bodies at sacred, open-air sites and roofless temples, and an implicitly illimitable ancestry represented on earth by stelae as formalised human figures sculptured in rock, large numbers of which survive to the present day. While there were surely universally pantheistic elements, the idea of an over-arching One-ness, not to be visualised, appears to have prevailed. (*See* 'Tengrism', *on page 91*.)

The stability of the Jeti-Su's twin Turkic cities of Tarim and Sogdia, attracted trade by the northern branch of the Silk Road, and helped to ensure the safety of caravans crossing the Tien Shan Mountains in the east by a route which avoided Persia. Meanwhile, it seems that the second half of the sixth century saw Istemi, founder of the Western Turkic Kaganate, ruling the area around the Volga south of the Urals. His campaigns against the Bulgar Turkic people and others led in due course to the Turks becoming overall masters of the northern branch of the Silk Road, much of it through the Steppe

and passing north of the Caspian.

From 630 to 682 AD the Eastern Turkic Kaganate – whose territory still included Mongolia – became subject to China. However, by 687, it had reasserted its independence. Soon thereafter, the Western Turkic Kaganate occupied part of the Eastern Kaganate and the territory from the slopes of the Karatau to Jungaria (east of the Altai). Under the Kagans' benign rule, various religious wisdoms spread and mingled their visions and dogmas in a spirit of mutual tolerance. Zoroastrianism, Buddhism, Manicheism, Nestorian Christianity and Islam, together with shamanic beliefs and practices, were all present and most likely enlightened one another, if at the expense of cohesive discipline among the common people.

Gradually, as the people of the Steppe became more literate, the Sogdian and Runic scripts came to be developed and put to use. At the same time the creation of petroglyphs, which had diminished during the Hunnic era was revived. Horsemen, costume and paraphernalia were depicted in

The natural Sogdian fortress (left) dates from the tenth century.

in rock etchings and this practice continued up to the time of the Mongol invasion, when such artistry ceased definitively.

For the security of its trade routes the Chinese Empire was trying to exert a measure of control over the lands of the Jeti-Su (i.e 'seven rivers', or Semirechie, the southern region of modern Kazakhstan), through which the most active Silk Road now ran. Additionally, political division within the Kaganate, together with poor harvests and a succession of famines, were

contributing to the weakening of the Kaganate's authority. Rule was reluctantly yielded to the Turgesh, headquartered at Shash, near today's Tashkent, who were able to sustain the independence of the Jeti-Su and its community of landowning nobles, traders, peasant farmers, nomadic herdsmen, and a professional warrior class.

This fresh consolidation was viewed as a threat to the Persian dynasty of the Samanids, whose rule was established in Samarkand and Balksh, northern Afghanistan. The Samanids sought good

relations with China, and gave battle to the various Turkic Kaganates ruling the southern regions of present-day Kazakhstan, spreading Jihad (Holy War) northwards. They captured Isfijab (near Taraz) which became a centre for the conversion of several of the nomadic tribes of the Kaganate. Across the Steppes further north had emerged the Karluk confederation, built by the latest wave of Altai Turks, which in due course subdued the Tushes, Chigils, Azkizhes, Halajes, Charukes and Barskhans. Under the Karluks, the fortified cities of Taraz, Isfijab (renamed Sairam) and Otrar bloomed.

Meanwhile, another dominion was growing east of the Samanid and Karluk spheres. The Karakhanid Turks expanded their territory from Kashgar and Cherchen (Qiemo), north of Tibet, as far as the Amudarya (Oxus) river in the west, and as far north as Taraz. After 922, the Karakhanids took city after city, gradually wiping the Samanids from the central Asian map and subduing the Karluks.

The Karakhanids were the most

The eleventh century Muslim ruler of Taraz, Karakhan, is memorialized by the mausoleum (above) built in his honour eight centuries later. Right is seen the tomb of the venerable Babaji Katun.

In the twelfth century, various religions jostled for the souls of the people of Kazakhstan – symbolized on this page by figurines of Buddhist provenance (left and above, left), a clay lid for a Zoroastrian ossuary (above, right), a stone communion vessel of Nestorian Christian fabrication (right), a minaret and Holy Koran (below) and an image of the Kazakhstan-born Islamic scholar and divine Al-Farabi, memorialized on present-day bank notes.

The Karakhanids were the most successful so far at establishing fiscal order in the central Asian region. Administrative and military authority were kept separate. Some nomads in groups took to settled cultivation. Settlements had grown up across the Jeti-Su; Otrar developed further on its well-defended land, as did Yassy (present day Turkestan). New cities, towns and villages facilitated the establishment of a more effective political system.

The very first Khanate of the Karakhanids developed Islamic literature in the prevailing Turkic tongue. These masterpieces have survived, among them are the works of Yusuf of Balasagun and Mahmud of Kashgar. They paint for us the transformations in economic and cultural life that were occurring at the time across southern Kazakhstan and across the central Asian Steppe.

Islam became the Steppe religion; Arabic script replaced Turkic. In the 930s, the Karakhanid state separated in two: the Western Khanate, based in Bukhara; and the Eastern Khanate, which had its capital city in Balasagun and encompassed Taraz, Fergana, Samarkand and Kashgar. A new era of statehood had dawned in Central Asia: Islamic, and was productive of a school of Sufic spirituality of profound and lasting significance, exemplified by the figure of Ahmed Yassavi, whose life spanned a century across the latter half of the eleventh and the first half of the twelfth centuries. It is no chance, also, that one of the great philosophers of mediaeval Islam, Al-Farabi, was born on Kazakhstani territory – at Farab.

Meanwhile the Khitans, a people of Mongolian origin, were establishing power between the Tien Shan and the China Sea. They were broken in 1125 by the armies of the Chinese empire. A formidable force of Khitans, however, migrated west towards the Jeti-Su. By remaining obeisant to the Khan at Balasagun at first, the Khitans were later able to capture Balasagun, de-throne the Khan and establish their own state. As

for the western Khanate, it was subdued by the ruler of Khorezm, Sheikh Mohammed. By 1212, Karakhanid rule was at an end.

The Khitans' Gurkhan – the title meaning 'Khan of Khans' – established tough military discipline, upheld law and order, and introduced standard taxes. Breaking with tradition, the Gurkhan – at least in principle – refrained from sharing power with his blood relatives, fearful of family rivalries.

The Khitans had come to align their Buddhist allegiance with Nestorian Christianity. Whereas the earlier Khitan Gurkhans had pursued a policy of tolerance towards Islam, the later rulers – after 1169 – persecuted Muslims. Consequently, in areas subservient to the Gurkhan, including the Jeti-Su, Muslim rebellions broke out. At around the same time Genghis Khan would impose his undeterred strength on the central Asian region.

We need here to underline the importance of the Kipchaks (otherwise known as Nogai). It is this element of the broader Turkic brotherhood to whom, throughout the rise and fall of other empires of the east, we owe the first written descriptions of the battlefields and of urban life. Their first home territory lay in the region of the Irtysh river and to the east of it – as far as the upper Yenisey. The Kipchak play a seminal part in the development of the Kazakh language and culture. Early runes from the Kipchaks tell of the Turkic Kaganate. Evidently prosperous and resourceful, the Kipchaks established extensive contacts in Europe. Their masterwork, the *Codex Kumanicus*, contains (among much else) a three-way dictionary, between Latin, Persian and Kipchak, a Turkic grammar, and fragments of the New Testament in Kipchak. It also entertains unrivalled accounts of Byzantine, Georgian, Hungarian and Russian life in the twelfth and thirteenth centuries. A line of Kipchaks later came to provide Egypt with its Mameluke dynasty which would continue to the nineteenth century.

Meanwhile, Kipchaks had risen to establish aristocracy within the Khorezm state.

The Mongols

The all-conquering Genghis Khan, in contemporary imagery.

'All who surrender will be spared. Whoever does not surrender, but who opposes with struggle and dissension, shall be annihilated.'
(Genghis Khan)

At the turn of the thirteenth century the Mongolian state was a conglomerate of tribes united under a certain Temujin, an hereditary warlord. Its territory encompassed approximately the region of today's Outer Mongolia, which is to say, that region immediately north of today's independent Republic of Mongolia, east of the vast Lake Baikal, and part of today's Russian Siberia. Temujin had inherited from this father most of the territory between the Amur River and the Great Wall of China. From this bleak and largely featureless homeland, severely cold in winter, Temujin was to create an empire of an extent and suddenness the world had never previously known. It was achieved by a mastery of the horse, perfectly adapted weaponry and armour, skilled military strategy engaging extraordinary speed, and a capable administration.

Temujin was quick to seize power in the lands nearest to him. In 1206, he was appointed Kagan of all the Mongols and accorded the title of Genghis ('most mighty') Khan. His precepts of conquest are quoted above.

By 1211, Genghis had seized the Khanates of the Kerait and Naiman Turks to the south of his territory, and had subdued the peoples of Siberia and China's Eastern Turkestan (today's Sinkiang). By 1215, he had captured Peking, and went on to take the land north of the Hwang Ho (Yellow River) in 1217.

Among those tribal elements to give him their allegiance and swell his Horde may be counted those identifiable in the ancestry of both the Kazakh and the Kyrgyz people of today. Following upon his successes in China and in immediate southerly Greater Mongolia, between Tibet and Lake Balkhash, Genghis entered the Ili valley, a site of prosperous settlement, where he destroyed the power of the significant Khan Kuchluk. From there Genghis planned his assault on Jeti-Su – and, further west, Khorezm, the heart of the Khitans' empire.

At this point, Sheikh Mohammed, ruler of Khorezm, was at the zenith of his authority, with the Indus, Iran, Uzbekistan and parts of southern Kazakhstan all part of his realm. Yet his was a vulnerable regime. The Kipchak aristocracy of Khorezm was undermining his authority. He was rivalled by his powerful Kipchak mother, Terken-Hatun, who had placed her blood-relatives in key political positions. She induced her Kipchak nephew, Kaiyr Khan, to attack her son's army. Mohammed won the battle; yet

*While perceived as a figure of implacable ruthlessness, as in the Chinese cartoon (**left**), or interrogating a captive (**right**), Genghis created and bequeathed a vast and coherent empire, to be divided between his sons.*

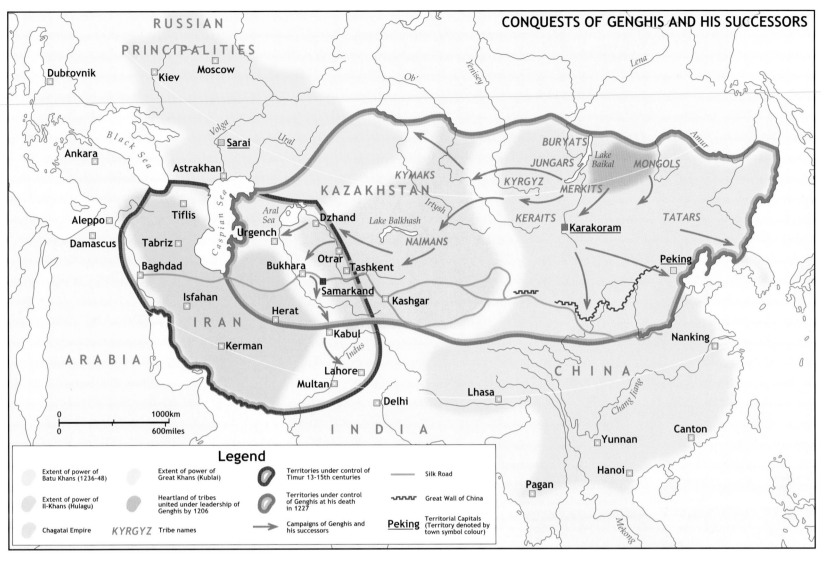

CONQUESTS OF GENGHIS AND HIS SUCCESSORS

RUSSIAN
PRINCIPALITIES

Dubrovnik
Kiev
Moscow

Black Sea
Ankara
Astrakhan

Volga
Ural
Sarai

Ob'
Lena

Yenisey

BURYATS

JUNGARS
Lake Baikal
MONGOLS

KYMAKS
KAZAKHSTAN
Irtysh
KYRGYZ
MERKITS

Aleppo
Tiflis
Damascus
Tabriz

Aral Sea
Urgench
Dzhand
Lake Balkhash
NAIMANS

KERAITS
Karakoram

TATARS

Baghdad
Caspian Sea
Bukhara
Otrar
Tashkent

Peking

Isfahan
Samarkand
Kashgar

IRAN
Herat

Kerman
Kabul
Indus

ARABIA

Lahore
Multan

Nanking

Delhi

Lhasa

CHINA

INDIA

Chang Jiang

Canton

Yunnan

Pagan
Hanoi

Mekong

0   1000km
0   600miles

Legend

Extent of power of Batu Khans (1236-48)	Extent of power of Great Khans (Kublai)	Territories under control of Timur 13-15th centuries
Extent of power of Il-Khans (Hulagu)	Heartland of tribes united under leadership of Genghis by 1206	Territories under control of Genghis at his death in 1227
Chagatai Empire	*KYRGYZ* Tribe names	Campaigns of Genghis and his successors

Silk Road

Great Wall of China

Peking Territorial Capitals (Territory denoted by town symbol colour)

A Civilised Flowering

The phenomenon of the nomadic Mongols' conquest bred a culture that was to adorn a continent (from the Taj Mahal to Kublai Khan's pleasure domes, recorded by Marco Polo). In Kazakhstan it produced the wonder of the Sufi Ahmed Yassavi's, mausoleum in Turkestan (*opposite* and *left*) of which Timur initiated the building.

Nothing today remains of Timur's own city of Otrar (of which the site is pictured *left*). Under such order and energetic trade, all crafts of porcelain, tile-making, stoneware, and metal work, such as those illustrated here, some of which pre-date the Mongol sweep, found their styles and flourished.

A fragment of a 12th century dastarkam

A 13th century ewer

Lid of an 11th century Jeti-Su pot

The incomparable wonder of the mausoleum for Ahmed Yassavi, mystic and poet, born in Sairam in 1103 and residing till his death in 1166 in Turkestan (the Kazakh town) was created on the orders of the Mongol Timur more than two centuries later on the site of his original tomb. This masterpiece of architecture, design and craftsmanship was no fluke, but the full blooming of a combination of skills and disciplines widely practised among the people of the region, drawing upon influences both from the Chinese east and the Persian south-west, to render an indigenous masterpiece. The dome, of a brilliant aquamarine, is the largest to have survived in Central Asia.

A 14th century Jeti-Su plate

Base of a 15th century Jeti-Su vase

An enamelled tile, South Kazakhstan

was nonetheless obliged to accept Kaiyr's appointment as governor of the Jeti-Su's capital city of Otrar.

Mohammed dispatched his ambassadors to Genghis in Mongolia. In reply he received the Great Khan's invitation to sign a peace treaty. This invitation was accompanied by a caravan of Mongolian merchants, which had to pass through Jeti-Su. Kaiyr Khan chose to suspect the merchants of espionage and ordered their execution, duly carried out. In response, Genghis demanded – through envoys – Kaiyr Khan's extradition to Mongolia. But Sheikh Mohammed, fearing an insurrection from the Kipchak nobles, refused to extradite Kaiyr and, what is more, murdered the Mongol envoys.

Genghis prepared his armies. In 1219 a Mongolian force under his son laid siege to Otrar. Kaiyr Khan's garrison held out for almost five months. After breaking through the city gates, the Mongolians met an almost completely deserted town. Both townsfolk and military had retreated inside the citadel, which was duly stormed and every soul massacred. Within a month, citadel and city alike were little no more than a pile of rubble. Meanwhile, Genghis' two other armies had swept on – one to Bukhara, under Genghis himself, and one to the Syrdarya basin.

Thereafter, the surge of conquest rolled south to Afghanistan and into northern India; and westwards, south of the Caspian, against a combined force of Kipchaks, Alans (the ancestors of today's Ossetians) and Russians, who were defeated near the river Kalka in the Ukraine. In 1224, north of the Caspian, Genghis' army crossed the Volga river from the west to eliminate the last of Kipchak power in the region east of the river. Southern Siberia had already submitted to Mongol authority. Thus, by 1224, Genghis had most of the Eurasian Steppe in his hold.

In 1227, the year of Genghis' death, the campaign against the Kipchak resumed. In 1229, command was handed on to Genghis' grandson, Batu Khan, who completed the conquest of the Kipchak lands along the Volga northwards (1232); driving westwards, he defeated the Bulgars, in due course overrunning Hungary and Poland, and, ultimately, moving southwards to gain a corridor to the Adriatic.

The lands of the empire were shared out among the three sons of Genghis. Joshi's vast region included most of what is territorial Kazakhstan today; but the key region of the Jeti-Su, the seven rivers, comprising the (northern) Silk Road, fell under the governorship of Chagatai. These two orders, or 'Hordes', came to be known respectively as the Golden and the Blue. The third region of rule by a son of Genghis was China and Mongolia itself.

The Mongol dynasties co-operated. The scale of this tripartite empire across half the globe had brought some unquestionable benefits. One was the security and range of international, not to say, intercontinental, trade. The Silk Road (or roads) flourished, carrying the silk, porcelain and spices of China to Europe. Exploration – of this time, west to east – exemplified by the Venetian Marco Polo's unprecedented return journey to China, between 1271 and 1295, was stimulated. Trading centres evolved comprising international and multi-cultural communities, and inspired not least by Genoa, at various points along the route. There was a contiguent interchange of ideas. Genghis' grandson, Kublai Khan, ruling China (1259-94), admitted Christian missionaries.

The administrative techniques of centralised power were introduced and developed. Numerous disorganised tribal units coalesced. A fifteenth century Chinese historian, Hen Zhu-Min, was to comment, 'Genghis Khan severed the frontier between west and east that had impacted economic and cultural relations. Thereafter, connections between east and west have become more prosperous than ever.'

Such a claim could still be made in spite of the considerable disruption of Timur's extraordinary military ascendancy of the previous century, when, between 1385 and 1405, after inheriting authority in Samarkand, as Genghis' supposed descendant, Timur – or 'Tamberlane' – reshaped the map of Mongol authority. He wrested his own empire out of Jeti-Su in the east to Lahore (today's Pakistan) in the south, and comprising all of Iran, the Caucasus and Syria to the Black Sea, and all of the northern shore of the Caspian.

Timur's ambitions and achievements were double-edged. The initial Mongol surge had been undertaken by an army obeisant only to their Khan and an elemental shamanic cult. Mongol rule was tolerant of the Islam they had overrun – tolerant, indeed, of all varieties of formalized religion provided they posed no threat to political authority. Khan Berke, however, governing the territory of the Golden Horde in the fourteenth century, recognised the value of Islamic adherence as a social discipline. He made Islam his empire's official religion. Timur went one further. Conquering the territory of the Golden Horde, he ordained the construction of a mausoleum for the remains of the saintly Ahmed Yassavi and magnificently adorned the glory of Yassavi's mentor, Arystan Baba. These superb architectural and decorative achievements (celebrated in this work in Chapter 6, on pages 220-3) live on today as central to Kazakhstan's cultural and, implicitly, spiritual heritage.

The opposite edge of Timur's imperial expansion was negative. It had disastrous consequences for the populations living on the Kazakh Steppe at that time. Tribes were scattered, their political consolidation retarded; grazing and cultivating communities declined; a fatal reduction in livestock ensued. Yet it may be said that these ferocious challenges, and the ultimate collapse of Mongolian authority after 1395, released the hunger of the indigenous people for self-determination and led to the emergence of the new Khanates, the Nogai 'Horde' based between the Volga and the Ural rivers, and the so-called Uzbek Khanate, controlling the length of the Syrdarya basin to the Aral Sea, and the Steppe northwards to the Irtysh river, neither of them precisely Kazakh.

The Kazakh Khanate Emerges

Gradual recovery from the Mongol conquest saw the growing influence of the local Turkic nobles and intensified the people's resistance to the feudal powers of the Mongol Khans on an ethnic basis. The Khanate emerging in the first half of the fifteenth century incorporated Dasht – I – Kipchak, the Ak Horde of Turkestan and the Khanate of Abul Khayr, comprising the Nogai Horde and the Jeti-Su area.

The revival of agriculture and the cities of southern Kazakhstan and the growth of trade resulted in closer links between the nomadic and semi-nomadic peoples of the central Steppe and the settled farming communities of the Jeti-Su who were related by origin, language and culture. Towards the middle of the fifteenth century there was a need for a stable union, which could safeguard the national identity and economic activities of the Kazakhs.

Under Abul Khayr, what was then known as the Uzbek Khanate ruled Khorezm and the whole Syrdarya basin. But Jungar incursions from greater Mongolia east of the mountains crippled Abul Khayr's authority, and in effect civil war broke out, with two great-grandsons

A Kazakh warrior of the later fifteenth century (drawn by K. Akhmetjan).

of Genghis Khan, Janibek and Kerei, championing a group of tribes of the old white Horde which was identifiably Kazakh. In the latter part of the fifteenth century they had moved their warriors westwards from the independent Khanate known as Mogolistan, which comprised the south-eastern region of Kazakhstan as we know it today, most of Kyrgyzstan, and the habitable territory on the east of the Tien Shan mountains as far as the Takla Makan desert. They now struggled for control of the cities of the Syrdarya and the Jeti-Su.

It was another period of grievous disruption for the indigenous, and essentially Kazakh, people. Khan Esenbuga of the Chagatai Ulus of eastern Kazakhstan offered these newly assertive Sultans certain swathes of his territory in a gesture of solidarity. With the progressive weakening of the Uzbek Khanate, a substantial portion of its territory was now giving allegiance to Janibek and Kerei.

By the 1490s the expanding Kazakh Khanate was incorporating the territory of the western Jeti-Su and the valleys of the rivers Chu and Talas. The major city

of Yassy – today's Turkestan – had become their capital. Progressively, all the tribes of southern and central Kazakhstan were cohering. By the end of the fifteenth century, the Kazakh Khanate was embracing the territories of the Syrdarya basin, the area around the Aral Sea, and north from there. The Kazakh Khanate was developing its own momentum, embracing the greater part of the territory comprising the transhumant patterns of life of those recognising themselves to be Kazakhs. It fostered relations with further central Asia to the west and north – the Khanates of Astrakhan and Kazan, and, indeed, Russia itself. Peoples of Nogai, Mongol and Uzbek heritage merged with it, expanding its territory.

The coming century saw the spontaneous evolution of the three Juzes. This was an essentially peaceable division of political management and second-tier allegiance. It would give further stability to Kazakh presence and authority across so vast and borderless a territory. This spontaneous resolution of issues of territory and society are further discussed below.

Each Juz was determined by factors of geography and rainfall, and hence grazing practices and economy; and by tribal alliance. Common ancestry was not the prime factor in the forming of the Juzes. Each contained summer and winter pastures. Under climatic challenge, each would aid the other. The so-called Great Juz comprised all that region of the previously identifiable Mongolistan lying west of the mountains, and therefore the Jeti-Su area, and north-eastwards to the region of the Ili valley and Lake Balkhash. The significance of Jeti-Su always remained crucial. As we have seen, the ancient history of Central Asia pivoted on the region where the Steppe met the cultivable areas and their settlements – indeed their cities.

Adjacent, and incorporating much of the lower basin of the Syrdarya, the territory immediately to the west and the north came to form the pastures of the Middle Juz. It took in the Kipchak region as far north as Siberia. The people wintered in the valleys, and summer pastures were provided by the uplands of what would become central Kazakhstan.

The third, or Junior, Juz incorporated

Time-honoured weaponry of the Kazakh warriors of the later mediaeval period included a sword designed for both piercing and *slashing, the ball-and-chain, iron shields, light chainmail and a light bow suitable for an equestrian archer.*

that region – much of it low and dry – west and north of the Aral Sea. In the summer months, the transhumant herders grazed the plains of today's Aktyubinsk Oblast. These Kazakhs of the Junior Juz bordered with the territory of the peoples of the Volga.

All the three Juzes shared a language, albeit with regional variations in styles of speech. There were other differences in domestic practice, clothing and folklore; yet these were insignificant. Every household had its herd of sheep, together with a small number of goats, some cattle, a few camels and many horses. The average per household was a few score of animals; the rich could own up to a thousand. In regions, seasonal migrations could take a tribe – a union of *auls*, or settlements – as much as five or six hundred miles, but most migrations were between the valley, the sheltered winter encampments, and the summer upland

pastures, for which the whole community would set forth after the spring thaw.

The enemy common to all was the weather – the treacherous cold which could bring the bitter Siberian *buran* winds, or the *jut* which, descending upon the ground waterlogged by the thaw, could trap the fodder under a sheet of ice and starve a herd. The parallel menace was drought.

The social and hierarchic pattern was also common to the entire Kazakh community. The most significant figure in any group was the Biy – best translated as 'judge', or 'arbiter'. The importance of those who filled this role in Kazakh society can scarcely be exaggerated. Biys were men invariably of natural authority and sagacity. They fulfilled administrative and judicial duties across each vast territory. Only a man wholly versed in the common law and respected among his people would be elected a Biy. The role

was not hereditary: appointments were (in the parlance of today) 'democratic'. The function of the Biys was unusually significant given the disputatious nature of the nomadic tribal life, and the co-existence of private property (as, for example, of animals) and selective rights to pastures. Next to the Biys as leaders among the community were the Batyrs – the warriors, or heroes, with their own military and chivalric functions, whose influence in relation to the Biys depended in practice on the cast of personality.

Theoretically superior to both Biy and Batyr, a dual nobility held sway. This aristocratic rank was known as the 'White Bone'. Such an aristocracy stood aloof from the tribal system – a factor essential to its status. As to the 'duality', the *Tore* were descended from Genghis Khan (or claimed such descent), and bore the title of 'Sultan' from birth. They inherited various privileges, including being

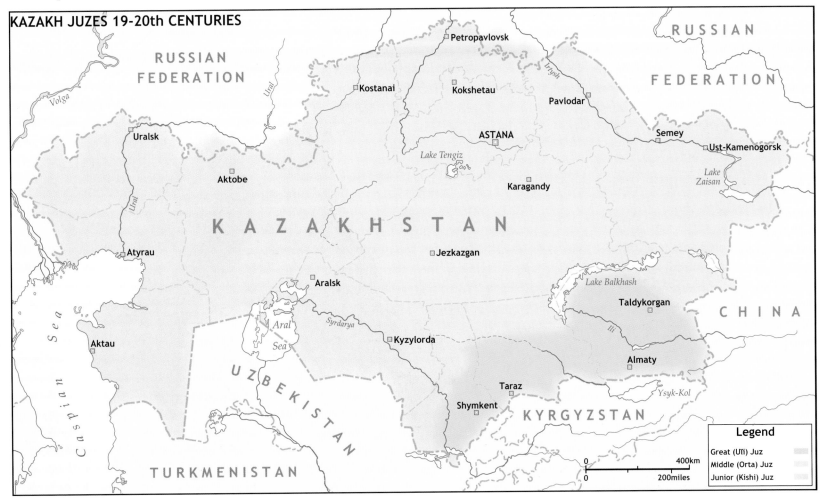

immune from corporal punishment; they were not indictable even by the Biys. The nobility of the *Khoja*, by contrast, stemmed from their spiritual authority. These were descendants of the original Muslim teachers and carried profound respect among the people, although with rights not as wide as those of the *Tore* Sultans. Those of the White Bone were instantly recognisable to each other across the entire breadth of the land, and across the divisions of the Juzes.

The middle caste – the Kara Suyek, or 'Black Bone' – was by far the most numerous section of society, beholden, of course, to the authority of the Biys, and also to that other senior category of command, the Batyrs, themselves of the Black Bone. This Black Bone body of Kazakh society comprised the general run of clansmen or tribesmen, mostly herders, who invariably felt superior to the settled cultivators. There was beneath them a lower caste, essentially slaves, and made up of captives taken in combat, or their descendants, and including Turkmen, Russians, Kyrgyz, and, not least, the Jungars, a people stemming from the northern region of Chinese Turkestan, just beyond the Altai range, who were coming to be the principal threat to security and peace of the Kazakh Steppe, particularly to that of the Great Juz. This slave caste was not numerous.

In the generality, an equality and harmony prevailed among ethnic Kazakhs throughout this communal period, until there began to arise – in the later sixteenth century – the two powerful contenders for mastery of the Kazakh Steppe, one on the west and one on the east: Russians, who had overwhelmed the Tatars in Kazan in 1552 and Astrakhan in 1556, bringing them to the edge of the territory of the Junior Juz; and the ever more assertive Jungars (or Kalmyks) from the east who, in the last three decades of the seventeenth century occupied most of southern Kazakhstan, overrunning the cites and wholly devastating Sairam.

The Kazakh Khanate under Threat

Jungar campaigns pressed on the Kazakh Khanate with a vengeance in the last years of the seventeenth century and the first decade of the eighteenth, the warriors flooding across from their heartland east of the Altai. The Jungars were aiming to occupy southern Kazakhstan and the trading towns on the banks of the Syrdarya as well as to assume control of the trading caravans' routes. In 1710, Tauke Khan summoned representatives of all three Juzes for a conference on how to organise resistance, meeting in the Kara Kum desert. For some six years the Kazakhs held back the enemy, repeatedly melting back into the Steppe: even there they were not safe.

The broad Kazakh political system rested upon the principle of the autonomy of each of the Juzes' territories. It was wonderfully suited to the management of internal problems. Ever since the reforms of the early seventeenth century, conflicts of clan and regional rights were invariably handled peacefully, using the judgement of the Biys. However, as the external threat sharpened at the start of the eighteenth century, the authority of the Kazakh Khanate was exposed as too decentralised to meet the challenge. Tauke Khan remedied that – but only briefly. After his death in 1715, certain Sultans began vying for the central Khanship. After long wrangling, Kaip was elected in 1715 and was at once obliged to confront the Jungars, who had resumed their assault.

Khan Kaip died in 1718. His successor Bolat proved weak-willed, unable to master the situation across the Khanate. Substantial parts of the Junior and Middle Juzes gave their allegiance to an alternative figure, Abulkhair, who would hold sway until his death in 1748. It may be said that this division sowed the seeds of the eventual demise of the Kazakh Khanate.

In the spring of 1723, a large Jungar force encroached upon Kazakh land from the east along the Talas valley, skirting the Karatau mountains. The Kazakhs at that time were preparing to migrate to their highland summer pastures. They were caught off-guard. Almost the entire Kazakh population of the Talas region was eliminated; those who survived were obliged to flee, abandoning their cattle and possessions. Vast numbers of suddenly destitute and hungry refugees crowded the oases of Bukhara and Samarkand. In 1724-25 the Jungars overran the cities of Tashkent and Turkestan, laying waste to both of them. These dreadful events are known even among Khazakhs of today as Aktaban Shubyryndy – 'running (*i.e.* fleeing) to the bone' (of the foot).

*Abulkhair Khan (**above**) had a testing role to play, with the threat of the Jungars in the 18th century, and an expanding Russia.*

*The revered protectors of Kazakh integrity and confidence of the period were the three Biys (**below**) – Tole, Kazybek, and Aiteke.*

The threat to national independence galvanised the Kazakhs into a united response. That next year, 1726, the combined armies of the Great and Junior Juzes at last inflicted a major defeat on the Jungars. Representatives of the three Juzes, each under the governorship of its Biys, gathered near Shymkent and elected a new commander for the Kazakh army in the person of Abulkhair, committed to the principle of strong central power.

A further victory by the Kazakh army in 1729 at a battle near Lake Balkhash should have cemented the union of the Juzes, yet once again rivalry among the Sultans frustrated it. Only the initiative of the three Biys – Tole, Kazybek and Aiteke, together with Sultan Abilmansur, known as Abylai – restored the essential unity. We shall come back to this remarkable Abylai below, after turning to the origins of the Russian protectorate.

Under sustained threat from the Jungars, Khan Tauke had already sent several embassies to Russia when, in 1694, Peter the Great proposed a treaty of protection and trade. 'This Horde,' he had noted, referring to the generality of Kazakhs of the time, 'is the key and the gate to all Asian lands. For that reason this Horde must be placed under Russian protection.'

By 1720 several Russian fortresses had been built – Omsk, Zhelezinka (north of Pavlodar), Semipalatinsk and Ust-Kamenogorsk. At the same time, Peter had devised and initiated the methodology of securing Kazakh compliance with Russian guardianship. His written instruction to his principal emissary demonstrated the significance of the protectorate for the Russian empire. 'If this Horde does not wish to become under the Russian shield, try everything, whatever the expense, be it a million roubles or more. For they must be under Russian protection.' He refers here to the cost not only of the protective role as such but of official bribery, in the form of gifts to the Sultans and others. A million roubles at that time was a very great sum indeed.

Peter's death in 1721 delayed the project. Yet it was to resume a decade later when, in 1731, the Russian envoy crossed the Kazakh Steppes persuading the White Bone and Black Bone leadership alike to swear allegiance to the Tsar. He used all the devices short of force – gifts, bribery, unfulfillable promises. By 1731 the Lesser Juz under Abulkhair, in their eastern and northernmost territory, had became subject to the Russian empire, with Russia having the right to approve the appointment of the Juz Khan in recognition of its role as the protector and defender of the territory from external threat. The truth is, the Lesser Juz had not been much threatened, and had not participated in campaigns against the Jungar. It was, instead, itself becoming something of a threat to the Middle and the Great Juzes.

Now, with renewed menace from the

Jungars, elders of the more easterly (and senior) Juzes expressed a wish for Russian protection – albeit without any formal submission as vassals of Russia. The purpose of this ploy was at least in part to dissociate the Great Juz and to some extent the Middle Juz from that effective submission that Abulkhair had chosen to accept, while at the same time being seen by the Jungars as a participant in the Russian sphere of influence. Abulkhair could not in such circumstances use Russian military power against his fellow Kazakhs.

The Middle and Great Juzes continued the struggle against the Jungars. The Russians, at least overtly, accepted the proposed formula; but it became the new template for an evolving Russian colonial policy. In 1741, the Jungars were again assaulting Kazakh lands, with no true leadership emerging among Kazakhs of the Great and Middle Juzes. Then, in 1748, Abulkhair was murdered by Sultan Barak, as a protest against his pro-Russian policy.

The restoration of Kazakh unity is indissolubly linked to the name of Abylai Khan, to whom we must now return. Born Abilmansur, he was a son of a Sultan, Korkem-Wali. In his youth, during one of the Jungars' invasions, he had fled to the Steppe and, concealing his parentage, worked as a simple shepherd. In the late 1720s he resolved to take part in the wars against the Jungars and quickly became one of the Middle Juz's most influential Batyrs, the Kazakh knights, taking the name of his grandfather Abylai, himself a famous warrior.

In 1739, the Jungars signed a peace treaty with the Ch'ing dynastic rulership of China. Two years later and taking advantage of divisions among the Kazakhs, they launched a fresh assault which ended in the total defeat of the Kazakhs and capture of Abylai Khan. Only at the price of the secession of the Middle Juz from Russian protection, and the

*Abylai Khan (**above**), as warrior leader and as politician, played the key role in unifying the pan-Kazakh territory and inspiring the nation, until his death in 1781.*

***Right** and **opposite**, the Kazakh way of life as seasonal migrants, imbued with their own indestructible discipline and elegance, in the period up to and after colonisation by Russia, was faithfully recorded by the brush of the artist Nikolai Khludov (born 1850).*

acknowledgment by that Juz of vassalage to Jungaria, was Abylai released. The switch of the Juz's allegiance at once provoked dispute between the Russian and Jungarian governments, and nearly led to war.

Long years of contention for the Jungars' throne led to China's occupation of Jungaria and to Chinese penetration of Kazakh territory, where the armies of Abylai Khan gave battle, wearing down the Chinese forces. In 1758-59, Chinese armies

finally destroyed the Jungar state system, although in doing so frequently intruded upon Kazakh land. Yet the Emperor was to make no territorial claim; what is more, he acknowledged the legitimacy of Abylai Khan's title and repeatedly invoked his help against the Russians.

For Abylai Khan to accommodate both his powerful neighbours – or play off one against the other – called for sustained skill and constant manoeuvering, which he conducted brilliantly. While preserving a formal allegiance to the Russian empire, Abylai Khan frequently sent his envoys to China to request their help against Russian colonial intrusion.

At the same time, Abylai Khan took steps to unify all territory occupied by Kazakh people. In 1740, the majority of clans of the Great Juz had sworn an oath of loyalty to their own Abilmambet Khan. On Abulkhair's acceptance of Russian protection, many of the clans of Middle Juz came to seek union between

Abilmambet Khan and Abylai, who in any case worked in close harmony. In 1759 the Tzarist administration proposed to Abylai that he replace Abilmambet and become the new, single Khan of all the Kazakhs, promising their support for him accordingly; the great man refused, while remaining the dominant figure. It was only on his death in 1781 that Abylai Khan achieved symbolic acknowledgement as the single leader and champion of the Kazakh people. This was when, at his burial in the mosque of Ahmed Yassavi, his body was ceremonially raised above the great concourse of mourners on a felt sheet. The event captured the Kazakhs' collective imagination to become the sustaining symbol of their potential unity and independence.

In the late eighteenth century, Russian colonial policy towards Kazakhstan was to become much more assertive and overbearing. The days of any presumption of Kazakh autonomy were numbered.

Tsarist Kazakhstan

The stationing of Cossack troops on a line of ten garrisons and fifty-three outposts between the Uil river, a tributary of the Ural in the north-west – the region of the Lesser Juz – and the Irtysh river in the north-east, may be counted as the first significant act of formal colonisation of Kazakh territory by Tsarist Russia. This was in the 1760s, when Catherine the Great was ruling. Ostensibly the garrisons were there to protect the indigenous Kazakhs. From the 1780s, in the years immediately following Abylai's death, Russia was strengthening in presence on the Steppe and in the forest land immediately to the north of today's Kazakhstani territory, in regions far beyond the Russian homeland – with garrisons at Omsk, Orsk and Orenburg.

St Petersburg was actively pursuing a policy of encouraging settlement by Russians on colonised, non-Russian land in central Asia, much of it Kazakh. Areas of territory were effectively cordoned off by the Russians, where the Kazakhs suddenly found themselves forbidden to roam or to

graze. Instead they were occupied by Cossack soldiery and their families, and cleared for settlement by ethnic Russians. The Kazakhs had indeed been restored to all their Steppe land west of the Altai and Jungar ranges since the removal of the Jungars; but Russian settlement constituted an intrusion of a different kind.

At first the Kazakhs responded by wilfully driving their cattle through the territories newly denied to them, then by attacking Russian (or Cossack) fortifications. A taste for defiance of Russia had been spread by those Kazakhs of the Junior Juz who had elected to join the short-lived rebellion of the Tsarist pretender, Emelyan Pugachev, creator of his own 'Kingdom' in the Ural River region in 1773-4. In the winter of 1782-3 the first Kazakh revolt broke out, headed by Syrym Datov. He and his horsemen sustained their campaign for a decade and a half, in a complex series of partnerships with both Kazakh and Russian factions, until he was killed in 1798 or 1799.

The Russian colonial hand, however, became progressively heavier in the first half of the nineteenth century, with continuing settlements and the migrants exempted from all taxes for the first five years. The Cossack mercenaries engaged in many forms of needling impositions on the Kazakhs, such as levying a charge on crossing rivers and capricious seizures of land. The Russian administrator Mikhail Speransky, Governor-general of Siberia, sought to codify the *adat*, Kazakh customary law, into a system of administration, for which Kazakhs paid a poll tax. He encouraged settled farming, as distinct from nomadism. Yet if not exactly in a role of vassals, Kazakhs found themselves second-class citizens in their own country. The Lesser and Middle Juz were 're-organised'. Nomadic Kazakh migrations across the Ural River resulted in outright fighting with the Russians in 1818 and between 1826 and 1828. Discontent amid the Junior Juz repeatedly flared.

A new wave of Kazakh indignation swept the Middle Juz until a fresh rebellion broke out in 1837 championed by Isatai Taimenov and Makhambet Utemisov and was snuffed out in little more than a year. There simultaneously erupted a far more substantial insurrection against Tsarist rule, this time under the command of a grandson of Ablai Khan – the charismatic Kenesary Kasymov – or Kenesary Khan. He rallied virtually the entire Middle Juz against the intruders, repeatedly outwitting and out-fighting them in daring raids on settlements and fortifications alike. He cast his own rifles. He established a refined legal system, combining Kazakh law with Islamic *shari'a*. In 1844 – after seven years of sustained rebellion – the Russian government sent a pair of envoys to Kenesary's headquarters offering an amnesty in exchange for the Khan's formal submission to the Tsar. He accepted, though himself departing to assist the Kyrgyz in their own fight for independence from Kokand: he died in battle, two years later. Three localised rebellions followed – in the north-eastern Caspian region, 1853-7; the Syrdarya basin, 1856-8; and in the Uralsk, Turgai and Mangyshlak oblasts in 1868-9 – which proved to be the end of Kazakh resistance.

Russia was now moving energetically to consolidate its rule. In 1854 the Russians founded Fort Verny, which would grow to be Alma-Ata (Almaty); and in 1862, Akmolinsk (today's Astana).

The imperial government relentlessly cut away at the authority of the Khans, until the role was totally abolished. By the 1880s colonisation by Russia was a wholly formalised reality, and the last decades of the nineteenth century saw the settlement of Russian peasantry proceeding on an unprecedented scale. In 1889, to ease a land crisis in Mother Russia, St Petersburg passed a decree for the resettlement of peasants from Russia in Kazakhstan, which resulted in the expropriation of lands of the nomadic Kazakh population on a massive scale – so great indeed that by the end of the century there had developed an acute shortage of farmland of the northern provinces of Kazakhstan. This prompted the Russian administrator to order the

Patriot and warrior, Kenesary Khan, kept the torch of Kazakh self-determination burning, as Tsarist Russia's colonial grip on the territory tightened in the nineteenth century.

mass migration of Russian peasants to southern Kazakhstan. The settlers were invariably armed.

By the early twentieth century, as much as fifty million hectares of Kazakhstan had been expropriated and settled by Russians and Ukrainians, who together made up more than one third of the population. Between 1895 and 1905 close to 300,000 foreigners were re-settled on the Steppe; by 1910 the figure had risen to 770,000; by 1916 the number of Russian settlers was 1.5 million. The entire national make-up of Kazakhstan had been transformed, by edict of the colonising power. At the date of the Revolution of 1917, Russians constituted 42 per cent of Kazakhstan's population. The practice of enforced movements of population was therefore by no means an exclusively Communist vice.

Nor indeed was Russia's practice of using the places of central Asia of which she had control as a dumping ground for citizens sentenced to 'internal exile'. By the middle of the nineteenth century, the Tsarist regimes had been engaging in these practices. Hence the exile of the

A rare photograph records a colonial court in session, evidently arbitrating in a dispute between (perhaps) a Kazakh and a Russian litigant, in the late nineteenth or early twentieth century.

Ukrainian artist and writer Taras Shevchenko to Orsk in 1847, and his later rearrest and exile in the Mangyshlak Peninsula on the eastern shore of the Caspian. A decade later, Feodor Dostoevsky also had a taste of exile for four years in north-eastern Kazakhstan's Semipalatinsk, where in 1862 he wrote *Memoirs from the House of the Dead*. There he met the Kazakh Orientalist and ethnographer, Chokan Valikhanov, who was to be a sustaining strength and source of knowledge for the novelist in his recovery from the shock of near execution and his ensuing exile, and was an outstanding scholar in his own right. There too Dostoevsky met and fell in love with Maria Isaeva, the wife of a Russian officer stationed in Semipalatinsk, who in due course would become his wife.

The benefit of education and dubious advantage of sedentarisation were being brought to bear on the nomadic Kazakh people by the Russians, to some extent by

(continued on page 132)

Russia's expansion into Central Asia involved not only colonial rule and settlement, but also internal exile as punishment for those regarded as politically undesirable. These included arguably their greatest nineteenth century novelist Feodor Dostoevsky (seen here with his Kazakh friend and mentor, Valikhanov), and the Ukrainian painter and writer Taras Shevchenko.

The 1916 Uprising

The economy of the Steppe was fast deteriorating in the years prior to the First World War. Land seizures were increasing. War led to the breakdown of the empire-wide market. Kazakhs and Russians alike were forced to trade their goods almost exclusively locally. This meant a sharp drop in the price of livestock and a variety of shortages. Kazakhs were 'requested' to make 'donations' of meat and hides and to provide horses to the imperial cavalry; in 1914 and 1915 alone some 260,000 head of livestock were taken with no payment. Taxes went up. Already by June 1916 the Tsar had called for conscription into labour brigades of the indigenous population, aged 18 to 43, to prevent the front against the Germans from collapsing. In Kazakh regions 87,000 men were to be drafted from Jeti-Su, 60,000 from Syrdarya, 50,000 from Uralsk, 40,000 from Akmolinsk, 60,000 from Turgai, and 8,500 from Semipalatinsk. Mobilisation began with the dissemination of the *ukase*, and so too did violent resistance. It took some time for word of the conscription order to spread throughout the Steppe.

Organised open resistance began first among the southern Turkestani population. The uprising quickly spread, first engulfing Samarkand then Tashkent and Fergana. By early August the uprising had spread throughout the Syrdarya Oblast, and detachments of between 5,000 and occasionally even 8,000 armed Kazakhs, Kyrgyz and Uzbeks attacked Russian troops along the Tashkent–Orenburg railroad. Russian troops battled the insurgents throughout September in Jeti-Su.

Kazakh resistance was even more widespread and better organized. On July 10, Kazakh representatives from eleven *volosts* gathered near the ancient city of Otrar to organise their plans for concerted attacks on Russian forces. At this same meeting the Kazakhs also decided to send thousands of draft-age men into exile along Lake Balkhash. Russian forces retaliated. Cossacks gathered from Perm, Kazan, and Saratov. The troops treated the native population of Jeti-Su harshly. Throughout September and October punitive detachments were sent from *aul* to *aul* to hunt out participants of the uprising and arrest draft resisters. In

Abdulghaffar Khan (right), leader of the Turgai, headed the rebellion in the central west region.

Amangeldy Imanov (below), co-rebel leader with Abdulghaffar, survived the revolt to welcome the Bolsheviks, before dying in 1919.

The First World War was to set in train a vast, albeit calamitous, upheaval in Kazakhstan from early 1916. It sparked rebellion – a freedom struggle – across the country in reaction to Tsarist Russia's attempt to mobilize thousands of Kazakhs for its war effort, coming on top of colonial oppression. Thousands of rebels died; thousands more fled... though some of those awaiting execution were saved by the peaceful revolution in St Petersburg of February 1917.

Amangeldy's militia (right) rallied the Steppe.

many cases whole villages were judged collaborators and all the yurts burned. The Kazakhs of the northern oblasts of the Steppe also offered substantial resistance to the Tsar's *ukase*. By mid-July disturbances had been reported across the eastern and the northern parts of the country. By September Kazakh resistance was fully organised: colonial officials in Omsk reported that nearly 30,000 Kazakh fighters were camped in the Akmolinsk region alone.

The Kazakhs made a major assault on the city of Akmolinsk on September 26-27, again on October 3-4, and a final attack on October 6. These attacks were repulsed by General Lavrentiev's expeditionary forces. Meanwhile the Kazakhs of the western Steppe had risen:

in Turgai, Irgiz, Aktyubinsk and Kostanai. Beside the tribal figures of Abdulghaffar Khan, the key leader of the revolt in the area was Amangeldy Imanov (1873-1919), later to become the first Soviet Kazakh hero because he commanded pro-Bolshevik Adigei troops during the Civil War.

By October 1916 the rebel army numbered some 20,000 men, of which 5,000 were under Amangeldy's personal command and the rest under a group of allied commanders. He was responsible for the greatest Kazakh victory of the uprising; on October 23 some 15,000 Kazakh fighters surrounded the city of Turgai, cutting off telegraph and railroad connections. The siege did not end

completely until mid-November, when Lavrentiev's troops arrived. The Russian army regulars launched a three-pronged attack on the Kazakhs and inflicted heavy casualties; by November 30 only about 6,000 Kazakh fighters were left.

The revolt proved to be very costly to the Kazakhs. For example, the population of the Jarkent *uezd* declined by 73 per cent in the period between the onset of World War One and January 1, 1917, in Przhevalsk by 70 per cent, in Lepsink by 47 per cent, in Verny by 45 per cent, and in Pishpek by 42 per cent.

Ultimately, the 1916 uprising accomplished little except, perhaps, that it signed in blood the Kazakhs' will to survive as themselves.

Paralleling the spontaneous popular uprising on the Steppes was the powerfully nationalist movement of Kazakh intellectuals, the Alash Orda. The movement included three elected Kazakh members of the Russian Duma (Parliament), pictured below.

Clockwise from above, left, are S. Koshegulov and Z. Shanturin, both of the Muslim Party, and A. Kamenov, of the Constitutional Democratic Party, all members of the Duma working for Kazakh self determination.

Following the Bolshevik putsch in St Petersburg in November 1917, and the outbreak of civil war across the Russian empire, Alash Orda survived to provide an independent political leadership for Kazakhstan, and succeeded in forming administrations in several major towns, before being eliminated by Lenin in 1921.

Alash Orda's leaders, pictured above and below, struggled to provide a popular political leadership during the turmoil of the civil war. All were executed or imprisoned.

force. The Russians made it a point of pride to bring their own form of civilisation to the Kazakh people. The Russian commander-in-chief of the Kazakh headquarters at Fort Verny in the 1880s is on record with a declaration: 'There is a requirement to admit with sincerity that our business here is a Russian one, first and foremost, and that the land populated by Kazakhs is not their own, but belongs to the State [*i.e.* the Russian state]. The Russian settled elements must force them off the land or lead them into oblivion.' Russian settlers were, likewise, to an extent, soldiers of the Tsar. 'As a general rule,' said a senior administrator, 'each [Russian] man here must be literate, and must be able to use weapons.'

Increasingly, in the early twentieth century, Kazakhstan came to be seen as a source of raw materials, for Russia and, indeed, of rewards for daring British and French entrepreneurs, who became the masters of coalmines in Kazakhstan and certain mineral mining enterprises. When the First World War broke out in 1914, the call upon these resources increased.

With the onset of war, things were about to change radically. In 1916, matters came to a violent head. A wave of self-determination swept across Central Asia. Wholesale mobilisation of Kazakhs as indentured labour backing up the front line against the Germans in the Great War ignited widespread insurrection. It was headed by Abdulghaffar and Amangeldy Imanov. In the desperation of a European war which threatened the

*The former life was about to be swept away – the Islamic authorities, pictured **left**, the tranquillity of old Taraz (**right**) and Almaty (**below, left**), and the Muslim medresses for boys (**below**), for whom Kazakh was taught in Arabic lettering.*

very existence of the Russian state, the resurrection was brutally suppressed. An estimated 150,000 Kazakhs were slaughtered and as many as 200,000 fled to China. Out of such massive disaster and suffering, the Kazakh nationalist party Alash Orda (first formed as a nationalist underground by educated Kazakhs at the start of the century) was ready to exploit a totally new and unexpected development.

The Russian Revolution and the Soviet Era

During the First World War, the whole Kazakh Steppe was engulfed in spontaneous anti-colonial uprisings, as already described, provoking ferocious Tsarist response. The mood of rebellion was unassuaged when the liberal revolutionaries of the Kerensky government seized power from the Tsars in St Petersburg in the first revolution, of February 1917. When Lenin's *coup d'état* took place in Petrograd (as the capital had been briefly renamed) on October 25, 1917 (November 7 by the Western calendar), the Kazakh nationalists perceived their opportunity: Bolshevik authority in Kazakhstan was virtually negligible.

The Alash Orda and Kazakh Islamacists made their bids for power.

Nonetheless, immediately following the so-called 'Great October Socialist Revolution', the Soviet congress in Kokand, in Uzbek territory, proclaimed the Autonomous Turkestan Soviet on November 22. Five days later, the Muslim congress, sitting in an extraordinary session, proclaimed their own independent Mukhtariat of Turkestan. The Mukhtariat was to survive scarcely a year. The entire forces the Soviets could muster in their own Turkestan, including units of the Cossacks, were flung upon Kokand; the

majority of the populace was killed.

In the far north of Kazakh territory, at Orenburg, the situation was rather different. The 'All-Kyrgyz Congress' (the term Kyrgyz at that time being synonymous with Kazakh) of December 5-12, 1917, passed two ringing resolutions, one declaring the foundation of independent statehood, another structuring its own military forces. An Alash Orda government was set to assume power. In reality the entire territory of the former Russian empire was now on the verge of a civil war which, ranging far and wide, would continue for another three years. By February 1918, pro-Bolshevik Soviets were claiming power in Kostanai, Turgai, Aktyubinsk, Akmola, Semipalatinsk and, indeed, in Orenburg itself. Even so, nationalist resistance

organised by the Alash Orda were still formidable. *De facto* Bolshevik authority did not apply beyond the occupied towns and territory bordering the railway lines. Most of the Kazakh Steppe acknowledged its preference for the Alash, committed to parliamentary government, and expressing qualified loyalty to a comparable regime in Russia which no longer existed. In the votes recorded in late 1917 for the Alash constituent assembly elections in Turgai and Uralsk, the movement had captured some 75 per cent.

By the summer of 1918 the tide of civil war on Kazakh soil had turned against the Bolsheviks: the Reds had been ousted from most of the towns they had claimed to control six months earlier, although they held on in the Syrdarya basin, Jeti-Su, and Almaty itself. By the autumn even those

*As the new order descended on the people, elders of the communities met to confer (sitting in judgement **above**). Most of the judges and volost governors, such as those pictured **right**, were replaced by Party adherents.*

Bolshevik enclaves were under threat from Alash, in their always uneasy alliance with the White army, under Alexander Kolchak.

It was not to last. In the early spring of 1919 the Fifth (Red) Army commanded by V. Frunze, under orders from Leon Trotsky in Moscow, began to turn this tide. Amid a situation of desperate famine in the south of the country, which the head of the Bolshevik Department of Nationalities, Natsotdel, valiantly strove to offset, the Reds threw ever greater numbers into the fight. The military fortunes of the Whites had collapsed by the winter of 1919-20, and by January a severely weakened Alash Orda was in 'negotiations' with the Bolsheviks.

After their definitive acquisition of power in the territory, the new government introduced impossibly onerous taxes and draconian laws across Kazakhstan. Popular disturbances persisted. Perturbed by such continuing protest, Moscow somewhat softened the laws in 1921, and saw to it that the lands occupied by Cossack soldiery were given back to the rightful Kazakh owners. By 1922, all remaining leaders of Alash Orda had been removed from their positions.

Two figures now appear in the story of Kazakhstan, whose names to this day provoke a sense of horror in the people's memory. They are Nikolai Yezhov, head of Stalin's secret police, the OGPU, despatched to Kazakhstan to consolidate the grip of the party; and Feodor Goloshchekin. The two men arrived in the Kazakh Republic in 1923.

Their first actions seemed innocent enough – although dictated by the interests of Moscow. The Kazakh majority of the Semirechie and Syrdarya Oblasts, which were until then included in Turkestan, were permitted to unite with their northern (and Kazakh) neighbours. Moscow also sought to partition the Turkestan Republic to the south and west, aiming to weaken

Kazakhstan's rail network, involving the linking of Tashkent and Orenburg by way of Shymkent, Kyzylorda and Aktobe, and the later link (below) via Almaty to Akmola and Petropavlovsk, became essential to the exercise of Moscow's new power, which involved mass immigration (lower picture) involving families of young children.

pan-Islamic and pan-Turkic sentiment in Central Asia. Chosen as the new capital of the Kazakhstan Republic was Kyzylorda (formerly Perovsk). At the same time, however, Orenburg was annexed to Russia itself.

Goloshchekin had been one of the perpetrators of the mass execution of the Tsar and his family at Ekaterinburg. He was now elected to head the regional branch of the Communist Party in Kazakhstan. Directed by Stalin, he immediately instituted a policy of liquidating social differentiation, and of changing irreversibly the nomadic way of life to an urban and sedentary one. Those who did not share his opinion were ruthlessly repressed. Arrests swiftly followed. Land belonging to the kulaks, the better-off peasantry, was divided among the

marketing and barter and, indeed, of husbandry. A policy of ferocious industrialisation descended upon Kazakhstan. A lead plant was established in Shymkent; at Balkhash and Jezkazgou copper was mined and smelted, as was zinc and titanium at Ust-Kamenogorsk (which was already taking place at Ridder – renamed Leninogorsk); coal at Karaganda; while major chemical works was set up at

Shymkent and Aktyubinsk. Oil production began tentatively in the northern Caspian, where Atyrau became a caviar centre. Sugar beet was planted and Taldykorgan and Taraz cities grew.

In 1928 came the decision from Moscow to collectivise agriculture. It was introduced under a regime of terror. The grain yield and flocks of sheep and goats further diminished. Hunger was rampant. Entire

As First Secretary of the Kazakhstan Communist Party, Feodor Goloshchenkin (far left) implemented – ruthlessly – the collectivisation policy of Josef Stalin (left) in which nearly two million Kazakhs died and half a million fled. Those that survived turned from the horse to the tractor (below).

poorest peasants – a move which produced none of the expected benefits. Cattle-owners were likewise disposed of their animals, and often banished; but the beneficiaries had neither hay nor the rights of pasture. In the winter of 1927-28 the malnourished animals endured a peculiarly evil *jut* – that climatic phenomenon where a freeze follows a thaw, and the animals' fodder, while visible, is unreachable under its layer of ice. Herds and flocks catastrophically diminished. At the same time, a monetary economy was imposed, disrupting the traditional methods of

flocks were obliterated when, to meet their wool quota, shepherds were forced to shear them at the onset of winter. In one year alone (1933) more than 33,000 men and women were convicted and sentenced (sometimes to death) for attempting to hide grain or meat for their own household. Mass re-settlement accompanied these appalling privations – including re-settlement onto collective farms. The effect was widespread starvation. In the decade up to 1939, somewhere between 1.75 million and two million Kazakhs died of starvation, epidemics, or execution – not less than 40 per cent of the entire indigenous population.

Several hundred thousand Kazakhs fled to China, Mongolia, Afghanistan and Iran, where their descendants remain to this day as Oralmans, although some are at last beginning to return to the land of their fathers.

The nomadic way of life had by now all but ceased to be except in remote corners of the country; and with it the entire culture of an ancient people. Of all this calamity the outside world knew almost nothing. Indeed, up to our own time, the record of this cruel period has been negligibly documented.

Stalin meanwhile was engaged in a reign

of terror throughout the entire Soviet Union on a scale unprecedented in the world's history. He was in the course of creating some 30,000 prisons and prison labour camps, the gulags. Kazakhstan was a favoured territory for the disappearance of those he deemed as undesirable. (Stalin had already despatched to Almaty, as an internal exile under house arrest, his earlier intimate co-revolutionary and head of the Red Army, Leon Trotsky – later to be assassinated on Stalin's orders in Mexico, where Trotsky had sought asylum.) The prison population in Kazakhstan was now to expand massively. Our map shows the

To stimulate the 'masses' into greater effort, the Soviet system offered the inducement of trophies like the red pennant (right). Moscow's national emblem for Kazakhstan closely approximated that of the Soviet Union, with its hammer, sickle, and wheat sheaves.

THE GULAG SYSTEM IN KAZAKHSTAN

Kurgan · Omsk · RUSSIAN FEDERATION

RUSSIAN FEDERATION

Kokshetau · Pavlodar

Uralsk

Semey · Ust-Kamenogorsk

Aktobe · Karagandy

Astrakhan · Atyrau

K A Z A K H S T A N

Jezkazgan

Aktau

C H I N A

Caspian Sea

Kyzylorda

U Z B E K I S T A N

Almaty · Bishkek

400km

200miles

Shymkent · KYRGYZSTAN

Tashkent

TURKMENISTAN

Legend
More than 25,000 prisoners ★
5,000-25,000 prisoners ★
Less than 5,000 prisoners ☆

sites of the largest prison and labour camps for political prisoners, established in Kazakhstan up to Stalin's death in 1953. Nobody was safe from suspicion, from denunciation, from capricious elimination. In 1937, all members of the Politburo of the Kazakh Communist party, including the Chairman of the Kazakh Sovnarkom – a figure equivalent to the Republic's Premier – were arrested and were mostly done to death. One of Stalin's prisoners to survive and to make Karagandy's gulag infamous throughout the world was a certain Alexander Solzhenitsyn, who described in his first novel, *One Day in the Life of Ivan Denisovich* (which Nikita Khrushchev, by then firmly in power in Moscow, allowed to be published in 1956), the reality of the gulag experience.

Nazi Germany's assault on the Soviet Union in 1941 gave rise to a fresh Stalinist policy, of devastating human consequences. This was the mass deportation of ethnic groups deemed to be potentially disloyal to Russia as Germany's Wehrmacht advanced eastwards, apparently unstoppable. Kazakhstan was once more Stalin's favoured dumping ground. The deportation of the Germans began in 1941, mostly from the Volga basin. Others were moved *en masse* from the Ukraine and from the Caucasus. A state edict entitled 'Migration of the Volga's Germans' was made public on August 28 1941: 'According to reliable sources discovered by the military authorities, among the German population on the shores of the river Volga are thousands and tens of thousands of spies and saboteurs, who are ready to set off explosions in inhabited areas, following the orders of Germany. We are undertaking punitive measures against the whole German population who live on the shores of the Volga.'

Apart from the Germans, substantial

*A Shymkent painter of the present day, Pavel Rechensky, who grew up in one part of Kazakhstan's gulag while his parents were incarcerated in another, exorcises his past by painting a satanically horned Lenin with his coven, and Stalin presiding over a 20th century 'El-Dorado' of drowning bodies. The poster, **right**, ridicules the 'capitalist' who would sneer at Communistic planning.*

Kazakhstan in the War

However severe the ordeals of Stalinism, a genuine patriotism for the defence of their own land was aroused by the German assault on the Soviet Union in 1941. Kazakhs fought willingly alongside their Russian fellows, not hesitating to endorse the struggle. During the war some 220 factories moved to Kazakhstan from elsewhere in the USSR, while another 200 plants were initiated in the territory. Kazakhstan came to produce 85 per cent of the lead, 35 per cent of the copper, and a significant proportion of other metals, as also of agricultural produce, for the whole Soviet Union. Over one million Kazakhs served in the Red Army.

The revered bard, Jambyl Jabaev, amid his Russian and Kazakh fellows in time of war, is 'armed' with his dombra.

An entertainment troupe from Kazakhstan is snapped, with members of a largely Russian serving unit in 1943.

Fighting the enemy – visibly, Adolf Hitler, in the poster right – was identified with ever greater economic effort. Meanwhile, Kazakhs were producing their own war heroes, honoured throughout the Soviet Union. Banjan Momyshuly commanded the Panfilov Brigade which with outstanding gallantry halted the German advance on Moscow.

Shells and bullets produced by collective endeavour send Hitler and his gallows flying.

Kazakh womanhood became identified with the struggle against the invader – and a handful emerged as iconic figures for their feats of courage.

Certain Kazakh women became unerring marksmen.

Momyshuly, hero of the Soviet Union, from a contemporary newspaper clipping.

*Manshuk Mametova (**above**) and Alia Moldagulova (**above right**) were made heroines of the Soviet Union.*

Deportation

Dispersing the unwanted – or patriotically untrusted – to the presumed oblivion of Kazakhstan was a sustained Soviet policy from the early 1930s. The Second World War accelerated it. Many nationalists and, in all, hundreds of thousands, were involved – leaving modern Kazakhstan with a diverse plurality of whom many have returned to their countries of origin while others have stayed as loyal Kazakhstani citizens, while preserving their varied cultural inheritance.

A dismayed family of Polish deportees was captured by the camera (**in the top picture**) on their arrival in the 1930s. The pictures **left above** and **left** are of a family of Chechen deportees, and children engaged in a piece of Chechen theatre. The centre picture **above** is of deported Volga Tatars. **Above right,** Japan's wartime alliance with Germany resulted in the deportation of tens of thousands of Koreans to Kazakhstan who, like the Georgian Greeks below, have assembled for a wedding.

communities of other nationalities were deported *en masse* to Kazakhstan, among them Chechens, Tatars, Ingush, Kalmyks, and – from the Far East, where a triumphant Japan was allied to Germany – Koreans. Many of those deportees' descendants are still in Kazakhstan, loyal citizens of an independent Kazakhstan. In all, some 50 nationalities shared the destiny of the Volga Germans as forced deportees into Kazakh territory.

Kazakhstan's perceived remoteness within the Soviet Union, and its isolation from the outside world, opened another page of Soviet inhumanity during the mid-century period. In 1949, the Soviet Union announced its first nuclear test explosion. This had taken place in what was to be known in the Semipalatinsk Polygon, the principal site (although there were five others in Kazakhstan) for testing Soviet nuclear weapons. President Nazarbayev of Kazakhstan revealed something of the reality in his speech to the United Nations General Assembly on June 23 1997: 'The biggest nuclear polygon in the world, enough to comprise the territory of several countries – 18,500 square kilometres – saw 470 explosions, some 70 per cent of all nuclear tests conducted by the Soviet Union, bringing colossal damage to people and to nature.'

A witness of those times, Yuri Belikov, has described the way the policy worked. 'When in August 1953, the train hurried people off

*Nikita Khrushchev (**centre**) reviews the Virgin Lands scheme for Kazakhstan, launched in the mid 1950s. Leaning forward on his left is the future First Party Secretary, a popular Kazakh, Dinmuhamed Kunaev.*

to the Kazakh Steppes, almost no one had any idea that in a week or two all of its passengers would become guinea pigs for the testing of hydrogen bombs. The train was a sort of Noah's Ark: there were not only people but horses and sheep, dogs, snakes and lizards, even specially packed insects.' We inspect this dread reality further on page 149. The authorities of Semipalatinsk at the time would advise the school teachers to oblige their pupils to come out of the school buildings to gaze at the explosions, with the intention of observing the reaction of the eyesight and the human body down the years to such exposure to radiation. Those human experiments led, indeed, to the development of widespread illness, mostly involving cancer in one form or another, and to an

immensely high rate of suicide, extensive deformities and abnormalities of birth, and many young people discovering on reaching adulthood that they had been made impotent.

In 1958 Nikita Khrushchev announced extensive plans to boost agricultural productivity throughout the Soviet world, and in particular the Virgin Lands scheme for Kazakhstan. The intention was to establish vast wheatlands, created by ploughing up the Steppe of north-central Kazakhstan. The 'lands' of course were far from 'virgin' in the sense that they had for centuries been grazed by Kazakh transhumants, although collectivisation had effectively depopulated large areas. Yet there was not sufficient rainfall nor an

Kazakhstan's own astronauts of the 1980s, launched at Baikonour, became national heroes. Baikonour saw the launch of all of the USSR astronauts, beginning with Gagarin in 1961, who so captured popular imagination.

The agricultural lady Stakhnovite and her companions on the official poster promoting the USSR's wheat growing scheme for Kazakhstan's 'Virgin Lands' gives little indication of Kazakh ethnicity.

inherent fertility for the scheme to flourish in the long run; and while great crops of wheat were initially produced, yields dropped off and the region soon turned into a partial dustbowl. Khrushchev's man in Kazakhstan was none other than Leonid Brezhnev, and it was he who coined the slogan 'All – to the Virgin Lands!'

Kazakhstan had become a site of major heavy industry for the Soviet Union, and above all of mining. Kazakhs had for some time been a minority in their own country; and politically the supposedly autonomous Republic had stagnated. The new constitution of 1977 had dared to announce that the building of 'developed socialism' had been realised. It proclaimed 'sovereignty' for the Republic, basic human rights and freedoms (which did not include political choice or freedom of expression), and interestingly enough the Republic's theoretical right to leave the Union, as well as to conduct its own foreign policy. There were no mechanisms for such developments. Yet the First Secretary of the Communist Party was, at last, a native Kazakh, and a close friend of Brezhnev, Dinmuhamed Kunaev, who ruled the country according to Moscow's wish but was perceived locally as a protector of the Republic's interest.

Hopes stirred with the accession to power of Mikhail Gorbachev in 1985. Yet within two years of Gorbachev's arrival, a

mass spontaneous demonstration had been provoked by the move to foist a Moscow appointment, Gennady Kolbin, a man virtually unknown in Kazakhstan, in succession to Kunaev. On the night of December 16 1986, the crowds surged onto the streets and the main square of the capital Alma-Ata (today's Almaty) in protest – only to be ruthlessly beaten back by the police. Kolbin was to hold on to office for little more than two years.

His successor, a true-born Kazakh, Nursultan Nazarbayev, son of a herder, could not have reasonably foreseen what was to take place in less than a year of his assuming office in June 1989.

In the early hours of April 24, 1990, a meeting of the Supreme Council of Kazakhstan was about to hear a speech by S. Sartaev, rector of the Kazakh Institute of Law and International Affairs, defining the new role to be filled by Nazarbayev as 'President' under the Republic's slightly adjusted constitution. Nazarbayev himself received a telephone call from Gorbachev's principal aide: the issue of the role of the Presidency was to be deleted from the agenda. When Nazarbayev vouchsafed this to Sartaev, a silence fell. Sartaev commented: 'This is our last chance to head for independence.' Nazarbayev responded in Kazakh: 'Full steam ahead.'

The history of independent Kazakhstan was soon to begin.

The Ethnic Mix Inheritance

The *raison d'être* for the Republic approaching independence could not but be that it was the immemorial homeland of the Kazakh people. Yet the truth was that, as they neared their release from Moscow, the Kazakhs themselves were a minority in their own country. In 1991 they were not even the largest single ethnic component of the population: that distinction belonged to the ethnic Russians – themselves just under half of the total population of 16.2 million. Within a year that situation would already have changed, with the Kazakh element already reaching 52 per cent; and by the turn of the century the Kazakh proportion of the overall population would be a comfortable majority, almost certainly increasing with the vigorous indigenous birth rate and the continuous inflow of those Kazakh exiles who – under the collective name of 'Oralmans' – were responding to the national call to return to the land of their fathers.

At the attainment of formal nationhood, the policy of the new leadership was to be consistently one of tolerance and ethnic inclusiveness. Yet not unnaturally, with a Kazakh ethnic predominance in government and the certainty of a sustained Kazakh leadership, those nationalities of non-Kazakh origin looked back towards the land of their own ancestral origin. Independence was to be followed by a significant spontaneous exodus – westwards. A notable exception was the Jewish community which continued to flourish *in situ*.

By far the largest non-Kazakh ethnic component was Russian. Indeed just two generations earlier, in the 1950s, Kazakhs had comprised scarcely more than 30 per cent of the population of their own so-called Kazakh Soviet Socialist Republic. On independence, there were some seven million ethnic Russians in Kazakhstan, and over 400,000 ethnic Germans. The surge of exodus by Russians and Germans during the early years following Independence was to reduce the population of Kazakhstan by seven per cent during its first decade. By 2003, that exodus was to have dwindled to a trickle: that element of today's population that is Russian – a significant 30 per cent – are set to stay, continuing to build their lives in an independent Kazakhstan, comfortably settled into an increasingly homogeneous population, and contributing markedly to the national weal with skills and a relatively high level of education. By a small margin, the majority of them are still countrymen, as distinct from urban dwellers.

The Russians had come to Kazakhstan in the first place to man the colonial authority from the middle of the eighteenth century. There was always a measure of settlement, even from the days of Catherine the Great (1761-96). There followed several waves of Slavic – largely Russian – migration up to the end of the nineteenth century. When, soon after the revolution of 1917, drought hit much of agricultural Russia, a substantial stream of immigrants moved, under Soviet protection, to Kazakhstan for a supposedly better life.

To the Russians thus resident – including a notable proportion of the survivors of Stalin's gulags sited on Kazakh soil – life in Kazakhstan seemed like a permanency.

The accession to nationhood in 1991 was to pose no threat to the ethnic Russians; and yet a country which had been for the better part of two centuries progressively Russified was clearly to be intent upon an assertion of its Kazakh identity. That 30 per cent of today's population comprising the ethnically Russian element recognises that they belong to Kazakhstan on Kazakhstani terms; and the symbiosis, indeed the integration, of the two communities is proving a successful and an easy one, culturally fertile, and with intermarriage between the communities on the increase. The effective secularisation of the community has diminished, if not eliminated, the religious context of difference.

By contrast, the German element had always been, and so remains, more self-contained; and the exodus of Germans from Kazakhstan since Independence was to be proportionally greater than that of the Russians. While there were some 900,000 Germans in Kazakhstan according to the census of 1989, a decade and a half later there remained not many more than 300,000. Like their Russian counterparts, Germans had begun to enter Kazakhstan as long ago as the eighteenth century, they were drawn from that long-standing German-speaking community present in Mother Russia since as far back as the eleventh century and forming the significant community of Volga Germans following the reign of (German-born) Catherine the Great – who offered a haven along the Volga to the (pacifist) Mennonite Christians when Prussia introduced compulsory military service in the late eighteenth century. Volga Germans continued to speak their own German in the home. In the early Soviet days, in the 1920s, the German contingent was still quite small, and was allowed its own schools teaching in the German medium. By the end of the 1930s that policy had changed. Then, with the Nazi German assault upon Russia, Stalin engaged in the wholesale deportation to Kazakhstan of Volga Germans, deemed to be unreliable in their loyalty as the German Wehrmacht captured more and more Soviet territory.

After Stalin's death, an easing of policy permitted the appearance of a German newspaper, even though not more than two per cent of Kazakhstani Germans were able to study their own language in the schools. Yet the Germans held on to their traditions, and kept their culture and identity alive in a wide range of associations. German radio was permitted in Kazakhstan under the Soviet rule.

The first surge of German emigration after Independence was to provoke alarm in Germany itself, which demanded a halt to the wave of ex-Soviet immigrants. Berlin limited the quotas, complaining at the migrants' weak knowledge of the German language in written form. But in Kazakhstan, a dozen or so years later, things had settled down and the preservation of German identity was encouraged. Ethnically German associations – like the German House in Almaty – was fostered by the Kazakh Government and by the Ministry of Internal Affairs in Germany itself. German societies such as Wiedergeburt – 'Rebirth' – flourish in several Kazakhstani cities.

The Kazakh people, and notably the students, took to the streets in Almaty on the night of December 16, 1986, demanding – as the banner demands – each nationality to be governed by its own kind. Retribution was brutal. It has become a day of national martyrdom.

The Rocky Road to Independence

Kazakhstan both reflected and played a part in the events which culminated in the break-up of the Soviet Union and its own independence.

From the moment Mikhail Gorbachev took over as Secretary of the Soviet Communist party – on March 11, 1985 – he knew that the USSR could not continue as it had for the previous nearly seven decades.

Yes he intended it to survive. *Perestroika* – reconstruction – was inescapable. But the manner of reconstruction was to prove indefinable. It was to involve devolution, yes, and a wider measure of consent; it was also to admit *glasnost* – 'openness' – which is to say the transparency of authority and a (relative) freedom of popular expression. But the combination of those two forces were not envisaged as being incompatible with the centralised *imperium* of Moscow, political and economic.

The people of the Soviet Union knew differently, albeit instinctively. Gorbachev's placeman in Almaty, Gennady Kolbin, was appointed to introduce the new liberality: his regime was born in the teeth of mass, mid-winter demonstrations in the capital, on December 16, 1986, which provoked a characteristically Soviet-style response. Many scores of those prominent in the essentially spontaneous popular protest in Brezhnev Square (as the plaza overlooked by the Central Committee's building was

known) were arrested; several (to this day the number is imprecise) were made to disappear, two were killed on the streets and some two hundred injured by snow shovels and truncheons wielded by those in uniform. Dozens were imprisoned, and some two thousand may have been otherwise punished or dismissed from their jobs.

But the seeds of a specifically Kazakh self-determination and democracy had been sown. And in the summer of 1989, the 49-

Glasnost brought free speech and free speech brought popular protest at Semey against Russian nuclear testing – protest voiced in this picture by the influential journalist Heinrich Borovik.

year-old chairman of the Council of Ministers of the Kazakh Soviet Republic, Nursultan Nazarbayev, took over the top job – as Party leader.

Soon enough (by April 1990) the leaders of all the constituent Republics had become their countries' nominal Presidents. Yet the momentum was far from spent. The conversion from a centralised to a free-market economy was proving far too cumbersome and universally damaging, with rocketing prices in the shops and a dearth of staple consumer items. Already, five years to the day after Gorbachev's accession to power – on March 11, 1990 – Lithuania had announced its independence, to be followed by Latvia and Estonia, in spite of the activity of Soviet tanks and a final scattering of martyrdoms in the cause of nationhood in the streets of their capitals. The previous year, the Soviet satellites of East Germany, Poland, Hungary, Czechoslovakia and the Balkan States had abandoned their subservience to Moscow,

whether as democracies or as indigenous tyrannies. The centre was manifestly no longer holding.

In Moscow, the former Party chief of the city, Boris Yeltsin, had emerged as the overwhelmingly popular and defiant champion of a speeded-up dismantling of the economic apparatus of the State and the acquisition of democratic freedoms. Under the constitutional reforms of 1990, he had become President of Russia. Meanwhile, in September 1990, the Kazakh Parliament drafted a declaration of sovereignty, asserting the authority of its own laws over those of Moscow.

Gorbachev, as President of the Soviet Union, vacillated. A reformer at heart, he nonetheless recoiled at what he saw as impending chaos. Early in 1991 – again in March – he attempted to ban the Moscow rally called by Yeltsin. The entire apparatus of the State was now aware that jobs were at risk. That June, the Union treaty with the Republics was scheduled to be rewritten, vastly diminishing Moscow's formal authority. Gorbachev was warned of a reactionary conspiracy, but disregarded the warning. In the high summer, he took his wife Raisa on holiday at the presidential dacha at Foros, in the Crimea. It was August, 1991.

On August 17, a Saturday, Yeltsin had flown to Almaty for discussions with Nazarbayev. On Sunday, the plotters in Moscow, bent on the restoration of Soviet authority throughout Russia and the empire, made their move in secrecy and silence. In the Crimea, Gorbachev discovered that all five telephone lines at his disposal had been cut off when his chief of staff, Valery Boldin, entered his room unexpectedly to tell him that he, Gorbachev, was to sign a decree declaring a State of Emergency giving power to an Emergency Committee, headed by Gennady Yanayev, the Union's Vice-President. Gorbachev refused. He and his wife were under virtual arrest: anything could happen.

That evening, in Almaty, Nazarbayev

and Yeltsin were oblivious of these events. Yeltsin was due to return for the three-hour flight to Moscow leaving Almaty at five p.m. The flight path traversed the skies above the Soviet Army's base at Aktobe, where a special detachment had been instructed to shoot down the aircraft passing overhead at the anticipated hour of six p.m. Kazakh hospitality providentially delayed the Russian President's departure until eight p.m.; and when at last the aircraft overflew Aktobe at nine p.m., the would-be gunners

had been stood down.

At 6.30 a.m. Moscow time the next morning, the plotters announced the take-over by the 'Emergency Committee' on the grounds of Gorbachev's incapacity through 'sickness'. Back in Almaty, Nazarbayev and his wife heard the news on a radio bulletin from Moscow. Within half an hour, Nazarbayev was on the telephone to Yeltsin, who was not yet detained. The Russian said, 'I will try to go down to the White House [the site of Parliament]. We should take a stand together against this State of Emergency Committee.' Yeltsin indeed made it to the precincts of Parliament, where a vast crowd had begun to assemble. He clambered atop a tank to address them. Ex-soldiers, students, the common people from priests to pensioners, responded to his call to besiege the White House from where the plotters presumed to exercise their Union-wide authority.

That afternoon, Yanayev's group of eight

appeared on state television, claiming State of Emergency authority but manifestly nervous. That same evening Nazarbayev went on state television in Kazakhstan to denounce the *coup*.

At Yeltsin's request, he had telephoned both the Deputy Defence Minister of the Union and the head of the KGB to give his own views and those of his fellow Republican leaders whom he had already consulted by telephone – views to the effect that support for the plotters against the

Gorbachev (left) backed Nazarbayev's accession to Kazakhstan's pre-independence Presidency. But as the USSR disintegrated, Yeltsin (right) swept to power in Russia, welcoming the Kazakh leader as an equal.

people would not be accepted or indeed tolerated by the Republics.

By now, the people of Moscow were swarming the streets. The Emergency Committee curfew that night was disregarded. The military were visibly beginning to turn. By the Wednesday, Yeltsin announced that the *coup* leaders were on the run. One of them, Boris Pugo, the Union's Interior Minister, shot himself. The others were arrested. Yeltsin sent to fetch Gorbachev from the Crimea. Gorbachev, reconnected with the outside world, had already telephoned Nazarbayev, who has recalled that 'when the long awaited call came through from Foros, my joy knew no bounds. I find it difficult to reconstruct that conversation, so powerful were the emotions that I felt at that moment.' Gorbachev had asked Nazarbayev to thank the people of Kazakhstan for their loyalty to the principles of freedom and democracy and to

their lawfully elected representatives.

The Soviet leader was to remain in formal office for another sixteen weeks, but essentially powerless. By the end of August, Yeltsin had signed the decree 'suspending' the activities of the Russian Communist party. The failed *coup* had effectively overtaken the impending revision of the Union treaty.

Those ensuing weeks were filled with intense activity for Kazakhstan and its leadership in the dismantling of empire and the establishment of its own true governmental autonomy. Yet once again events – and Boris Yeltsin – were to upstage a relatively orderly process leading to sovereignty for the twelve remaining republics of the Union.

' As late as the second week of December, it was widely expected – including in Almaty – that the Union would remain as some sort of entity. Yet on December 8, arriving in Moscow, Nazarbayev was to receive a telephone call from Yeltsin, then in Belarus. 'Come over and join us,' said the Russian President, referring to himself and Leonid Kravchuk of Belarus. 'We have just created the Commonwealth of Independent States.' With characteristic impetuosity Yeltsin urged Nazarbayev to fly in and countersign a document of total devolution there and then, virtually unread. Yet key issues – the army, citizenship, and not least nuclear weapons – had been scarcely addressed.

The Nazarbayev Story

Nursultan Nazarbayev has grown into the role of President of Kazakhstan with impressive sureness of touch. He is far from infallible, but he has shown himself swift to learn from experience and to make good his own mistakes or the mistakes of those beholden to him. His is a double role, familiar to the leaders of republics everywhere. He is the chief executive of a political and administrative machine and accountable to the people, and at least theoretically removable at their will; he has to be that same people's figurehead and exemplification of their sovereignty – their inspiration and their face in the outer world. To serve as a constitutional Pharaoh is to operate a contradiction. Such a role is bound to provoke complaint and invite criticism. The President receives both: much of it is less than fair.

Moreover, his is a country which is all but brand new, still rubbing its eyes in the hard light of its own emergence into genuine sovereignty. This new-born Kazakhstan pulses with expectations from a centre which seeks to devolve the fulfilment of expectations upon the people themselves. It is a country ethnically varied, part Euro-centric part Asia-centric, and still uncertain as to its preference for the often meretricious liberties of western polity over the stabilising restrictions of Asian and indeed Islamic obediences. The still-sleeping natural treasures of the place are as much a source of restlessness and vulnerability as they are of prosperity and ease of heart.

The President was born into a family of transhumant herders in the foothills of the Tien Shan Mountains (which this book celebrates pictorially) in July 1940. It was a tough existence made triply hard by the grotesque requirements of a Marxist-Leninist ideology as interpreted by Stalin and by State quotas. His mother's greatest fear was of wolves, lest they stole a sheep

and she would be condemned to ten years in a labour camp for lack of vigilance. She tended and harvested her hectare of beet with her own hands, only to pass the entire crop to the collective for a reward of one and a half sacks of sugar from the local mill.

Young Sultan, as they knew him, got to school, drove himself hard, setting out through snow (for half the year) before five a.m. for the six-kilometre trudge and returning to feed the cattle before he did his homework. He then got himself to boarding school at Kaskelen, forty miles west of Almaty. Next he seized the chance of a job at Temirtau (near Karagandy) where, in the late 1950s, one of the biggest

At Temirtau in the 1960s, the young furnaceman Nazarbayev – seen here second from the left with team-mates in the steelworks in 1961 – rose swiftly to prominence and political authority.

steel mills in the USSR was being erected. His training took place in the Ukraine, at Dneprodzerzhinsk, where he discovered for himself the extreme privations of the industrial workforce under Soviet rule. When in 1959 the workers of Temirtau rose in mutiny at their conditions, and scores were shot down by troops and hundreds more arrested and jailed, the impressionable nineteen-year old was sharply alerted to the reality of naked State power. He worked at the blast furnace, joined the Party, became a central committee member of the Young Communist League and – biting the bullet of obeisance to the Party – became Party Secretary of the Karaganda metallurgical Kombinat.

He first met his bride-to-be, Sara, at the plant when, covered in soot and grime, he had worked for twenty-four hours non-stop following an accident at the smelter. It was a providential shaft of love. She was from a family of the Middle Juz, he of the Great Juz. Each could trace their ancestry to seven generations – trace them with old-fashioned Kazakh pride. Bringing him one step-daughter, she was to bear him two more daughters and to be a life-long strength and source of sound judgement. The eldest was to prove thrusting and influential – as a figure of the media; but their father was no Lear. When in 2001 one son-in-law was to fly too high, father

in-law famously clipped his wings.

At Karagandy he was on the up, ambitious, disciplined, trustworthy, intelligent and personable. Step by step he was entering public life. In 1967 he graduated from the Karaganda Polytechnic; in 1972, he was Party leader of Kazakhstan Magnitka. Let us note that because of Nikita Khrushchev's Virgin Lands scheme (launched in 1953), the Politburo and the Kremlin took detailed notice of Soviet administration in Kazakhstan, designated as the breadbasket of the Union. Khrushchev's *protégé* Leonid Brezhnev was made Party Secretary – the top role in Kazakhstan – in 1955; and when he, Brezhnev, took over the first Secretaryship of the USSR, he became aware of the capabilities of the young Party worker in Temirtau, as indeed did Mikhail Suslov, the Soviet Union's leading ideologue.

In 1976, Nazarbayev became a member of Karaganda Oblast's Party Committee; in 1979, member and Secretary of the Kazakh Communist Party; in 1980 Secretary of the Central Committee of the Kazakh Communist Party; in 1984, Chairman of the Council of Ministers and thus, effectively, Prime Minister at 44, of Kazakhstan under Kunaev's leadership. This next year, Mikhail Gorbachev took over in Moscow. He liked Nazarbayev and

> *He is widely recognised as a Kazakh patriot, as a symbol of national unity, and as a fierce guardian of the country's looming prosperity.*

backed him. It was widely believed that, while he could still entertain hopes of the survival of the USSR, he envisaged a role for the young Kazakh leader as his deputy.

It was a remarkable trajectory. Nazarbayev by now had first-hand experience not only of the production and distribution of the products of industry, but also of the flaws and deceptions of the system. He was aware of the dead hand of Moscow's centralising authority and most likely influenced Gorbachev on the imperative of devolution. In 1992, he had submitted a doctoral thesis to the Russian Academy of Management on the strategy of resource saving and the development of market relations.

Thus, when his time came for real power in 1991, he was wholly familiar with the machinery of government as it was, and perceptive as to how it might be reformed.

Yet the mindset of the entire apparatus needed to change, and needed time to change. 'Post-Soviet Mentality' was a condition of inertia, of awaiting direction from on high, of an absence of initiative and lateral thinking and commercial imagination, which was vividly evident to foreigners experienced in commerce and economics entering the newly-opened corridors of Kazakhstan's bureaucracy and supposedly liberated economy. Political and economic freedom was a wholly novel reality for both President and people. Yet how to exploit such golden freedoms?

A measure of popular disillusion was inevitable after Kazakhstan acquired independence in 1991. The early setbacks are discussed elsewhere in this book. Yet after the President's candidacy in 1991, supported by 98.7 per cent of those voting, the referendum to approve the constitutional changes of 1995 extending his term of office and strengthening Presidential powers was again substantially approved by the electorate. Nearly four years later, in January 1999, his re-election was massively endorsed by the vote. The people as a whole are unquestionably glad to have him.

He is widely recognised as a Kazakh patriot: whatever his own ambitions, he is known to have the interests of the country at heart. He is seen as wise in the handling of the country's highly significant ethnic minorities (notably the Russian element) and to be a symbol of national unity. He is a fierce guardian of the potential for prosperity offered by the country's vast hydrocarbon reserves.

Internationally, he is respected for his decisive rejection of what might have seemed a nuclear option, and as a force for Central Asian stability. He is known as a daring bargainer – not to say a brinkman – for the best possible deal from the multi-national commercial interests with which he must work to exploit his country's wealth and build its future.

Nazarbayev is as yet a stranger to the caprice of the democratic whim. He has signed up Kazakhstan to the democratic and humanitarian premises of the European community. He is still unpractised at the skills and style of handling dissent in an open society, and perhaps supposes that his Kazakhstan, albeit coming of age, has not yet attained to the political maturity of brooking an active and organised opposition, as among the western democracies with their vaunted electoral choices and their supposed transparency of government. He knows there is 'jam tomorrow' in Kazakhstan. He will not want to pass on his power to others before

Kazakhstan's First Lady, Sara Aplysovna, pictured with her husband and President in 1996, has vigorously championed the rights and health of children. She is the mother of three daughters. The couple are now grandparents of a clutch of small children.

his people have experienced in their homes and lives the benefits of his economic strategy and he has felt the brush of a genuine kiss of popular gratitude. His constitutional term as President is due to end by 2006.

The Soviet Legacy

It is helpful to distinguish between the Soviet experience in Kazakhstan and the Soviet legacy. The experience entailed suffering on an appalling scale, most of it unnecessary even in terms of Marxist-Leninism's own idealistic purposes, and the consequence of crass implementation, wilful indifference to the effect on people, and institutional cruelty. Millions gratuitously died, every death a personal tragedy, millions more were subjected to fundamental upheaval – uprooted, dispersed or imprisoned. In the years following the later 1920s an entire culture was virtually obliterated, by the forcible destruction of a pattern of life of immemorial antiquity, by the dismantling of structures of kinship, by official scorn and denial of its worth, and by the falsification of history. The Islamic religion which in critical ways reinforced and deepened that culture, and bore its own truths, was suppressed to the point of near extinction; a parallel elimination was meted upon the Christian – substantially Russian Orthodox – element of the population. For at least two generations, traditional culture and religion alike were cast as causes of shame: as 'backwardness' and 'superstition'. Where that which purported to be the cultural inheritance was at length permitted to reappear, it could only be a pastiche of its former reality – decorative, dumbed-down, folkloric, voyeuristic – essentially nullifying the validity of whatever it might purport to symbolize: a nomadism, and all of its crafts and arts, and a spiritual reading of existence.

Lenin's paradise did not materialise for these 1950s toddlers.

Such was seven decades of Soviet existence in Kazakhstan. Yet it has to be said that in the same period – say, between 1920-90 – across the face of the earth, and virtually irrespective of the political regime, the nomadic way of life came close to extinction, peasant craft and genuine folk art – decorative, implemental, bardic, musical – had declined, and religious observance had widely retreated. Whatever Kazakhstan was, prior to the onset of Leninism, was in any case destined for radical change as to the shape and practice of society, and in personal and collective aspirations. For Kazakhstan to have remained more or less as it was would have left it a backwater. At the start of the period, industrial activity was negligible – a few mines, a scattering of cultivated crops, some fishing in the Caspian, the Aral, and Balkash. In terms of measurable output, by the date of its Independence (1991),

Kazakhstan's product had increased 900 times. Its industries may have been monolithic and outworn, but they were there. So were their Russian markets. However, 'sedentarised' and urbanised, and however wastefully and restrictively, every employable man and many women had a job. They also had had a solid education within Marxist limitations. At the start of the period, some seven per cent of the Kazakh population could read and write – read, that is, mostly in Kazakh, and write mostly in Arabic. By the end of it, 95 per cent of Kazakhs were literate, albeit most of them in the Russian language and the Cyrillic script. Women occupied a range of roles unmatched in the non-Soviet Islamicised world, not excluding Turkey or Bangladesh.

There was a factor of change constituting the legacy of Kazakhstan's sovietization more fundamental still – a factor bearing on the very existence of the Republic itself. Under the Tsars, that great swathe of colonisation of central Asian 'Turkestan' was being subjected to a progressive Russification not only in the institutions of its governance but in human settlement. Under Sovietization, colonisation by Russian settlement indeed continued. But the Leninist theory of recognisable nationalities – of collective man's inherited territorial and ethnic allegiance – bore upon the Soviet imperial structures. Kazakhstan was from the start a Soviet in its own right, and nominally and still perceptibly a Kazakh one. Albeit very soon the Kazakhs becoming a minority in their territory, that territory's *raison d'être*, under Communism, was as a Kazakh place, attaining for the first time its distinction from the catch-all term Kyrgyz. Marxist-Leninism presumed, of course, the eventual withering away of national distinctions in a synthetic global brotherhood (run from Moscow). The trick that history was to pull, of course, that December of 1991, was a sudden withering away of the imperial centre. What was left was a precisely definable Kazakhstan over which, true to the Leninist premise, ethnic Kazakhs were in charge. And they were Kazakhs of capability, moderation, foresight and patriotism.

The experiential cost of Kazakhstan's emergence into viable independent statehood had been terrible – proportionately, it might be argued, as terrible as Israel's. But it had the legacy of Marxist-Leninist tyranny to which to attribute the fact of that viable independent statehood.

The Environmental Legacy

The incipient yearnings for greater self-expression amongst the Kazakh population were already evident in the Almaty demonstration of December 1986. However it may have taken just two particularly powerful nuclear explosions on the Semei testing grounds in late 1988 to galvanise people into action. On 28 February 1989 the Nevada-Semei Anti-Nuclear Movement was founded by Kazakh poet and writer, Oljas Suleimenov (born 1936) who for some years had been a leading advocate of improved civil rights. This was in direct response to a particularly insensitive – not to say wicked – regime of testing. The Movement sought to articulate ordinary people's resentment at the continuing use of Kazakhstan for nuclear testing. It was remarkably effective, first in mobilising over one million signatures and then in bringing about the closure of the testing grounds in October 1989.

Nuclear testing was but one aspect of the Soviet environmental legacy. There were many others. Much of the environmental damage in Kazakhstan was not caused deliberately. The general attitude amongst Soviet planners coming from the relatively cramped cities of European Russia appears to have been that, here in Kazakhstan, space was simply boundless. So too was Nature's propensity to absorb pollution. Kazakhstan had so much open space and so few people that it could take whatever Russia threw at it. Many skilled engineers were not aware of the environmental impact of industrial processes. They had not been taught this at the Institutes of Metallurgy.

The draining of the Aral Sea was, of course, a deliberate act. However it was not done with malice aforethought. It was done for macro-economic reasons. The welfare and product of millions of cotton farmers using irrigation water upstream was put above those of a few thousand fishermen on the Aral Sea. It was as simple as that.

However when the Soviet Union collapsed at the end of 1991 so did this system of exchange --- and very abruptly. A good example of this is the railway wagons factory at Kazalinsk in Kyzylorda. It employed 5,000 workers and exported railway wagons all over the Soviet Union. It brought wood from Latvia and steel from Ukraine.

It always paid in railways wagons. A factory producing rubber tyres in Saran in Karagandy Oblast, and employing 8,000 people, was in much the same position.

Despite Kazakhstan's pre-Independence isolation, the international community was not entirely unaware of or unconcerned by what was taking place in the newly independent Kazakhstan. Just over a year after Independence in 1993 the United Nations Development Programme (UNDP) established its offices in Almaty. Some of UNDP's tasks were to mobilise international support for a humanitarian aid programme for the Aral Sea region and for environmental planning support for the Semei nuclear site. UNDP was followed by the World Bank, the Asian Development Bank, the European Bank for Reconstruction and Development (EBRD), the European Union and others. The Turkish Government became a prominent player on the diplomatic scene because of the strong linguistic and cultural ties between Kazakhstan and Turkey. Indeed Turkish investors in business, construction and supermarkets are some of the most visible throughout Kazakhstan today.

It will take many years to assess properly the impact of foreign aid on Kazakhstan after Independence. However it is safe to say that, so far, the United Nations has done much to raise awareness of environmental issues and of participatory democracy amongst ordinary citizens.

The World Bank has concentrated on privatisation, fiscal reform and social protection, i.e. building up the national system of pensions. However the Bank has been financing one project involving the rehabilitation of the Aral Sea where a dam is being constructed between the northern and southern parts of the Sea in order to stabilise the inflow of water. In its first nine years of operation in Kazakhstan, the Bank was to lend Kazakhstan over 1.3 billion dollars. The European Bank for Reconstruction and Development has financed the oil and gas sector, transport and industry. Its lending scheme to small and medium scale businesses is said to have been outstandingly successful and includes over 30,000 loans totalling 200 million dollars to small businesses through locals banks. Kazakhstan has not found it difficult to find foreign donors or investors. Because of its great revenue potential from the petroleum sector the country has had to develop a negotiating skill rarely called upon in newly independent nations.

Despite the verdict of time, Lenin in granite still dominates Karagandy's skyline.

Independence

Independence was met with euphoria amongst Kazakh people. The streets changed their names from Lenin, Soviet, October Revolution and Communism to legendary names of Kazakh batyrs, khans (like Abylai and Kenisary), the famous judges of three Juzes: Tole, Aiteke, and Kazybek, and prominent Kazakh leaders, writers and artists. The cities and settlements got back their original names. Nauryz, the celebration of Kazakh New Year, became an official holiday. Several newspapers in Kazakh began to appear.

The new-born Kazakhstan was swift to conjure its symbols of statehood – flag, emblem and hymn. In September 1992 the first World Kurultai (Congress) of Kazakhs took place in Almaty. The ethnic Kazakhs from other countries (Oralmans) who left the country during the revolution or Stalin's purges started to return to Kazakhstan – by 2001 more than 215,000 of them.

The nation's security and international recognition were the main priorities of sovereign Kazakhstan. International prestige gained by its closing of the Semipalatinsk nuclear base in August 1991 resulted in all official nuclear countries providing security guarantees to

The snow leopard, accorded its Scythian wings, has come to be Kazakhstan's symbol of power, in its sparkling new capital of Astana.

Kazakhstan. President Nazarbayev devoted much time to neighbourly relations and inter-ethnic solidarity. The balance between free-for-all democracy and security was solved in favour of security, although the basic democratic principles and safeguards were introduced by the new Constitution without delay. The first year of independence was marked by Kazakhstan's entry into the UN, OSCE, IMF, the World Bank and OECD, and to the signing of security agreements within

the CIS, Europe and Asia.

During the first phase from December 1991 to November 1993 Kazakhstan depended on Moscow's decisions. The Government had little power to influence macroeconomic policy: money was issued in Moscow. The inflation rate at the end of 1992 was 3060 per cent. Exports were controlled by the government monopoly. Most commercial transactions were done by barter and mainly with CIS countries. During 1990-94 the industrial output fell

The President of young Kazakhstan moved swiftly to impress the fledgling Republic on the world's consciousness with visits to the world's established figures of the early 1990s – President Clinton of the US (left), and the author of 'Thatcherism' and the gospel of the free market, Margaret Thatcher of Britain (right).

Nazarbayev makes his vow before the flag as he takes office as President.

128 per cent in 1996. Foreign commerce was liberalised. Kazakhstan was emerging as an international trader. (Inflation today is negligible.)

The scale of privatisation can be grasped from the fact that in the early '90s almost all production was created by state enterprises, while by the end of 2001, 74.4 per cent of GDP was produced in the private sector – 99.2 per cent in agriculture, 84.9 per cent in industry, 40.3 per cent in construction and 96.5 per cent in services.

By 1996 and 1997 economic growth was reasserting itself. Then, the Asian and Russian crisis caused a fall in oil and mineral prices and, therefore, a drop in production in Kazakhstan in 1998. The country was swift to overcome difficulties using market tools: devaluation of the tenge, regulation of money supply, increase of interest rate and monetary intervention. Every cloud has a silver lining: as result a number of improved programme documents were adopted, and institutional reform was deepened. The significance of gold and of foreign currency reserves was asserted.

Meanwhile, Kazakhstan was pioneering pension reform by introducing accumulation and investment functions for pension funds, and stimulating the private

by half, transportation by two thirds, and wage and pension arrears became grave. There was a real threat of hunger and freezing. Then in November 1993 the national currency – the *tenge* – was introduced. The liberalisation of the economy had started, the state reduced its role as a manager of enterprises, opened the country for foreign investment, and introduced stock exchanges.

In 1993-95, untrammeled democratic activity and economic reform were at odds.

The legislative bodies were dissolved twice as a result of inability to provide for economic reform. Using emergency powers granted him upon the dissolution of the Parliament, Nazarbayev reappointed Prime Minister Kazhegeldin who triggered privatisation, developing of tax and custom, banking and budgeting regulation. In 1995 more than 140 Presidential decrees (valid laws) were issued to provide for the market economy. The tough anti-inflation policy resulted in decreasing inflation by

*As pictured **left** with the his neighbouring Central Asian Presidents, Nazarbayev insists upon regular consultations. Meanwhile, in the eyes of President Putin of Russia, with whom he shares a ski-lift (**right**), Nazarbayev is outstandingly the foremost figure in the region.*

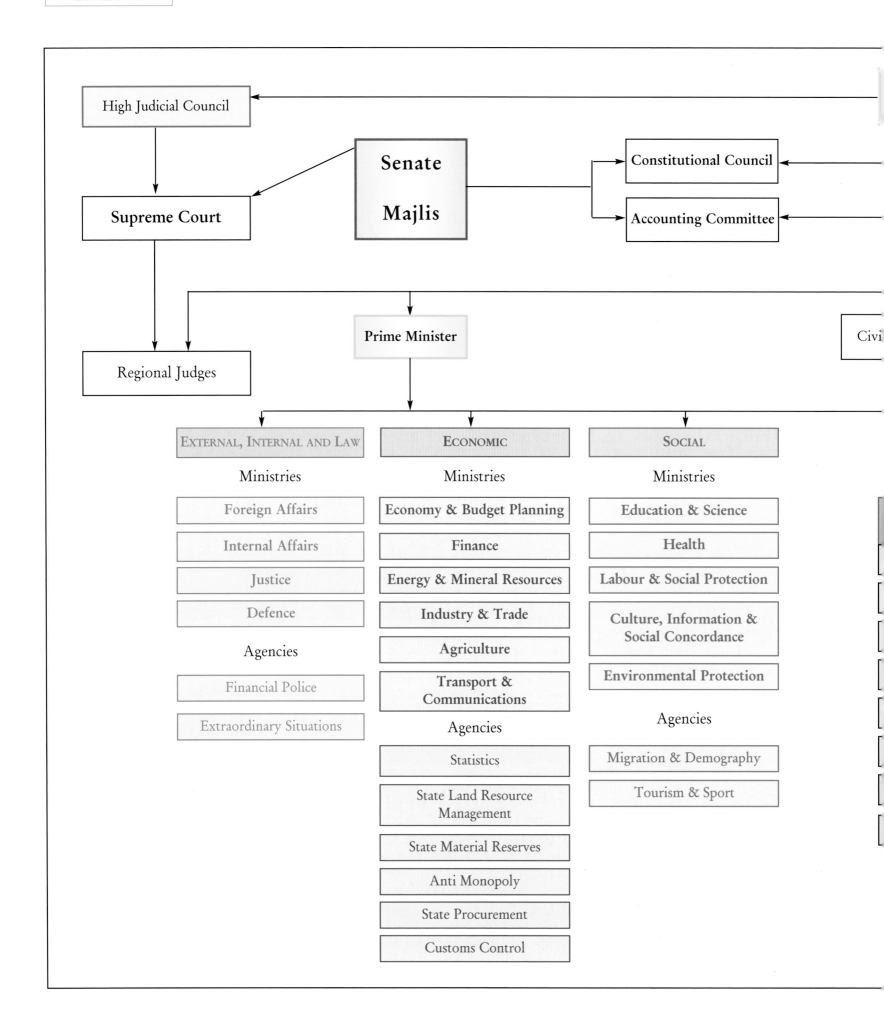

High Judicial Council

Supreme Court

Senate

Majlis

Constitutional Council

Accounting Committee

Prime Minister

Regional Judges

Civi

EXTERNAL, INTERNAL AND LAW

ECONOMIC

SOCIAL

Ministries

Foreign Affairs

Internal Affairs

Justice

Defence

Agencies

Financial Police

Extraordinary Situations

Ministries

Economy & Budget Planning

Finance

Energy & Mineral Resources

Industry & Trade

Agriculture

Transport & Communications

Agencies

Statistics

State Land Resource Management

State Material Reserves

Anti Monopoly

State Procurement

Customs Control

Ministries

Education & Science

Health

Labour & Social Protection

Culture, Information & Social Concordance

Environmental Protection

Agencies

Migration & Demography

Tourism & Sport

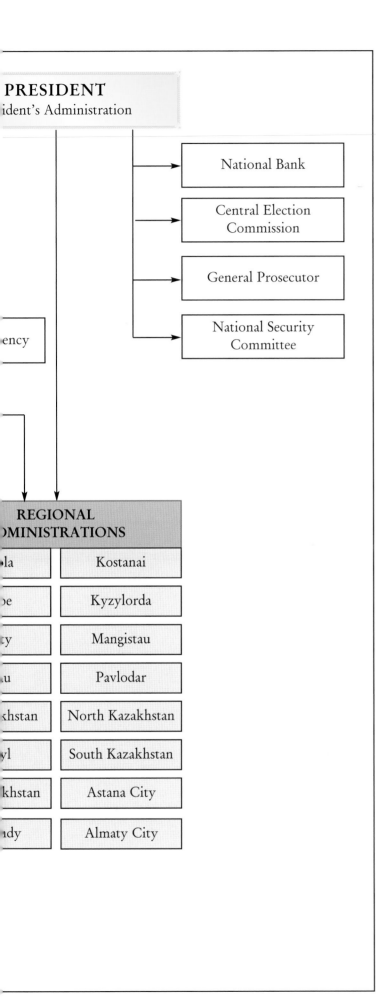

PRESIDENT
ident's Administration

National Bank

Central Election Commission

General Prosecutor

National Security Committee

ency

REGIONAL DMINISTRATIONS

·la	Kostanai
be	Kyzylorda
ty	Mangistau
.u	Pavlodar
khstan	North Kazakhstan
yl	South Kazakhstan
khstan	Astana City
idy	Almaty City

sector to enter education and healthcare sectors. Stimulated likewise were privatisation in housing and business, and the banking and insurance system. Macroeconomic stability and improved financial regulation facilitated cuts in the interest rate and, therefore, a dramatic growth of the long-term loans. Introduction of the Deposit Insurance Fund and amendments in bank secrecy regulation resulted in doubling the increase of bank deposits.

In September 2002 Kazakhstan, first amongst CIS countries, was ranked by Moody's Investors' Services at Baa3 by bonds, at Ba1 by foreign, and Baa1 by national currency deposits. All ratings have a stable forecasting. That meant low risks and widening investment. The National Fund was launched to protect the Kazakhstani economy from the global price volatility. The Kazakhstani Development Bank sought to expand long-term investment, and to motivate domestic production.

The number of small enterprises grew dramatically during the first years of independence and today the share of small business in GDP is 17 per cent. Kazakhstan has taken the lead in reforming the administrative sector. For example, in 1997 the number of government bodies controlling business activity was reduced from 47 to 25.

By 2000, economic growth had risen to 9.8 per cent, and in 2001 to 13.5 percent, while foreign direct investment in the country reached $4.5 billion. The number of definable 'poor' fell from 38.3 per cent in 1997 to 28.4 percent in 2001. Per capita income is today growing annually by ten per cent. In 2000 the European Union and in 2002 the United States rated Kazakhstan as a 'market economy', the first among all so-called transition states.

The Presidential Constitution

Kazakhstan's first constitution was adopted in 1993, two years after Independence. It gave Parliament extensive powers. In 1995 Parliament and the Constitutional Court were dissolved (*see* Chapter 4, History) and the President ruled by decree until a National Referendum approved a new Constitution, which was modelled on that of France's Fifth Republic. Under this new Constitution stress is laid on Kazakhstan as a unitary state, with a presidential form of governance. The President is the ' head of the state, its highest official who defines domestic and foreign policy' and 'provides coordinated functioning of all branches of authority'.

Under the Constitution the President is not assigned any of the organs of government as such, although in practice he acts as an executive in many circumstances. He appoints the Prime Minister and the cabinet, the Chairman of the Constitutional Council, all heads of law enforcement bodies, the Chairman of the Accounting Committee, and the Chairman of the National Bank. He heads the High Judicial Council, and is overall Commander-in-Chief of the armed forces. It is he who defines the structure of the Government.

There is no total separation of powers between judiciary and executive, in that the President chairs the High Judicial Council, and appoints not only the Chairman of the Constitutional Council but all local judges in the country. His authority over the Parliament is enshrined by his right to dissolve Parliament in various circumstances (should, for instance, Parliament pass a vote of no-confidence in the Government, or following Parliament's twice refusing to approve the President's nominee for Prime Minister, or should there be a political crisis). The President appoints all regional heads

President Nazarbayev vows to uphold the Constitution.

(*akims*), to ensure that his domestic policy is implemented at the grass roots. He also appoints seven senators (out of a total of 47) for the full parliamentary term (of six years), and the Chairman of the Election Commission.

At the first general election on 1 December 1991 the President was elected to remain in power until 1996. Later by the Republican Referendum of April 1995 (and 91 per cent of the votes) his term was extended to run until 1 December 2000; then, in January 1999, he was elected for another seven years, by 80 per cent of the votes. According to the 1995 Constitution

the President has a right to serve two terms in succession.

The Executive

The President functions by issuing decrees, defining priorities and policies, appointing all key figures and guiding them, and directing the country's management in the terms provided him as Chief Executive. The President's administration serves as a policy maker and watchdog of the Government operation including regional administrations and, to some extent, of the judiciary and legislature.

Fifteen bodies report directly to the President, including the General Prosecutor, the State Election Commission, the National Security Committee, the Accounting Committee, and the Civil Service Agency. Several advisory bodies are contained within the Presidential office, including the quite powerful Security Council, the Anti-corruption Commission, and the Supervisory Council of State Mass Media.

The Government as headed by the Prime Minister handles day-to-day administration of the country's affairs. It consists of the Prime Minister, four Vice

Prime Ministers, departmental Ministers, the Head of the Prime Minister's Chancellery, and the chairmen of the agencies. Unlike European countries, members of the Cabinet are appointed by the President from outside the elected parliamentary chambers. There are fifteen ministries, with thirty-three committees reporting to them, and ten agencies.

Legislature

The right to initiate bills belongs to Members of Parliament, and particularly to members of the Majlis. The President has a right to prioritise bills and to insist upon Parliament debating a bill within a month. Alternatively the President may issue a decree to stand in place of a piece of legislation until it had been endorsed by Parliament.

Parliament consists of two houses: the Majlis or lower house, and the Senate or upper house. The Majlis is a popularly elected body. Sixty-seven members of the Majlis are directly elected for five-year terms from single-member constituencies, with an additional ten members from political parties selected on the basis of proportional representation. The Senate is partly appointed and partly elected indirectly. Forty senators are indirectly elected by local legislators and seven are appointed by the President. Senators serve six-year terms, with half of the Senate facing re-election or re-appointment every three years.

The Parliament enacts laws, appoints and dismisses Supreme Court judges and endorses certain appointments; it approves the Government Programme and the National budget, receives the report by the Accounting Committee on budget implementation, and can raise questions about this report. The budget, however, is prepared solely by the executive. Parliament makes decisions on State borrowing, international agreements, and the amnesty of offenders. The Senate can withdraw

Parliament as a building rises higher than the President's headquarters as both fine structures overlook Republic Square *(above)* in the heart of Astana, but their respective authority is a matter of checks and balances. *Below*, the President presents his government's legislative programme to Parliament.

immunity of the General Prosecutor and Supreme Court Judges. Majlis has a right to bring a charge against the President.

Parliament appoints four delegates to the Accounting Committee (two from each House). It may appeal to the President to dismiss a member of the Government. The President, Prime Minister, National Bank Chairman, General Prosecutor and the National Security Committee Chairman have a right to attend any Parliamentary session.

legitimacy of elections of the President and Parliament, and of referenda. The Council officially interprets the Constitution and reviews draft laws in the context of their compliance with the Constitution.

The Chairman of the Constitutional Council is appointed by the President. The 1995 Constitution adopted a new procedure for appointment of judges. The Chairman, board chairmen and judges of the Supreme Court are recommended to

Council. The system has been changing from the Chairmen of the Collegiums being responsible for assigning individual cases to this or that judge, to automatic distribution of cases. The lower (district) court judges are also appointed by the President, following recommendations from the Ministry of Justice which are in turn based on the Qualifications Collegium of Justice.

All legal cases are first heard before district courts. Ninety per cent of civil and

The structure of precedence is as follows:

The Constitution; Laws amending the Constitution; Constitutional Laws and Presidential Edicts having the force of a constitutional law; Codes; Laws and Presidential Edicts having the force of law; Presidential Edicts; Parliamentary Decrees; Government Decrees; Ministerial Orders; Decrees of State Committees; Orders and Decrees of other central Government organs; Decisions of *maslikhats* (local legislatures); *akims'* decrees and decisions.

Judiciary

The judicial system is represented by the Supreme Court and local courts. By the Constitution of 1995, the Constitutional Council is not a part of the judiciary, although it solves disputes on the

the President by the High Judicial Council, nominated by the President, and appointed by the Senate. Chairmen and judges of regional courts are appointed by the President according to the recommendations of the High Judicial

The Supreme Court (above) and in session (above, right) is aptly guarded by the great 18th century Biys in bronze. The poster (right) exhorts the citizen to fulfil his national duty as a loyal taxpayer.

criminal cases are settled by such one-man courts. Because of the growing number of commercial disputes, specialised economic courts have been introduced in all oblasts since 2002. Courts dealing with civil, public order and employment issues are being introduced, with juvenile courts anticipated. More substantial cases are heard by regional courts. 'Supervisory collegiums' have the power to review both civil and criminal cases. These collegiums can serve as courts of the first instance, depending upon their jurisdiction, or as courts of appeal.

The Supreme Court is the highest judicial body for civil and criminal cases. The Plenary Supreme Court reviews the findings of the lower Court in line with standard judicial practice. As a rule the Supreme Court acts as a court of appeal, although in certain instances it too can operate as a trial court.

The independence of judiciary was enhanced by the transfer of the administrative concerns from Ministry of Justice to the Judicial Administration Committee of the Supreme Court, and by improved financing of the judicial system. Since the year 2000 the Supreme Court submitted its indents for funds direct to the Ministry of Finance. At the same time, the procedure of recruiting and selection of judges became standardised and more

Specialisation is a central policy in the defence of Kazakhstan, which today looks beyond Russia, to NATO countries, including Britain, for some equipment and specialist training of its forces.

by the Atyrau local authority's penalty for 'environmental hazards', that 'there is law and justice in Kazakhstan... We are satisfied with the outcome of a trial that lasted for a whole year.' The finding of the Court resulted in a reduction of the penalty from $71 million to $7.1 million.

Defence

Statistics of Kazakhstan's armed forces are a state secret. The country is, however, protected by a substantial, well equipped and trained army, an airforce using mostly

transparent. The number of officials who could influence court decisions – officials from the Ministry of Justice, and the Procuracy, and the Office of President – was sharply reduced. The quality of justice has benefited.

Significantly, in April 2002, the Supreme Court ruled in favour of a

branch of commercial company on all significant issues in a case arising from a $29 million tax demand by the Ministry of State Revenue. This was a sign of the genuine independence of the judiciary from the executive. Another case – in March 2003 – convinced a multi-national oil TengizChevroil company, confronted

Russian-built combat aircraft and attack helicopters, and naval vessels, including minesweepers, on the Caspian Sea. The Republic has no nuclear weapons or nuclear ambitions. The President is, *ex officio*, Commander-in-Chief. In 1992, he established the Republican Guard, beholden directly to himself.

Chapter 5

In Kazakhstan today it may sometimes be not so much a matter of 'Stop the bus, I want to get off,' as 'Stop the world, I want to get off.' For the scene is beginning to change almost breathlessly, with accelerating urbanisation, widening horizons, the consumerist appetite. Many of the active and ambitious are filling their waking hours with more than one job, and throwing in a further educational course as well, to improve a skill or add a fresh qualification. There is a vibrancy in the air, a 'can-do' mood, and when a little gap for leisure opens up, it is seized upon with gusto – not least for sport.

The Social Scene

While the family car may belong to the next phase of social evolution, the ubiquitous bus is unquestionably a boon today.

Two particular features of life in Soviet Kazakhstan before 1991 made it difficult to have fun. Firstly life was often heavily regimented by employers, by local government, and by the State. People did what they were told and took what was on offer. This made for security, but not for *élan*, for *joie de vivre*. And security, in the natural state of affairs, is not always what young people make their priority. Secondly there was a culture of secrecy. It was wise to watch what you said, what music you listened to and which celebrities you admired. Because of this, the young and indeed the older generation too, often felt excluded from the mainstream of world culture.

With Independence came a sea-change. The younger generation in Kazakhstan today have little conception or understanding of the very real and pervasive restrictions which bore down on their elders even as recently as the 1980s.

Relishing the joy of life can often mean, above all, simply having freedom of opportunity. Freedom to travel, for instance. People in Kazakhstan who can afford it now travel overseas on holiday to Europe, to America, to South-East Asia or the Middle East. It also means freedom to communicate. Internet cafés all over Kazakhstan allow people to communicate with new friends across the globe, to start new friendships, to develop new hobbies.

Having fun also means having the freedom to import new ideas and pastimes, and discover what preoccupies the rest of mankind.

Not so long ago, leisure was highly organised, often with the aim of producing 'model' citizens. It was grindingly moralistic and depressingly uplifting. Now people are free to look for fun the way they fancy it, and find out for themselves what works for them and what does not.

Western-originating and Russian music and rock bands are widely popular. Open-air rock concerts attract thousands of young on Saturday nights. Night clubs and discos have sprung up in all the main towns. Bowling is a popular pastime. Shopping (or window-shopping) in the spanking new malls of Almaty or Astana is something everyone takes pleasure in, seeding aspirations, the urge to get ahead. And those of more serious bent fill the concert halls where a new generation of classical and traditional musicians are honing their talent.

Independent Kazakhstan has let the genie out: a zest for life.

*Astana's Ishym river (**above**), an ice playground in winter, is just right for a Sunday dip in summer. **Below**, Saturday night and it's good to be alive – for sure enough there will be a party to attend or a rock concert for the young in the city's main square.*

Speaking Freely

The law of July 23 1999 guaranteed freedom of expression. Further, it guaranteed equal opportunities between state-owned operations and for those independently owned. In broadcasting, the transmission on local channels of material originating from abroad was limited to 20 per cent of airtime, the changes made to prevent excessive reliance on foreign – particularly, Russian – television and radio programmes, and news coverage. The law also limited the number of foreign shareholders in Kazakhstan's media enterprises, so as to preserve a measure of loyalty to the country. Since, however, Kazakhstan is a signatory of several international agreements and organisations – OSCE (the Organisation for Security and Co-operation in Europe) in particular – international law is the final arbiter.

Most of the media in Kazakhstan is privately owned and managed. In common with the rest of the CIS, the Russian language is used more than any other. Thirty-five per cent of all mass media uses Russian only; 35 per cent use both Kazakh and Russian and 18 per cent uses exclusively the Kazakh language.

The heritage of Kazakh-only newspapers goes back to 1888, although such publications were often closed down for political reasons. Approximately 12 per

A vast range of publications is on offer for the Kazakh who seeks to keep up with the times. **Above**, *Almaty's citizens gather to celebrate beneath the fearsome war memorial in Panfilov Park, named after the 28 heroes who died to stem the advance of German tanks closing on Moscow in 1941.*

cent of the media serves the other ethnic minorities in their own languages.

The Kazakh Government insists on television and radio stations using Kazakh in over half of their broadcasting time, but no such obligations apply to print or electronic mass media.

Many of the minority peoples – Tatars, Ukrainians, Uighurs, Germans and the others – have their own media. Special attention given to English, as the language of international communication, has led to

Motherhood

A surging birth rate among the Kazakhs has given the country, statistically, one of the youngest populations in the world. Big families reflect the source of looming prosperity. This in turn has stimulated the provision of services and facilities for the young – crêches, kindergartens, playgrounds, and maternity and medical services.

The pictures illustrate the scene with shots of a young mother from Taraz (left), a horse-drawn buggy in Shymkent (centre), and (far right) a life-size toy buggy with its real-life young passenger in an Astana amusement arcade for the very young.

Womanhood's widening horizons

The women of old Kazakhstan used to say that the men did the talking and the hunting and the herding of the flocks and the women did the work. In the Kazakhstan of today women are most emphatically contributors to the work ethic of the country, yet with ever more opportunities open to them as education spreads and deepens.

The pictures here give a taste of the scope – from stallholders in Shymkent's market (left), an Aktau fishwife, and a busy waitress, to a paediatrician, an optician and a young wife whose family income has brought her a fur coat of environmentally respectable nylon (far right).

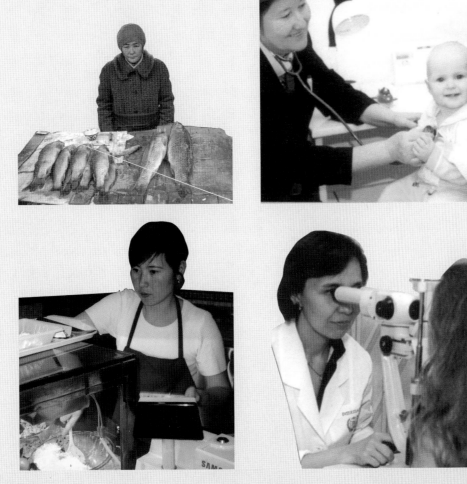

*In a world of new horizons, some like the Karagandy student of English and Italian (**left**) snap up their opportunities. Meanwhile the young teenagers **below** weigh their options amid the lures of globalised consumerism.*

the appearance of newspapers, magazines, TV and radio channels using English alongside Russian and Kazakh. The *Almaty Herald* publishes weekly.

News agencies are the sources of much information for television and radio channels. Most newspapers publish once a week. The most important State-owned paper *Kazakstan Pravda* and a handful of privately-owned journals – *Time, Express K, Egemen Kazakstan* publish either daily or several days a week. Newspapers in English are on sale only in the biggest towns or by subscription.

The principal broadcasting channels transmit throughout Kazakhstan. There are the State channels Kazakhstan and Habar, with its entertainment offshoot El Arna; private channels include KTK and NTK. The major Russian channel ORT is represented in Kazakhstan by its Kazakh subsidiary Eurasia. All nationwide channels are based in Almaty.

Every town has its local television channel. Almaty offers a wide choice. Kazakh Radio is the only channel to carry 'official' information. The rest are music channels.

Kazakh Fashion

Kazakhstan's new bourgeoisie can afford it. Brand names like Dior, Bzioni Kiton, Givenchy or Paul Zileri are a common thing among certain circles of the Kazakh scene nowadays. Other international companies, a little less up-market (such as Clarks, DKNY and Kappa) also stimulate a fashion sense, sponsoring all sorts of

competitions – like Miss Model of Kazakhstan – and exhibitions, like MODA Kazakhstan.

International shows are bringing Kazakh *haute couture* to the world. The Kazakh Fashion House 'OXI' was invited to participate in the *Haute Couture* Week in Rome in July 2003, the very first such invitation for a country of the CIS. The main device of the national couturiers is the apt use of traditional materials like fur and ancient Kazakh metal motifs – as ancient as the Sak period – of which examples are shown here. Some of the fashion houses such as Kuralai or Makpal are thoroughly committed to an identifiably Kazakh range of ideas in clothing. The Italian designer Lorenzo Riva has acclaimed those Kazakhstan themes as fitting well the European industry.

Kazakh women of today are much more interested in how they look than their mothers or grandmothers were. The masculine, robust and sturdy woman of Soviet posters is in the past.

In the main cities one can find fitness and beauty salons. The new Kazakh woman has the same elegant look as her Western counterpart.

*Good food and good wages are increasingly the norm in Kazakhstani industry as recovery gathers pace – particularly in the oil and gas sector of the West of the country (as **right** at Atyrau) on the Caspian.*

*For most, living is best done in a cosy flat (**below**).*

The Urban Transformation

As we have seen (in Chapter 3) the twentieth century changed Kazakhstan radically from a society which was still foundationally a pastoral and nomadic community to one of permanent settlement and widespread and usually rather gruesome industrialisation.

The brief period since the coming of independence at the end of 1991 has heralded, or indeed already brought about, a further transformation, perhaps no less fundamental although not so outwardly manifest – a transformation engendered by a free market, an enterprise economy superseding a ruthlessly monolithic command economy. And again, as we have seen, it has engendered, and still engenders, its hardships, although nothing like on the scale of the earlier transformation.

The present change, in its way no less

*While mastery of the computer is an essential skill in the power station (**right**) and in countless other modern professions, the meeting of true minds (**below**) is better done by intellectual debate between friends in a Shymkent street.*

***Below**, flats soar high over Karagandy's main avenue.*

sudden in its impact, has two faces: what one may call the existential and the economic – or, alternatively, the self-view and the means of survival and advancement.

The existential, or self-view, re-assessment concerns the citizen's view as to his or her responsibilities, both to himself or herself and those to whom the citizen is committed by love or family tie or dutiful practice. For the first time in some 70 years, it fell to citizens to look to themselves in the first place, for their own welfare, their employment, and their progress through life and, it might be said, the health of their souls. For the 'State' was no longer there to guarantee the citizens a job, a meal ticket, or indeed an ideology. All were back in the hands, or the hearts, of the individual. And individuals found themselves at once at the untender mercy and unpredictability of the market place and a global economy which offers nobody a free lunch.

Survival – individual or familial – became at once demanding in a new way: demanding as to hard work, ingenuity, competitiveness, the securing of key qualifications, and so on. It was instantly, in its way, a tougher socio-economic environment. At the same instant, life was arguably more meaningful.

For almost simultaneously the opportunities – which for a moment seemed invisible – began to appear. Wages, even for those with significant and hard-earned qualifications in, say,

teaching and medicine, were unconscionably low; but the rewards from second jobs made survival at an acceptable standard of living possible... if at the cost of hard work, a high level of alertness and (often enough) long hours. In the later 1990s, it was not uncommon for the energetic and resourceful in the major cities to be holding onto, and holding down, not two but three jobs in any single week.

The lure of what higher rewards could buy were all around – more spacious, better

appointed apartments, a smarter wardrobe, a range of stimulating and glamorous sports, a

While the new economy left some jobless for a while, there are many now who take a second job to boost the family income.

break at a health clinic or hydro, a holiday abroad, even a motor car.

New blocks of flats were, and are still, going up at a rapid rate, many of the first wave being erected by Turkish contractors to whom Kazakhstan became synonymous with a quick buck. Corners were sometimes cut; but building quality has steadily improved and standards are now being more rigorously upheld.

For there is money about for better quality, and the new shops show it. The trumpeted if deceptive egalitarianism of economic Marxist-Leninism has been replaced by the confessed amorality of the free market and commercial opportunism, which is bringing to the smart or well-placed few of Kazakhstani society newly-gained riches, sometimes of a high order. Thus Kazakhstan has been experiencing a multiplying 'skill base', and a fresh indigenous work ethic such as is set to exploit the impending accessibility of new wealth deriving from the hydrocarbon treasures of the Caspian region and the country's other mineral resources. By 2003 standards of living – already

The pictures tell the story of changing times – fast food (US style) wrist watches (Swiss style) 'kiddies' bow ties, velvet in fashion, shopping malls, an English pub (in the heart of Astana, no less) – and a cuddly toy to be the pride and joy of a Semey toddler.

Modern flats are home for a rapidly increasing population of Kazakhs these days, as the countless tenaments and bungalows built a couple of generations ago (recalled in the picture **below**) become a thing of the past. The urban population either walks to work – perhaps along the river front in Astana (**above** and **opposite, below**) – or takes the bus or, in Almaty, the tram (**right**). Aktau's high-rise flats – the better the view the higher the price – overlook the Caspian (**opposite**), while Shymkent's artists' colony (**centre, below**) looks down on college campus fields.

respectably high in the new western towns of Atyrau, Aktau, and Uralsk – were noticeably climbing in Astana and Almaty.

Beyond the enticement and excitement of rising living standards and personal amenities – the acceptable face of 'consumerism' – and the consequent expenditure not only of money but time and energy, must be seen the opportunity for Kazakhstan's coming generation for a greater leisure and the deeper rewards of the human spirit in reflection and creativity.

Literacy is remarkably high – 99 per cent is claimed.

A little sled is useful for the downhill run to home, where a sister practises on her Kazakh kobyz.

Almost all schools are for boys and girls together.

Education

In the brief period since Independence, Kazakhstan has managed to carry out major educational reforms, despite a quite severely restricted national budget.

In the new national model for education as world-wide, a large role is allocated to pre-school training. But in the 1990s Kazakhstan's complicated economic situation, many children's educational establishments were closed down, creating significant difficulties for the first year pupils and their teachers. The general improvement in the country's economic situation since the end of the 1990s has brought positive changes. At present about 150,000 children are being taught at pre-school, making up about 15 per cent of the numbers of children of pre-school age. More than two thousand pre-school classes or groups have opened in which 82 per cent of future first year pupils receive basic preparation before entry into primary school. The process of rehabilitation continues, as does the opening of new nurseries, innovative teaching pro-grammes, the raising of qualifications of nursery school and primary school teachers, and the training of teachers, all in collaboration with UNESCO, UNICEF, 'Step by Step', and the 'Soros-Kazakhstan' Fund.

At the secondary level, between the age of six or seven to 17 or 18, there are 8,334 schools, including 108 gymnasiums, 63 lycées, and 170 private schools. Teaching is conducted in eight languages: Kazakh (3,632 schools), Russian (2,199 schools), Uzbek (82 schools), Uighur (13 schools), Tajik (three schools), Ukrainian (one school). In 2,062 of these schools, teaching is conducted in two or more languages. At the basic level compulsory subjects take up 75-80 per cent of the teaching time. The rest of the time is given for a specific national and regional sphere of study, and extra subjects chosen by the participants according to their interests.

Higher level completes secondary education, taught at secondary comprehensive schools, in evening schools, professional schools, lycées and colleges. Special subjects are on offer: physics, mathematics, humanities, aesthetics, and others.

Besides the comprehensive schools, there are 103 specialist educational establishments in which around 23,000 children with development difficulties are taught. Around 4,000 children who are unable to attend ordinary schools because of health difficulties are taught at home through a special programme.

Playgroups, with a learning bias, begin at three or four.

Innovative teaching programmes, and the raising of teaching qualifications, all in collaboration with UNESCO, UNICEF, 'Step by Step', and the 'Soros-Kazakhstan' Fund, are rehabilitating the nursery schools.

The process, begun in the middle of the 1990s, of a general reconsideration of the educational content and methods of the Republic's schools found its real embodiment in the new generation of the Kazakh textbooks.

Electronic variants of textbooks on geometry, physics, biology, the history of Kazakhstan, the Kazakh language and other subjects have been developed. At present they are having a trial period in the Republic's experimental schools.

All schools in Kazakhstan are equipped with computer classes of various modifications; the process of gradually linking all schools to the Internet has begun. Within the programme 'Internet to Schools', 1,130 schools were connected to the above network by the beginning of

An older pupil brings his friend to secondary school on his first day.

Graduating students at 18 learn the hard – or uplifting – truth about their examination results.

Specialist academies have nurtured outstanding talents, especially in music, here at the Kazakh Music Academy.

South Kazakhstan's State University bears the name of the distinguished 20th-century novelist Mukhtar Auezov.

2003, out of which more than 300 are village schools.

Elementary professional education training involves studying at professional schools for two to three years, in specialist lycées, of which the total number is 304, including 26 private schools. Around 90,000 students attend these schools. Professional education can also be implemented directly at the factory.

The training of specialists takes place in around 200 government and more than one hundred non-governmental establishments, situated in practically all regions of Kazakhstan, and also 63 colleges attached to higher education colleges. Such students number 125,000. Professional courses run for three to four years. Moves are underway for grants and credits on a competitive basis. The gradual increase in the number and variety of establishments is explained by the growth in the market sector of the economy, accompanied by the appearance of new professions – management, marketing, banking activities, insurance and accounting, customs and tax services, economics, finance and others. There is a growing demand for specialists with a command of foreign languages and computer literate book-keepers, chief clerks, and qualified clerks for the growing number of private business undertakings in the Republic. There is quite a high level of demand for service workers: qualified seamstresses, models and shop assistants, and so on.

The education system is producing plenty of lawyers and economists; the great demand is for high grade technicians and scientists – civil, mechanical and electrical engineers, plumbers, welders, artisans of all kinds – even chefs. The wages are there to pay... but the vocational training is not widely available in Kazakhstan. Many such roles are filled by skills temporarily imported from abroad.

Meanwhile major reforms have taken place in the sphere of higher education. This process is aimed at creating a system capable of providing departmental training for a dynamically developing country. Of 170 higher educational establishments, 122 are private: traditional universities, specialist universities or academies and also institutes linked to higher teaching schools of the university type. Out of 48 state institutes, there are 28 universities, 13 academies, and seven institutes. Eighteen regional universities are functioning. Around 40 per cent are taught at private universities. There are 298 students for every 10,000 of the population of the Kazakhstan Republic. Courses last four years leading to a 'bachelors' degree; four years or more, leading to a diploma; or a higher scientific-pedagogical education degree, with a training period of two years. Such higher education can be obtained by correspondence and evening instruction, and also through long-distance learning and external studies.

One of the significant achievements of the higher education system recently is the creation of procedures in teaching students in the Kazakh language. There is now a new generation of Kazakh text books in use. Another priority in the education system is the computerisation of schools.

An important trend in the development of higher education in Kazakhstan is the reinforcement of international co-operation, founded on international talks, agreements and conventions.

Many major universities have direct links with their foreign counterparts. At present more than 5,000 citizens of Kazakhstan are studying in more than 35 countries around the world. Three international universities are functioning in Kazakhstan: the Kazakhstan-Turkish University, the Kazakhstan-British Technical University and the Russian-Kazakhstan Contemporary Humanities University.

High standards of education are required of those training to be officers of the armed services.

Astana's new 'Eurasian University' overlooking the Ishym (right) reflects the country's double continental role.

Astana's grandly-entitled Palace of School Children (left) has established its reputation as a font of educational enjoyment.

The sound of music sweetens the grind of hard book-learning.

Charting the route to raising the level of health and treatment

The acquisition of more sophisticated, state-of-the-art equipment for tackling illness has been possible only recently in Kazakhstan's major hospitals. All citizens receive free treatment, but average State spending per head of population on health was no higher than about $25 in 2002, representing 1.9 per cent of GDP. The system is only now recovering from a post-Independence crisis.

*The famous surgeon, Mukhtar Aliev, attends upon a patient (**right**) in his own Almaty hospital. Many of today's large-scale employers operate their own systems of regular check-ups for their staff (as in the pictures **below**), which are followed by treatment at the company's own clinic.*

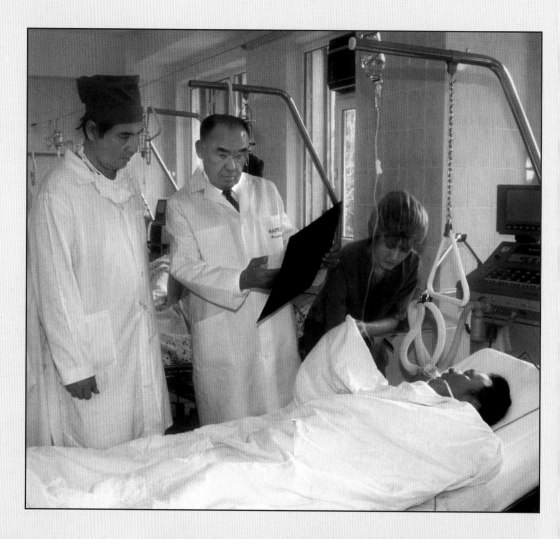

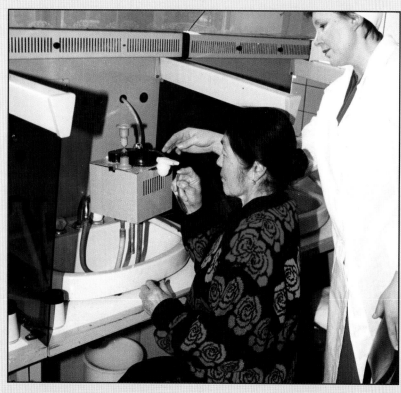

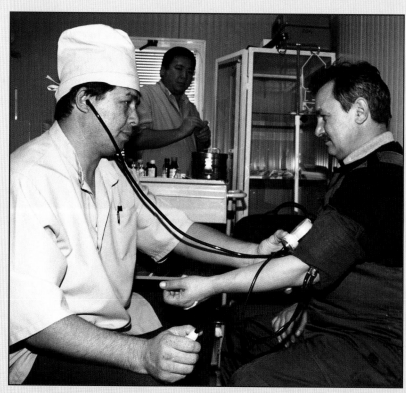

The statistics indicate that there is a doctor for every 280 people in Kazakhstan – a respectable average; and one hospital bed for every 91 citizens. But life expectancy is a lot lower than, for instance, Western Europe: 58 years for men, and 69 for women, and the infant mortality rate is grave – almost six per cent. This is partly attributable to the factor of pollution, above all nuclear, inherited from the Soviet period, the proportion of still births is particularly severe in Oskemen.

The Ministry of Health Report of 2002 found that as many as 45 per cent of school pupils were in imperfect health. The scourge of tuberculosis – a curable condition – is especially severe in the south-west of the country. There are 621 state and 89 private hospitals. The Health Ministry's budget was sharply increased in 2003.

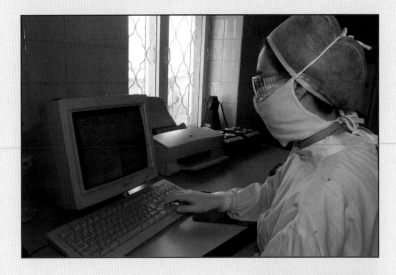

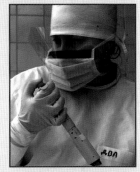

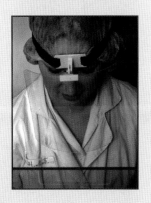

To heighten the quality of medical care, standards of qualification were sharply raised in 2000. The down-side was a reduction in the number of young qualified specialists. But within three years the shortfall had been repaired.

The health-giving effects of a plunge in cold water have been boosted by the championship of the President's wife, head of the Bobek Foundation promoting good health for the young.

Health farms and private sanitoria, like the one below near Jarkent, deep in the country, are widely patronised.

A talent for space

Coming quite late in their history to the requirement to build new cities, Kazakhstan's planners have blessed their country with a wonderful lavishness of parks, botanical gardens, zoos and arboreta. The Russian colonists began well with the confident planning of Fort Verny, which was to grow into Almaty, with its trees and fountains. That same city rejoices in its zoo large enough to get lost in, and parks like Panfilov, site of the Cathedral of the Transfiguration, and Gorky Park, its largest recreational area.

Astana, the new capital, would not be outdone by its precursor, and so has a wonderful spread of open spaces and the river too, all represented on these pages. Astana has actualised the remarkable idea of reproducing in miniature the entire country, in three dimensions, in the 'ethno-memorial' Atameken Park. With its amusement park Fantasy World, Astana has a talent for brightening its winters with brilliant inventiveness with ice sculpture and faery lights in all its open spaces.

A young pigeon-fancier in Almaty's Panfilov Park is counter-fancied by the pigeons.

Wit and wonder are the hallmark of Astana's winter sculptures of ice.

What is good for the capital, Almaty, goes too for all other major cities – for Semey, founded on its present site in 1770, which still names its central park after Lenin; for Shymkent, with its rambling zoo and Memorial Park, with its soaring monument. Children's playgrounds abound in Kazakhstani cities, with their swings and pony-carriage rides and decorated Christmas trees.

Below, Astana's monument and park also honours the nation's victims of repression.

*Astana's open spaces (as **above**) vie with Almaty's (**here**) for grace and imagination.*

*Shymkent's soaring monument to victims of oppression (**above**) stands in its own grounds. The city's zoo (**below**) sprawls imaginatively across many acres.*

The Islamic Underpinning

While Kazakhstan is built as a secular state in which obeisance to religious structures has no formal role to play, that which underpins the morality of society is Islam. And beyond the moralities of human conduct, Islam remains at hand throughout the country to provide the matrix of spiritual awareness. There is a mosque within every community and each mosque has its mullah, its Koranic doctrine, and its body of scriptural wisdom. Regular worship may be the practice of only a minority; yet that minority (as also in the nominally Christian West) by and large carries respect, and there cannot be many Kazakh families without its members of Islamic adherents.

Kazakhstan's constitution guarantees the freedom of religious practice, and since Independence religious groupings have proliferated. The substantial majority are the adherents of Sunni Islam, which as this book relates, entered Kazakhstan some 12 centuries ago to give a fresh coherence to the existing spiritual heritage we know today as Tengrism, and so forming a spiritually workable syncretism that has survived the swirl and tempests of history.

*Islam is a faith which seeks to eschew man-made hierarchies, and Kazakhstan's benign Mufti (**opposite**) would consider himself no more than first among equals. Worshippers at Almaty's Grand Mosque (**opposite, top**) are seen at prayer (**right** and **above**). Kazakhstan's Jeti-Su, in the south, has long been its Islamic heartland. The lower picture (**opposite**) is of Shymkent's Amali-Salikh mosque.*

__Left,__ the devout ladies of ancient Otrar leaving their site of worship, combine Islamic commitment with their gifts as baksy, *shamans.*

In the Sufic school of the Jeli-Su – the 'seven rivers' of the south, Kazakhstan's Islam reached its apogee, led and exemplified by Ahmed Yassavi. That was in the twelfth century. That same sublime Sufic adherence and practice is present in Kazakhstan today – in Shymkent, Taraz and Turkestan. Sufi mysticism always was, and is, tolerant in its very essence, aware of each individual route to God. 'Accept this

advice from me,' Yassavi would tell his disciples. 'Imagine the world as a green dome in which there is nothing but God and you, and keep reflecting on God until the theophany overwhelms you and frees you from yourself, and nothing remains but God.'

Marking the end of the long blight of Marxism under which many were executed for commitment to their faith, the Spiritual Directorate of Muslims was established in 1990, under the presiding influence of Kazakhstan's Mufti. It is the vehicle of contact with the international Muslim world. There are some 1,400 mosques in the country, the Central Mosque in Almaty – opened in 1994 – with a capacity for 3,000 worshippers. There is an Islamic University, and a flourishing Islamic press.

Christianity and Judaism

Not surprisingly, the first Abrahamic religion to penetrate the territory of Kazakhstan was Christianity – Christianity in the Nestorian mode, brought by those who accompanied Shah Kavad I to Turkestan to evangelise the Hephthalite Huns, north of the Oxus (today's Amudarya) River in 498. Nestorian Christianity claims St. Thomas as its founder, Nestorius himself being a Constantinople patriarch who took exception to the Alexandrians' appellation for the Virgin Mary as 'Mother of God'.

Long after the conversion of the majority of Kazakhs to Islam, the Russians brought their own Russian Orthodoxy with them, as the colonising power.

The mainstream of Christianity in Kazakhstan today is thus Russian Orthodox and beholden to the Moscow Patriarch. The 'Turkestan' diocese (containing all of Russified Central Asia) was established by Moscow as late as 1871. By 1898 there were 5,340 parishes with 360 churches in Turkestan serving 391,000 Christians.

In the year 1917, the Bolshevik seizure of power in St Petersburg (soon to be renamed Leningrad) proclaimed an atheistic statehood and all confessing believers of any religion were either persecuted or prosecuted. It is enough to say that in 2000 the Council of Russian Orthodox Church canonised as martyrs more than 1,000 priests and clerics executed over the years of repressions, several of whom had been working in Kazakhstan. Priests were shot, hanged, buried alive, and beheaded. The churches, cathedral and monasteries in Kazakhstan that were not destroyed were converted into barracks, stores, or occasionally museums.

By the time of the Soviet Union's collapse, the situation had been transformed. There are today twenty-two churches, cathedrals and monasteries in Kazakhstan, serving a substantially secularised Russian population yet with a significant proportion of loyal worshippers.

Aside from Orthodoxy, there are some 300,000 Roman Catholics, mainly Germans, Poles and Ukrainians, served by 250 parishes, three bishops, more than 60 priests and 70 nuns.

Kazakhstan's valuable (and valued) Jewish community is served by eighteen synagogues. It retains its cohesion, and Jews play an organisational and financial role in a country refreshingly free of religious or racial intolerance.

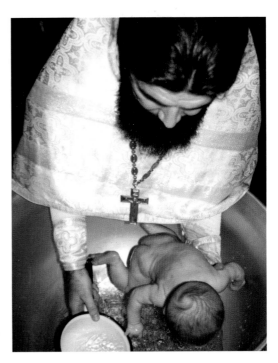

*Almaty's Russian Orthodox Cathedral of the Transfiguration (**opposite**), built in 1904 to H. P. Zenkov's design, was one of the very few buildings to survive the 1911 earthquake. Like other major Orthodox places of worship – in Uralsk, Semey, Astana and elsewhere – it is a spiritual centre for Kazakhstan's large Russian community, whose Christian exemplar is the Patriarch (**left**). **Centre, above,** holy scipture is read, while (**right**) a young priest baptises an infant into the faith.*

*To snatch a piece of cord from the ground (at full gallop), to pursue and whip one who has done you wrong, to wrestle your rival into submission, are all classic tests of Kazakh physical and equestrian prowess. If all else fails, then race your camel (**below, right**). Yet – disappointingly for any Kazakh – camels will not gallop.*

Indigenous Sport

With the Kazakh's mastery of the horse recently endorsed by the findings by archaeologists that the wild horse was first domesticated by inhabitants of the Kazakh Steppe, it can be no surprise that the national sport of Kazakhstan centres upon horsemanship. The Steppe horse is endowed with outstanding stamina and hardiness, and certain breeds are exceptionally swift. All true Kazakhs love the horse. In past times, prowess on the horse won young men their chosen brides. Kazakh festivities between springtime and autumn feature equestrian contests, and the popular heroes are the Kings of *Kokpar*.

Kokpar may be likened to a kind of polo

in its wildest form. Participating riders can number a thousand. The *Kokpar* pitch is as wide as the Steppe. The winners are those who can take possession of the carcase of a goat, hurled into the equestrian *mêlée*.

Then there is *Andaryspak*, in which the contest is between two riders, often galloping at full tilt, who seek to pull one another out of the saddle. It involves exceptional strength and dexterity.

Next is *Kumis Alu* – in which the test is to snatch from the ground a small object like a coin without leaving the saddle and at a fast gallop. It deeply impressed Alexander the Great, when his army swept through the southern Steppe 2,300 years ago.

The context of *Jangshty* involves the pursuit of an imagined enemy to whack him with a whip – the pursuer sometimes being a woman avenging a faithless lover. Then there is *Kazaksha Kures* comprising a match between two mounted wrestlers.

Kazakh equestrian sport is far from a mere physical matter. It demands pluck, craftiness and stamina, of which the severest test of all is the *Alaman-baiga*, a race covering up to 80 km.

The Kazakhs' national sport of Kokpar (below) is an equestrian free-for-all, involving mastery of your horse, great strength, daring and ruthlessness... to capture the goat's carcase.

No less than *Kokpar* and the equestrian contests, he who hunts with eagles – the *berkutchy* – is supremely, and uniquely – a Kazakh. In this work it has already been touched on (pages 88-9) as an integral feature of Steppe life, a tool of hunting game for the pot, and a means of protecting flocks from predators like wolves or foxes. In modern times, it has gained the status of a sport of rarity and high distinction.

The distinction stems from the training and mastery of this vast raptor. Many still practice the art of falconry throughout the world: peregrines, merlins and goshawks for the pursuit of smaller birds or small terrestrial game.

None but the Kazakhs made use of a bird with a wingspan of some three metres and a weight of seven kilos. To have such a sharp-beaked and taloned creature bating on one's wrist out on the snow-bound, wind-swept Steppe is a

man's task. So is the training, calling for endless patience. But first the eagle chick must be purloined from its remote eyrie in the Jungar or the Altai mountains.

To be any kind of falconer (there is no such English word as 'eagler' for a *berkutchy*) is a life's profession, and in Kazakhstan as elsewhere, often an hereditary one. The relationship of the bird and its master is constant, and all-consuming. In the training of a young bird, the falconer must sacrifice his sleep for nights on end. For weeks, the growing bird is rendered sightless under its hood: dependence on its master becomes total. Then that intimacy must be turned to lifelong trust – twenty years or more, with a healthy bird.

And it is said that as the man trains the bird, so does the great bird train his man, the *berkutchy* famous in Kazakh life on the Steppe for his inner resource, longevity, and perfect posture.

*A bating eagle, hooded, on the wrist, is a formidable and volatile burden at a canter on the Steppe. The hood removed, the eagle sights the hare and captures it, before the falconer dismounts (**far right**) to resume command.*

The Sporting Life

*Almaty's ski resort at Chimbulak is good for championships, a family schuss (as **left**) or paragliding (**opposite**). Kazakhs excel in snow and ice, and at wrestling, not least Kazaksha- kures, **below**, and water-polo too.*

Blessed with a fairly extreme continental climate, the people of Kazakhstan enjoy both winter and summer sports. The country has competed in both the Winter and the Summer Olympics. Thus Kazakhstan has produced world-class cross-country skiers, speed skaters and ice-hockey players brought up in the cold plains of northern Kazakhstan. The superb ski resort of Chinbulak, within easy reach of Almaty, draws skiers from around the world to the Tien Shan mountains. Overall, Kazakhstan promises to become pre-eminent as Asia's ski centre. In cross-country skiing, Kazakhstan's Vladimir Smirnov won the Olympic gold at Lillehammer in 1994, the 50 km *langlauf* being one of the world's most physically demanding sports contests. Cross-country skiers are an increasingly common sight in Astana and Karagandy every winter.

Speed skating is another popular competitive winter sport being taken up by more and more nations. Many world speed records have been set at Almaty's superb open-air Medeo Skating Rink, set at 1,800 metres in the foothills of the Tien Shan, about half an hour from the city's centre.

Kazakhstan has top-rated boxers, weightlifters, cyclists and westlers.

One of the greatest sporting achievements by a Kazakhstani in recent years was the sensational win by Olga Shishigina of Almaty in the 100 metres women's hurdles at the Sydney Olympics in 2000. At the age of 32 Olga rounded off a long career by taking Kazakhstan's first Olympic gold medal for a track event. She retired through injury two years later. Olga's glory was matched by two Kazakhstani boxers, Bekzat Sattarkhanov (featherweight) and Yermahan Ibraimov (light middleweight) who took gold medals in their respective divisions. Kazakhstan rounded off a highly commendable Sydney Olympics with a further four silver medals in boxing (two), cycling and wrestling.

Sports of strength – weight-lifting and men's wrestling – have always been popular in the nomadic societies of Central Asia, and Kazakhstan has produced its fair share of champions. Daulet Turlykhanov is one of the best known. An Olympic champion in Graeco-Roman wrestling at Seoul and

*Ice is the breath of life at Medeo's spectacular arena (**right**) – where the Olympic champion Lyudmila Prokasheva trained. **Below**, sailing the Caspian is a joy in summer. In winter, half of it freezes.*

Barcelona, he has been coach of the national wrestling team for many years and an inspiration to all.

Like most of the world, football (soccer) has probably become the most enthusiastically followed spectator sport... in spite of the Kazakhstan Super League attracting no more than a few thousand to its biggest fixtures. The harshly freezing and snowbound winters confine the season to April through September. Twelve teams from all over the country take part. Jenis ('Victory') of Astana and Irtysh of Pavlodar have been among the top teams. To gain greater international exposure Kazakhstan joined the Union of European Football Federations (UEFA) in 2002, and Jenis played in the UEFA Champions League whilst Kairat Almaty and Atyrau played in the UEFA Cup.

Before Independence, sport was often organised on Soviet lines, with sports facilities being provided and encouraged by employers. Since then, however, sport has had more of a private, individual character, although it has become more commercialised. This means that neither employers nor the Government are any longer building sports stadia as they used to. Today they often leave it to the private sport and leisure industry.

The break with the Soviet Union in 1991 had as profound an effect on sport in Kazakhstan as it did on other cultural activities. People found less time for it, as they concentrated on making a living. Now that prosperity in the country is beginning to grow, and leisure is becoming more generally available, the signs are that taking part in sport (and watching it) is again becoming important to ordinary folk. The new profit-inspired sports stadia completed recently in Astana and other cities bear witness to this expectation. (*See also* 'Tourism', page 250.)

Hockey is on ice – and fast, as this goalie knows.

Festivals

What Kazakhstan chiefly celebrates on the national holidays is their recent history – and with that recent history, shifts of history and heroism of long ago.

Which festival takes precedence? The Kazakhs' Day of Independence, December 16, is of course a national holiday. Both that day and the Day of the Republic, October 25, likewise a holiday, are celebrated in the central square of every city and every small town, with parades and bunting. Independence Day also recalls the critical events of December 1986, when thousands of young people massed in Almaty in protest at Russia's appointment of a non-Kazakh to take charge of their country, and a few were martyred. That event bites deep into popular memory.

Then there is the traditional New Year of the Steppe-dwellers – Nauryz, on March 22, when the big melt should have started. Nauryz can upstage Mayday – Europe's ancient pagan spring festival on May 1, which Lenin successfully appropriated as a kind of international Workers' Day, and is today designated 'Day of Unity of the People of Kazakhstan', with an ethnic unity implied. Lastly, there is Constitution Day.

At all such celebrations, the people caparison themselves in traditional costume. Yurts appear in the squares, and low dining tables, and *dastarkhans* – long tables laden with good Kazakh things to eat and drink, horseflesh and *kumys*... and musicians playing all the old instruments, the *dombra* and the *kobyz* and all the percussion. There are the equestrian contests, and fairground tests of strength and of accuracy with a rifle.

On all these days Kazakhstan's ethnic minorities – Russians, Uighurs, Koreans, Greeks, Ukrainians, Germans and all – celebrate alongside the host community, in their own manner and with their own symbols.

*A simulacrum of the Golden Man – high art in every sense – presides upon the Nauryz festival in Almaty (**left**), while others gather at the foot of Astana's elegantly soaring pinnacle to life and light (**right**).*

*Opposite, the pageantry takes off in the plaza, while (**below**) the Kazakh festival dancers take off their shoes.*

All circuses seek to amaze...
Kazakhtan's Grand Circus,
celebrated throughout Asia and
Eastern Europe, amazes in the heart
of Almaty in its own purpose-built
'big top'. Circus acts are hereditary
skills – the equestrian stars, the
acrobats, the animal trainers, even
the clowns, learn the craft from the
family.

State money customarily backed
the circuses of Russia and the Asian
republics throughout the Soviet
period. They won worldwide
acclaim for the daring, inventiveness
and professionalism of their acts.
When that backing shrivelled to
nothing, hard times ensued; the
troupe was reported to be spending
its own meagre savings to feed the
animals. But to be a circus artiste is

a vocation: they could not let it go. At last help from abroad came to the rescue, with investment from such entrepreneurs as Giovanni Giarola from Italy.

  Today once more Kazakhstan's Grand Circus flourishes: a major attraction to visitors from all over the world, which it plans to tour anew. Meanwhile, in Astana, a competitor wins audiences – the Baldyrgan Circus, established in the late 1960s.

Dudar Hojaev the clown (below), is a star known through the land, the fourth generation to follow the family calling.

Chapter 6

For immemorial generations the people of the Steppe carried their civilisation within themselves in word, in song, the stringed instrument, the flute, the woven rug or garment, the tool, the yurt strip, the vessels or utensils, the piece of harness, perhaps the weapon. Nothing they treasured could be other than portable – preferably in the heart and head. Yet they always had their treasures, and what they treasured – by virtue of its inwardness and portability – was imperishable. In a brief century the old life has all but gone for ever, and what passes for the civilisation of the global village is crowding in. Many a Kazakh knows today that if his creative energy is to find its true expression it will stem from his Kazakh roots.

The Creative Force

The paradox exemplified: amid a nomadic culture, where all is portable, stand monuments of such eternal artistic verity as the Ahmed Yassavi mausoleum at Turkestan.

Music and Song

'If trouble comes stand up to it, be strong,
If happiness – then welcome it with song.'
Abai

'The mother slipped rings decorated with little silver bells, *konyrau*, onto the fingers of her right hand. In her left, she took up a tiny instrument, the like of which can be found the world over, and here called *shan kobyz*. She raised it to her lips and tapping gently and plucking the metal tongue of the *shan kobyz*, and ringing the bells, started playing and singing over her infant's cradle. When the infant grew older, his father made him a simple musical instrument called a *tyaktas* from two small foal's hoofs which, when tapped, could reproduce the ambling clatter of a horse's hoofs in such an amusing manner.' Thus wrote Yuri Aravin, musicologist. The traditions of Kazakh music are rooted in the distant past, as archaeological finds and cultural artefacts from the first millennium BC testify. In Kazakhstan discoveries have been made of rock-carvings of four or five thousand years ago with depictions of people playing music, and of musical instruments.

The archaic plucked stringed instruments most resemble the Kazakh *dombra* and Kyrgyz *komyz*. Excavations at Khorezm have unearthed terracotta figurines of musicians playing two-stringed instruments sounded by plucking, made two thousand years ago by the Sak nomadic tribes – a prototype of the Kazakh *dombra*.

There are distinctive regional differences in the *dombra*'s design but the one most superbly simple in form comes from Western Kazakhstan. Its rounded, egg-shaped body and slender neck epitomises Oriental elegance and grace. The *dombra*'s strings used to be hand-crafted from goats' guts but nowadays they are made of nylon.

Many musicologists consider Central

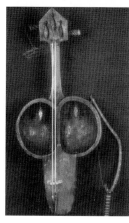

The intimacy of the yurt was – and is – the setting for the stringed kobyz *(left) and* narkobyz *(below it), and* dombra *(below) to join the bardic voice.*

Asia to be the birthplace of bow instruments. According to legend, the first bow instrument, the *kobyz*, belonged to Korkyt. He was a man who dared to search for immortality and he travelled the world. Having failed in his quest, he returned to his homeland and the shores of the Syrdarya. After sacrificing his female camel, Jelmai, he stretched its skin over the lower part of the instrument he had hollowed from a single piece of juniper wood. He made the strings and the bow from horse-hair. And the sounds of this hitherto unknown instrument rang out as wonderfully as life itself. But one day when Korkyt grew weary from playing and fell asleep, Death, disguised as a snake, bit him and he died. Ever since the Kazakhs have believed that the sounds of a *kobyz* protect

a person from death and drive the evil spirits out of their dwelling places and souls. This is no surprise: the sound of a *kobyz* is quite special, now recalling a human voice and now a swan's cry.

For many centuries only *baksy* (shamans) were allowed to play the *kobyz*. Later on story-tellers known as *jyrshy* performed to its accompaniment. In the nineteenth century the *kobyz* began to be played in everyday settings and in the last century it took up its well-deserved place in orchestras of Kazakh folk instruments. Young players have been equally successful in using the *kobyz* to perform both classical European orchestral works and create contemporary compositions.

The first collection of musical instruments, comprising 150 items, was

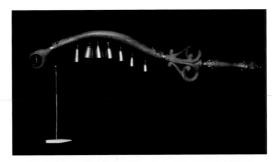

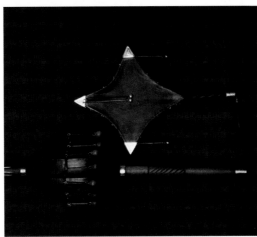

*Above and **right** the instruments give the beat – perhaps to the tinkling zhetygen (**beneath**). **Below,** a 1910 itinerant troupe, and **left** a similar ensemble today.*

compiled by the musicologist B.S. Sarybayev. All Kazakh instruments can be divided into three main categories: stringed, wind and percussion. The oldest folk instruments include the *sokpan* (rattle), *saz syrnai* (clay whistle), *sybyzgy* (reed flute) and *daulpaz* (drum).

The mediaeval period is also regarded as a golden age for music in Central Asia as musical theory then developed at the same pace as the performing art. Al-Farabi (870–950), Avicenna (died 980) and Safied-Din (1414-1452), all heirs of Greek philosophy, succeeded in enhancing the mathematical study of musical language.

Kazakhs have the nomadic tribes to thank for their original and rich musical heritage. Life in constant motion and the wide diversity of environment helped to elaborate a special strategy in assimilating the world. The ancient nomadic way of life in Kazakhstan penetrated social consciousness and ideology. The nomads' aesthetic world was of an ideal nature and not grounded in material things. Instead, the Kazakhs had music and poetry, the most crucial elements in integrating a communal system of beliefs through culture. In a musical culture with purely

oral traditions, they became an irreplaceable means of assuring continuity from one generation to the next. Music and poetry permeated literally every area of human activity. The first compiler of folk music, A.V. Zatayevich, called the Kazakh Steppe a 'sea of music'. No young girl had the moral right to wed without composing a song first. It was inappropriate for any young man to confess his love in commonplace prose. Wedding ceremonies included recitals of lengthy musical and poetic scenes, and a person's death brought new songs to life.

Musical and poetic traditions are unimaginable without improvisation of impromptu verses and music on a given theme. Many people used to be able to compose impromptu quatrains or a simple *kui* or song. The Kazakh musician is an artist who creates in public, and his creative works come into direct contact with his audience. He is therefore able to observe the impact of his art on his audience, who express their approval through various interjections such as *ei, eai, oi-duniya,* and *barekeldy.*

A revered and honoured place was occupied by the *akyny,* poets and musicians skilled in the art of improvisation who used to perform at *aitysy* (poetry and song contests) and at *toi* (popular gatherings) on behalf of a particular family. They had a good grasp of the history and culture of their people and of politics and geography as well. While an *akyn* represented a particular Kazakh family, a *jyrau* performed on behalf of an entire people. The *jyrau* was a revered man, and sometimes a military commander. The *jyrau* were advisers to the khans. They recited epic stories, one of the favourite genres of folk culture. Over a hundred epics, each comprising a thousand verses, have been recorded from the folk story-tellers in Kazakhstan. The recital of an epic was accompanied by a *dombra.* The heroic epics are based on the exploits of a *batyr* (warrior) and his struggle to liberate his

The sweetness of the plucked dombra, it is told, made Genghis weep. The instrument is to be heard in many a Kazakh household (as far right, opposite) and is experiencing a revival. Such music is widely broadcast. One of the greatest exponents of the instrument, as accompaniment to her own voice, was Dina Nurpeisova, who was immortalised in bronze after her death in the early 20th century (opposite).

homeland (*Yer Tartyn, Kambar, Alpamys* and *Koblandy*, to name but a few) and the lyrical epics of love and the family (*Kyz Jibek, Kozy Korpesh, Bayan Sulu, Sulushash,* and others).

The Kazakh epic consists of myths, legends, lyrical poetry and heroic songs. In the eighteenth century, the *jyrau* was superseded by the *jyrshy* who performed epic works. Both had extraordinary memories and were gifted singers, story-tellers, actors and musicians. In order to perform an epic one had to know the text of the stories, have a beautiful voice, accompany oneself on the *dombra* and

looked and behaved in a distinctive manner and their clothes and horses' decorations were always strikingly colourful and elegant.

The songs, *terme* (musical recitatives) and *kui*, were constantly being performed in everyday life. There would always be a *dombra* hanging from the *kerege* (the lattice lower wall) in every yurt. Virtually every Kazakh was a musician. Just as before, songs of various genres are still performed by the poet-singers of the Kazakh Steppe for weddings, funerals, family celebrations, and also social protest and historical record. Imprinted on popular memory are

Akhan, Isa, Mukhit, Shashubai, Jambyl, Kenen and other singers. Also alive during this period were the musicians and composers Tattimbet, Dauletkerei, Kazakngap, Ykylas and other unique composers who unleashed powerful songs and music on the world. The creative work of these musicians had the effect of a Renaissance, transforming the nation's spiritual and cultural world. The revived art helped into the political arena rebels such as Isatai, Makhambet, Kenesary and Nauryzbai who took up the struggle for the independence of the Kazakh people. The Renaissance began with Kurmangazy,

improvise. The Kazakh people are carefully preserving the art of such as Bukhar-Jyrau, Aktamberdy-Jyrau and Dosmambet-Jyrau.

Music and the spoken word are inseparable not only in the recitative art of the *akyny, jyrau* and *jyrshy* and in songs but even in the performance of *kui* which were always accompanied by legends and preceded by stories about their creators and author.

A special place in Kazakh culture is occupied by musicians known as *sere* or *sal* who were singers, story-tellers, wrestlers, magicians, trick riders and jugglers. They

events connected with the campaigns of Alexander the Great of Macedonia, the formation of the Kazakh khanate, and the onerous period of the Jungar invasion. Instrumental music is equally diverse and includes ancient *kui* for the *dombra* and *kobyz*, and lyrical and historical *kui* such as '*Erke atan*' (favourite camel), '*Akku*' (swan), '*Alatau*' (Alatau mountains) and many others.

Composers and singers of the nineteenth and first quarter of the twentieth century laid the foundations of professional folk art. It is hard to imagine contemporary Kazakh songs without Aset, Birjan,

symbol of *dombra* art, and Abai, as poet, philosopher and composer. Abai's songs can be heard in every Kazakh family and the song '*Kozimnin karasy*' (Apple of my eye) is known by all. A considerable role in the development of music in Kazakhstan was played by women musicians such as *akyn* Sara, the singer Maira Uvalieva, the *dombra* player and composer Dina Nurpeisova, Kulyash Baiseitova, and of great women of the Steppe such as Tumar, Boryk, Terken, Aiganym, the women founders of the Yenen tribes, Domalak *yene* and Nurbike, and the wives of the *batyrs*, Barakshy, Taidella and Baiali.

No *living art stands still. Kazakhs and Kazakhstanis have established their reputations in dance ensembles (this page) of a Kazakh inventiveness: others (opposite) have become stars in their own right – (anticlockwise from beneath the orchestra) the internationally acclaimed maestro Marat Bisengaliyev; Maria Muhamedkyzy, opera singer; the international conducting prodigy, Alan Buribayev; Aiman Musakojaeva, classical violinist; Ermek Seikebayev, baritone; Bibigul Tulegenova, pop singer; Batyr Shukeynov, pop singer; Alibek Dnishev, opera singer, and top right (with her venerable guest) singer Rosa Rymbaeva.*

The Jubanov music school, Baiseitova music school and the Kurmangazy National Conservatory which was founded in 1944, all provide specialised educations for the would-be professional musicians.

The work, emotional life and environment of Kazakhs were also embodied in dance. Ancient hunters' ritual dances may be seen in rock-carvings dating from the Bronze Age. People still remember the themes and movements of the dances. A horn-shaped pattern known as *koshkar muiiz* (sheep's horns) is reproduced in the steps of many dances.

A choreographic institute was founded in Almaty in 1934, linked to the name of the choreographer A.V. Seleznev. Along with classical ballet the institute also has a department of folk dance, created on the initiative of Shara Jienkulova. Graduates work both in Kazakhstan and abroad. The celebrated 'Gulder' (flowers), 'Saltanat' (triumph), and 'Altynai' (my precious) dance ensembles are imaginatively developing the traditions of the Kazakh folk dance.

The Abai State Academic Theatre of Opera and Ballet, founded in 1933 as a music studio, is at the forefront of the music scene in Kazakhstan, winning wide acclaim not only for its classical opera but also for national works such as Brusilovsky's operas *Abai*, *Birjan and Sara* and *Dudarai*, and for ballets.

The musicians and dancers of Kazakhstan are honoured in the names of streets and the Republic's banknotes carry their portraits.

Literature

The Kazakh word for literature – *adebiet*, borrowed from the Arabic – is linked at its root to education and morality. The concept of *adebiet*, as distinct from the word 'literature' of Western cultures (including that of Russia), gives equal value to both the oral and the written word.

The Oral Tradition

From ancient times, the art of words and music has had a special place in the life of the Kazakh people, fulfilling the role of 'art' in all its forms for nomadic and settled folk alike. The Kazakh ideal always presupposed a mastery of the word. Language, rhyming and rhythmical – in the majority of cases to the accompaniment of the two-stringed *dombra* – had to flow from the lips easily and lightly, as well as making an impact. The ancient Turkic saying *Ardam bashi til* ('In the word is the height of virtue') found a response in the Kazakh *Oner aldy – kyzyl til* ('Eloquence is the height of art').

Descriptions of literary duels, in which the participants astound listeners by their inventiveness, perceptiveness and figurativeness, feature prominently in Kazakh legends and stories. To judge from the texts surviving from ancient times the majority of Steppe poets composed verses about nature and love and were masters of the art of sung improvisation.

There were three types of Kazakh poets who combined a gift for poetry with musical talent: *akyns* (poet-improvisers); *jyraus* (minstrel-bards); and *olenshi* (performers of songs and poems).

Over the centuries, an original canon with a definite rhythm and song structure was created in Kazakh ceremonial songs, such as *toi bastar* (a song of praise, performed at the beginning of a marriage ceremony), *synsu* (a song of the bride, leaving her native land), *jar-jar* (a wedding song competition performed by maidens and *djigits*), *bet-atar* (the revealing of the bride's face – a wedding song, containing advice to the bride), *joktai* (a mourning song), and *koshtai* (a farewell to a dear and native land). The canon survives to this day.

Narrative songs and verses, to the accompaniment of musical instruments, are at the heart of Kazakh epic literature – a colossal verbal canvas, giving a vivid picture of historical events, and the everyday life and culture of the nomadic people. Texts of the epic poems which have survived reflect events which took place in the fifteenth and sixteenth centuries: the decline of the Golden Horde, the conflict with the Kalmyks/Jungars, the break-up of the Kazan khanate, the internecine battles of the Crimean khanate. The epic narrative poems of these times have entered the literary treasury not only of the Kazakhs, but also of neighbouring Turkic peoples: Karakalpaks, Kyrghyz, Tatar, Uzbek and others.

The epics *Batyr-Koblandy*, *Er-Targyn*, *Alpamys*, *Kambarbatyr*, *Er-Kokshe*, and *Er-Edige* tell of the life and victories of the Steppe warriors – the Batyrs. Among the Kazakhs the most famous heroic epic is *Batyr-Koblandy*, which descended through many generations of orators to the present day, and is about 6,500 lines long.

The epic's main character always embodies the nomadic ideal: Koblandy is so strong and skilful that he can take on forty thousand soldiers with one hand; his life's main work is to serve his people and defend his kinsmen against enemies; his life's code reflects the ethic of his native people.

Both the ancient spirits of nature and the Muslim saints are involved in the hero's birth. Koblandy's father – the revered Toktarbai – had remained childless until he was eighty years old, and bitterly lamented the fact. But after he had visited all the famous graves of the saints, met with the family of the *pirs* or Elders (the holy Sufi fathers, spiritual mentors), sacrificed a horse to the spirits of the saints, and sacrificed a ram to the evil smallpox Korasan, twins were born to him: a son, Koblandy, the 'lion', and a daughter, Karlygash, the 'swallow'.

The heroes of the epics grow not by the day, but by the hour. From the age of six, Koblandy began 'learning the knightly code' from the brave Estemes. The first public acknowledgement of his prowess was a competition in the camp of the Kyzylbash (a neighbouring Iranian tribe) for the right to marry Kortka, the daughter of their leader Khan Koktim Aimak. However much Estemes tried to dissuade his pupil from taking part in the contest ('You are still young, your ribs are not yet strong, your spine is not yet developed'), Koblandy wouldn't budge, trusting to the protection of the seven Elders. So Estemes gave him his blessing, saying: 'I entrust you to the one and only God.' Koblandy won the contest, receiving the beautiful Kortka for his wife. His odyssey in most versions ended successfully – the one and only God, the seven Elders, the ancestral spirits, and nature itself all protected Koblandy, making him his people's liberator, and the nomadic ideal for many centuries.

A traditional feature of nomadic poetry was the description of the hero's horse. The ever-loving Kortka, having seen a pregnant mare in Koblandy's uncle's herd, guessed that the foal was destined to become a magnificent steed worthy of Koblandy. She raised the foal Taiburla with great tenderness and care until it grew into a noble horse, possessed of magic strength and speed, its master's faithful servant. With Taiburla, Koblandy embarked on a march against the Khan of Kyzylbash Kazan, who was menacing the Kipchaks, and won a victory over him.

But any action unworthy of a Batyr would result in failure: when Koblandy, on his way to his friend Karaman, made a raid on the pagan Kalmyk Khan Kobikti's herd, he was captured and put into prison. (Incidentally, when he was preparing to commit the raid, Koblandy had forgotten to ask for help from the seven Elders.)

In difficult situations a beautiful woman would come to the hero's aid. Kobitki's daughter, Karlyga, whose mother was Muslim, fell in love with Koblandy at first sight, helped him to escape from captivity and ran away with him herself. When Khan Kobitki tried to stop them, Karlyga betrayed her father, who was killed by Koblandy.

Meanwhile another Kalmyk Khan, Alshagyr, conquered the land belonging to the Kipchaks and forced them into captivity. Koblandy's march against Alshagyr was difficult, but ended in victory, and Koblandy's kinsmen were set free. In the battle, the help that Karlyga gave to Koblandy was decisive, and she saved him from certain death more than once. When Koblandy's army was forced to fight the army of Batyr Birshimbai, Karlyga's blood brother, she killed her brother with a spear.

On more than one occasion, Karlyga begged Koblandy to take her as his second wife; but Koblandy, while acknowledging her beauty and courage, refused to marry her, saying that he couldn't trust a woman who had betrayed the two people closest to her – her father and her brother – one to the mercy of Koblandy, and killing the other herself. However, at the end of the story, Koblandy changes his mind and marries her. The epic concludes with a description of Koblandy's happy life with both wives.

Just as European chivalric tales gave rise to the courtly romance, an alternative to the Kazakh heroic epic was the lyrical epic, describing lovers who overcome the vicissitudes of fortune, whilst striving to be with one another. The epic poems *Kozy-Korpesh* and *Bayan-Sulu*, *Kyz-Jibek*, and *Kul'she-Kyz* are the best-known in this genre.

The traditions of ancient Turkic Tengrian, Persian Zoroastrianism, Islam, Buddhism, and Kazakh beliefs in ancestral protection are all fully reflected in the old Kazakh epics – a synthesis that has come about because of the geographical distribution of the Kazakh tribes who migrated across wide distances, making contact with settled people who prayed to different gods. In the Kazakh epic, the various gods do not contradict one another: they join forces in difficult times to send the people saviours, supporting them when they behave righteously and punishing them when they err.

In keeping with the nomadic ethic, there is a didactic purpose to the old stories and parables about powerful Batyrs, clever beautiful heroines, wise sages and 'humanised' animals with a mastery of human speech, who are both intelligent and cunning.

Historically, individual works by Kazakh poets are known from the eighteenth century onwards, beginning with Bukhar-Jyraiu (1693-1787), whose works reflect events which happened in the reign of Ablai Khan.

The annexation of Kazakh land to Russia in the 1730s brought significant changes to the life of the Kazakh nomads and immediately became the dominant theme in poetry, changing the emphasis from the fight for land to the defence of the social interests of its tribes and people. The poet Batyr Makhambet Utemisov (1804-46), whose poetry dealt first and foremost with the interests of the people, worn down by injustice and poverty, was held in high regard at the time of Khan Zangir.

The social theme was also taken up in the verses of Sheniyaz Jarylagasov (1817-81), the *aitys* of Suyumbai Aranov (1827-96), and the verses of the poetess Almajan Azamatkyza (born 1823), praising Isatai Taimanov, the leader of the Kazakh national liberation movement. The poets Dulat Babataev (1802-71), Shortanbai Kanaev (1818-81), Murat Monkin (1843-1906) and others turned in their songs to the spiritual values of Islam, identifying these with the best of Kazakhstan's heritage, and expressing misgivings at the annexation by Russia, which the Kazakhs found alien and difficult to understand.

Many poets sensed the difficulty and inevitability of developments in the Kazakh Steppes in the nineteenth century. Accustomed to expressing big emotions in poetic form, they immersed themselves in verses and songs about the coming of a new epoch. It is impossible to count the names of all the people who did so. But it is in the work of Abai that nineteenth century Kazakh literature reaches its fullest and most spiritual expression.

Abai

The beginning of a new written Kazakh literature is invariably associated with the name Abai (Ibrahim) Kananbaev (1845-1904). The son of a Steppe aristocrat, Abai received a traditional Muslim education as a child, but also went to a Russian school. As a young man he helped his father in his work for the government. By the age of thirty he became a volost chief (governor of the smallest administrative district of Tsarist Russia), and by the time he was forty he was in charge of a convention of a hundred volosts, and the author of a 'Statute on criminal matters for Semipalatinsk Kazakhs'.

As a young man Abai wrote verses and songs in the tradition of Kazakh poetry. His early works are already distinguished by their wisdom and elegant style. The images of his pastoral lyrics have something in common with the images of ancient Turkic poetry. This is especially clear in the poems dedicated to the seasons, and the description of a magnificent horse. The horse celebrated by Abai is so

Abai

handsome that it ranks with Koblandy's steed, the legendary Taiburla, with Alexander the Great's Bucephalus, with the great racehorse from the poem of Imryyl Qais, the inspirer of ancient Arab poetry, and with some of the finest horses in ancient Turkic poetry. His neck is high, his shoulder powerful, his hindquarters wide, his belly thin, with a mane like silk and a courageous look; he is fleet of foot and faithful to his master.

In Abai's descriptions of nature there is a new quality, enriching the more ancient poetic traditions. If the old Turkic texts provide us with a beautiful landscape as a portrait of changing nature, then in Abai's poems about seasonal changes there is always a depiction of a Kazakh *aul* (or village), since for Abai, nature is inseparable from people.

In his metaphors one can find a link with the ancient images of sunworshippers: in the poem about spring the sun is the long-awaited bridegroom of his bride, the earth, bringing lifegiving light and warmth with him. Abai exclaims like a true Muslim: 'How can you not trust in the mercy of Allah, once he has breathed life into the earth with spring?' 'You follow your great Creation, astounded by its perfection, enraptured by its beauty.' The taboo on singing a hymn to the sun that was present in orthodox Islam did not exist on the Kazakh Steppe – here the worship of Tengri, the god of heaven, and the spirits of nature also enhanced the Islamic creed, creating no contradiction between the one and only God and the forces of nature. Poetic forms of the past were open to new themes and images, mixing a boundless range of characters.

The genre which won international acknowledgement and fame for Abai was the love lyric. Like the famous Arab poets of the Middle Ages who created the *ghazal*, Abai sings of love as a force able to carry man to the height of happiness and doom him to suffering. Images of the happy lover and the suffering lover created by Abai, are sanctified by the word. Love, endowed with intoxicating strength, needs adequate literary expression and only with the help of poetry is the lover able to survive, while the loved one must remain true to the image which has conquered the poet's heart. Abai's poems about love – 'An infusion to lighten the heart' – became the texts of songs which spread across the whole of the Kazakh Steppe. They are sung and read to the present day.

One of the most important sources of poetical inspiration for Abai was the literature of Central Asia in the Farsi, Arabic and Turkic languages, which were understood by the Kazakhs thanks to their proximity and their shared Muslim values. In his poems Abai turns for spiritual strength to Firdousi, Khafiz, Saadi, Navoi and Sakhali. These poets' works, distinguished by an especially elegant style and impeccable structure, revealed to the reader the reality of the ancient confrontation between Iran and the Turanian region in the pre-Islamic epoch, and also the spiritual heritage accumulated by the settled cultures of Central Asia over a century of Islam. Studying these works allowed Abai to present a detached view of his nation's history in terms with which the Kazakhs were familiar and could understand.

By projecting images of Muslim poetry onto the life of the Kazakh Steppe, Abai introduced into Kazakh literature elements of the *zukhdiiat* genre, especially prevalent in Sufi poetry. Its content includes the preaching of spiritual improvement, virtue and the search for the path to true happiness.

Visiting the town of Semipalatinsk (today's Semey), not far from his native *aul*, Abai became acquainted with the exiled Russian democrats – Mikhailis, Dolgopolov and others. Besides learning news about events in Russia following the abolition of serfdom, Abai found a new source of spiritual development – Russian literature. The works of Pushkin, Lermontov, Krylov, Tolstoy, and Bunin were of particular importance to him.

Abai translated a series of works of Russian poetry into the Kazakh language. These translations were not literal, but conveyed the character of the original, using the content and imagery of the Russian verses, while giving them a Kazakh expression of emotion. His translation of Tatiana's letter from Pushkin's *Eugene Onegin* was especially popular. Abai set it to music, and the verses were turned into a well-known Kazakh song. Another beautiful song created by Abai which became popular amongst the Kazakhs was based on Lermontov's poem *Mountain Heights* (in its turn an interpretation of verses by Goethe).

The ideas of the enlightened Russian democrats Chernyshevsky and Dobroliubov, carried by the exiles into the Kazakh Steppe, were in harmony with Sufism in their striving towards the collective search for truth, the dissemination of knowledge amongst the people, and the education of man in the spirit of humanism. These moral values became defining ones in Abai's work. Through the Russian language, Abai became acquainted with ancient Greek philosophy, which led to the study of the western civilisations that had done so much to shape Russia's morality.

The result of Abai's philosophical search was a collection of his maxims, written in prose and consisting of forty-five 'word' essays. Abai's maxims are created in the spirit of Muslim *rasail* – reflections and edifying thoughts which were especially widespread amongst the Sufis at the end of the tenth century. Beginning in the twelfth century, Islam penetrated nomadic Central Asia in a Sufi form, preached by wandering dervishes, whose graves would become places of worship. The dervishes themselves were greeted as spiritual mentors, or Elders – bearers of the truth and goodness, who, like Batyr Koblandy's protectors, were at the same time able to bestow supernatural qualities on man.

Ancient epic literature established the Sufi influence as a reality of Kazakh nomadic life, but in Abai's maxims the Sufi's overriding search for humility and asceticism as a way to attain the knowledge of God in eternal life after death, is seen as an outdated world vision, confining people to passivity. Assessing the *tarikat* (the Sufi metaphor for a life's journey, leading to spiritual perfection and humility), Abai writes: 'If humanity took the path pointed out by the saints – the *tarikat* – for its model, the world would have fallen into neglect. Who would have herded the cattle, who would have stopped the enemy, who would have sewn clothes, who would have planted the seeds or procured the riches of the earth?'

In the maxims Abai creates his own *adat* or ethical code for the Muslims of his time. Leaning on the Hadith, the account of the words and deeds of the Prophet Mohammed, Abai shows the necessity of renewing religious canons in keeping with the time. Abai's ideals are the striving for knowledge, charity and justice – qualities that the Prophet and the saints possess. However, Abai considers that love of the saints is 'enough only in order to show concern about life after death as they forgot or failed to take into account worldly joys.'

Abai sees the embodiment of his ideals in those who combine the spiritual quest with an intellectual one, in those 'who strive to attain an Allah commensurate to their reason, who search for the cause behind all phenomena and objects'. The practical experience of government, gleaned by Abai from his early years, and his knowledge of the basic needs of his kinsmen, rich and poor, place the earthly, worldly life at the forefront of his vision. According to Abai the work of 'seekers for truth' is to aim at earthly welfare. 'They will attain truth, righteousness and goodness in the interest of humanity; for them joys and pleasures do not exist in their life apart from their work. Were it not for these thinkers, walking the true path, the whole world might collapse.'

A real feeling for the changing times and an inspired attempt to capture its meaning make Abai's work a moral landmark for the development of Kazakh literature in the twentieth century. Within the framework of this single creative life, Kazakh literature found a synthesis of the ancient oral tradition, the wisdom of literature and philosophy of Islam, and the growing spirit of humanism in Russian writing, harmoniously combined in an overall view that aspires to the highest levels of knowledge and spirituality.

Contemporary Kazakh literature.

In the first decade of the twentieth century a whole pleiade of political thinkers and scholars formed in the milieu of the Kazakh intelligentsia. Well educated, they had played an active part in the stormy events of political life and they left a valuable literary heritage. Figures such as Shakerim Kudaiberdiev (1858-1931), Alikhan Bokeikhanov (1870-1937), Akhmet Baitursynov (1873-1938), Mirzakysh Jumbaev (1893-1938) and others collectively laid the foundations for the new Kazakh literature. Behind each of these names is an interesting creative life, affected by the revolutionary upheavals in Russia and the Kazakh intelligentsia's aspiration towards political independence for Kazakhstan. However, nearly all these lives were cut short because of accusations of nationalism and because of political repression, and they were expunged from the records by censorship until the end of the 1980s.

The literary figures Seifullin, Jansugurov and Mailin also perished as a result of political repression, but were rehabilitated post-humously in the 1950s and came to be acknowledged by Soviet literary critics as founders of Kazakh Soviet literature.

The author of some beautiful lyric poems, Saken Seifullin (1894-1938), would sincerely welcome the new way of life, guiding the hero of his poem Kokshetai away from images of folk legend and past events towards new realities, and dedicating the songs *Path to Happiness* and *Red Falcons* to the new order. His historical documentary novel *A Difficult Path, a Hard Transition* was also dedicated to revolutionary events happening in Kazakhstan. Another outstanding poet, Ilias Jansugurov (1894-1938), painted colourful pictures of folk life, using the imagery of ancient poets in his *The Steppe, Kyushi, and Kulager*. He would describe the transformation of the traditional landscape as it was forced to suit the demands of the new epoch. The talented writer Beimbet Mailin (1894-1938) created a vivid portrait of a poor peasant called Myrkymbai who agitated for the transformation of a Kazakh *aul* into a Kolkhoz. In the short story *Raushan, the Communist* he depicted the fate of a woman deprived of rights in the old days who with the advent of Soviet power becomes a worker for the new life in the *aul*.

Reading the works of such wordsmiths as Seifullin, Jansugurov and Mailin one does not have the impression that they are creating deliberate propaganda for Communist ideals, rather their works convey a sense of beauty and a feeling of joyous illumination, such as experienced by converts to a new faith. Their fate is all the more tragic because of this. All three were declared 'enemies of the people' and punished in the name of the same Soviet power which they had celebrated.

Of works about the war the best known are

Seifullin

Auezov

Jansugurov

Suleimenov

Moscow For Us by the writer/soldier B. Momyshuly, *Notes from the Front* by M. Gabdullin, and the war novels *The Soldier from Kazakhstan* by G. Musrepov, and *The Long Awaited Day* by A. Nurpeisov.

A major event in the history of Kazakh literature was the publication of the first Kazakh novel-epic *Abai* (1947), and *Abai's Path* (1956) by Mukhtar Auezov (1897-1961). One of the few survivors of the pleiade of the creative Kazakh intelligentsia of the '20s and '30s, the author's intention was to give the nation back its historical memory, successively destroyed by Soviet power, by recalling the nomads' high spiritual ideals and their expression. Auezov carefully modelled Abai's image, drawing on the rich possibilities of the Kazakh language and the traditions of epic narrative and folklore, and saturating the narrative with the names of story-tellers, poets, musicians, philosophers,

scholars, historians and political activists from many nations. The novel about Abai soon came to be known as 'an encyclopedia of Kazakh life'. Its high artistic standard and synthesis of Kazakh narrative traditions with the experience of world-wide writers gained him international acknowledgement. The novel won the highest state prizes of the Soviet Union and was translated into thirty languages.

Beginning in the 1960s (the time of the Khrushchev 'thaw' in the Soviet Union) Kazakh literature and the humanitarian sciences began to be concerned with reviving national history. By the '70s this interest in history became more conceptual than factual. Historical events, lavishly interpolated into literary works in the preceding decade, were considered in a wide human context, and the theme of contemporary life is set in relation to the past. The novel trilogy *Blood and Sweat* by A. Nurpeisov, *The Nomads* a series of historical novels by I. Esenberlin, *Spring Waters* by M. Magauin, and works by the commentator A. Alimjanov were the most famous prose works of this time. In poetry, works by M. Makataev, T. Moldagaliev, K. Myrzaliev and others were popular.

A new milestone in the development of Kazakh literature in the '70s was the work – in Russian – of Oljas Suleimenov (b. 1936). His crafted prose, in the composition *Az and Ya*, becomes a form of historical-linguistic enquiry, free of ideological prejudice and cliché, into the ancient sources of Turkic culture. With huge erudition and easy mastery of his historical material, Suleimenov was able to weave a thread linking Kazakh literature with older Turkic and pre-Turkic imagery, based on analysis of the monumental Russian twelfth century work *The Tale of Igor's Campaign* and the ancient Sumerian epic *Gilgamesh*.

Suleimenov's poem *The Book of Clay* revolves around cultural researches into the depths of world history. It produced a huge response in Soviet literature, inspiring a new generation of the intelligentsia in their search for a spiritual dimension.

Of most recent literary works, Suleimenov's artistic exploration *The Language of the Letter* (1998), dedicated to the problems of defining the origin of literature and language, and Nurpeisov's novel *Last Duty* (2000) about the extinction of the Aral Sea and people's tragedies at the start of the new millennium, are especially of note.

Film

It is a fact that Kazakh audiences are neglectful of their own Kazakh-made films. Why is this so?

First of all, only in the first decade of the twenty-first century were cinemas beginning to spread throughout the country. Secondly, the mass audience has become accustomed to American blockbusters, blinding them to the merits of talented low-budget films made in Kazakhstan. Thirdly, many talented Kazakh directors are too content to make

elite films, which are fine to watch at film festivals but are not suitable for popular cinema. A clear example is the director Darezhan Omirbaev who makes films in Kazakhstan, using money provided by France, which win audiences in Europe yet scarcely so at home. In recognition of his work, Darezhan has even received an Order of Art and Literature from the French Ambassador to Kazakhstan, Serge Smesov; while his film *Killer* was awarded a prize at the Cannes Film Festival.

Among other directors better known in

Europe than in Kazakhstan is Amir Karakulov. His recent film *Zhilama* – shot with technical support from the Danish director Lars von Trier – was awarded a prize for best director at Kinoshok, the film festival of the countries of the CIS. Besides this, a number of his films such as *The Rival*, *Leaves* and *The Last Holidays* have won prizes at European festivals. But the Kazakh cinema-goer hardly ever sees such works. Frustratingly, it remains unprofitable for distributors to screen Kazakh films.

The most important project in Kazakh

With the evacuation to Almaty in 1941 of Mosfilm and Lenfilm came the director Sergei Eisenstein (left) who was to film his double masterpiece Ivan the Terrible *in Kazakhstan. Films on Kazakh themes flowed from the Almaty studio of Shaken Aimanov, seen right, in a still from* Beardless Cheat; *and recently from the directorial hand of Amir Karakulov (opposite, left) and the versatility of stage and screen actors like Asamali Ashimov, far right.*

film since the turn of the century is the film *Nomads*, adapted from of Esenberlin's novel (*see* 'Literature'). The original idea was conceived in the mid '90s, but it only began to be realised in 2002-3. Kazakhfilm, the main film studio in the country, plans to launch this historical epic on world screens by 2004, and it should open a new era in Kazakh cinematography. Involved in the production were the American directors Milos Forman and Ivan Passer, as well as the Russian script writer Rustam

Ibragimebekov. The head of Kazakhfilm, Sergei Azimov, hoped the film would show Kazakhstan and its people to a world audience: 'Everyone in the world knows about American cowboys, Russian monks, English milords. *Nomads* will show the world what the Kazakh people are.'

The roots of Kazakhstan's film-making derive from the 1920s and the film *Turksib*, and the early gems of Almaty's first studio like *Rebellion*, *Jut* and *Amangeldy*. From 1941 to the war's end (1945) the Soviet film industry was evacuated to Almaty where

Sergei Eisenstein made his two-part masterpiece *Ivan the Terrible*, and V. Pudovkin and his brother, Vasilev, were at work. Kazakh film began to bloom in the 1960s with the work of the actor-producer Shaken Aimanov in films like *The End of Ataman* and *Kyz-Jibek*.

The Stage

In the story of the culture of the Kazakh people, the creative art of theatrical

drama has come late. The first sprouts of indigenous dramatic art were visible in the 1920s. The new name to emerge was that of young Mukhtar Auezov, with the drama *Enlik-Kebek*, staged in the recently-constructed theatre of the predominantly Russian (in those days) town of Semey. It was the Russianisation of the then colony of Kazakhstan that introduced the element of theatre into the indigenous creative spirit, and insisted upon the presence of a Kazakh stage – as theatre or opera house – in every significant city.

The heavy patronage which descended upon the theatre – as upon all aspects of the arts – was a mixed blessing, yet true talents were able to emerge. Soon Auezov's celebrity was joined by that of Jansugurov, whose play *Revenge* captured audiences in the mid-1930s. At the same time State patronage allowed (with the appropriate ideological restrictions) the emergence of a Korean theatre on Kazakh soil – reputedly the first Korean theatre anywhere – and also Uighur performances at their own theatre in Kyzylorda. Meanwhile the year

1934 was marked by a musical drama, *Aiman-Sholpan* in the newly-constructed opera house in Almaty, named after Abai. The libretto was written by Auezov – it was a skilled adaptation of Kazakh folk tales, with music by Ivan Kostiuk.

It proved to be a seminal performance, evoking talent in hitherto unfamiliar fields of all aspects of stage and musical drama and of theatre design. The soprano Kulyash Baiseitova leapt to national fame – an eminence remembered and honoured to this day. Other names to capture the public imagination were those of Kurmanbek Jandarbekov (singer and director), Kanabek Baiseitov (singer, director and playwright), singers Shara Jienkulova, Manarbek Erjanov; writers Gabit Musrepov, Sabit Mukanov and composer Evengi Brusilovsky. To the last-named can be attributed the foundation of Kazakh opera. And where there is opera there is ballet. It was in 1938 that, out of a performance of Tchaikovski's *Swan Lake,* a troupe of Kazakh ballet dancers emerged, and the Kazakh school of ballet may be said to have been founded. Stars of high talent at once achieved celebrity, including Shara Jienkulova. The same year saw the staging of the first essentially indigenous Kazakh ballet, *Kalkaman and Mamyr* by Velikanov.

The Second World War (the 'Great Patriotic War' in Soviet parlance) was itself to stimulate development of theatre in Kazakhstan. This was partly due to the fact that certain creative spirits still able to engage in the arts of the stage were moved to Central Asia and thus a reasonable distance from the theatre of war. For example, both Mosfilm and Lenfilm were to be provided studio headquarters in Almaty. The misfortune of a sentence of internal exile brought to Almaty the directorial and organisational skills of Natalia Sats, a figure devoted to the concept of children's theatre; and

indeed the Theatre for the Young Spectator flourishing today in Almaty was founded by Sats (with official backing) in 1944. The city enjoyed the presence not only of Sergei Eisenstein, the internationally celebrated film director, but also Nikolai Cherkassov, the actor; and Vera Maretskaya, the actress.

The immediate post-War period was to see the presentation of a number of dramas which have held their place in the Kazakh repertoire to this day, for example *Idris Nogaibayerv* and *Nurmukhan Janturin.*

Alongside the theatre there emerged wonderfully skilled – and internationally popular – troupes of Kazakh dancers, in refined versions of folk dancing. The Kazakh Kurmangazy was making his name as a composer of popular orchestral music in the Soviet world. The dancer Bulatkhanov was building a reputation which clearly played its part in the later emergence of leading male dancers from Central Asia that have made their reputations internationally in our own time.

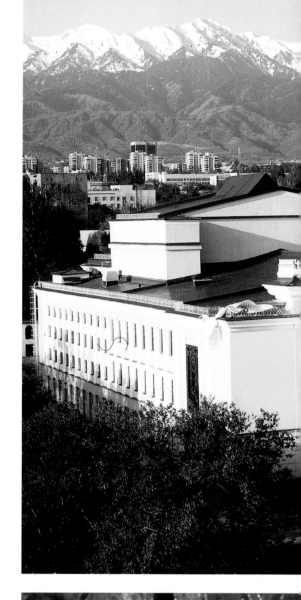

Ballet and Opera

Fine opera houses and theatres abound in Kazakhstan. No significant city is without at least one fine stage sufficient for a major operatic or balletic performance; in Almaty, Astana and elsewhere, there is a choice of theatrical venues. All – by and large – fill their seats, perhaps most infallibly by the art of the dance.

As we have seen, Kazakh ballet has inherited great traditions of Russian ballet, and down the years Kazakh stages have been graced by such stars as Anna Pavlova, Vazlav Nizhinsky, Galina Ulanova, Mikhail Baryshnikov, Rudolf Nureyev and Maya Plisetskaya, whose current partner is the Kazakh dancer Usman Khasanov. A substantial contribution to the formation of Kazakh ballet was made by Ulanova (who was dancing on the stage of Almaty Theatre in 1943), by Tamara Khanum and A. Seleznev, who was to found his choreographic school here. The pioneer of male Kazakh ballet dancing is the ballet-meister Dauren Abirov (b.1923), who emerged in the early 1950s and has since created many ballets and many dance episodes in theatrical and filmic contexts.

The factor of Kazakh tradition in indigenous ballet is central. That was clearly expressed by the launch in 1995 of the International Ballet Competition in Almaty and its 'Award for Traditions'. Today, Kazakh ballet has squared up to the financial challenges of the times and is nurturing a new generation of dancers. Kazakh competitors participate in all important international competitions and – invariably – are either winners or centres of attention in the media as significant contributors to the art of the dance. For example, young dancer Serzhan Kaukov not only won the Maya award, but during the competition was offered a contract by the *maître* of France's Young Ballet, Robert Bertier. Many young ballet dancers are moving on from Kazakhstan to Europe and the US and onto the international scene.

Yet there remain many wonderful dancers in Almaty and Astana Opera Houses, in whose repertoire are more than twenty ballets.

An outstanding contribution has been made by the relatively new ballet troupe Young Ballet of Almaty, established by Bulat Ayukhanov in 1968. This is a ballet loyal to the classical tradition, yet open to the idea of modernist dance. Most critics agree that this collective is more neo-classical than contemporary. This ballet company is frequently on tour, performing in Europe, India and throughout the CIS.

Meanwhile, performances of opera – both 'classical' (and often by the Russian masters like Borodin, Rimsky-Korsakov, Tchaikovski and Mussorgski) and essentially Kazakh musical dramas – fill the auditoriums, especially in Almaty's and Astana's several big-stage venues. A new school of popular Kazakh musical drama, retelling episodes of Kazakh folk history, has emerged, bringing to flower new talents in composition and the vocal arts.

*Anti-clockwise from the top left are pictured on these pages Astana's Opera and Ballet Theatre, Kanysh Bayev Musical Drama Theatre and Russian, Drama Theatre; the prima ballerina Leila Alpieva; a scene (**bottom centre**) from the Kazakh classic* Kyz Jiebek *stage drama; a scene from an Almaty performance of* Eugene Onegin (**below**); *Karagandy's Japanese theatre; Almaty's Auezov Kazakh Drama Theatre, and the city's Abai Opera and Ballet Theatre.*

A work by Aimagul Menlibayeva.

Bapishev's Symbol of Fertility.

A work by Salihitdin Aitbayev.

Modern Art

A spirit of uninhibited creativity in the visual arts of Kazakhstan began to emerge on the eve of *perestroika* in the mid-1980s. Alongside the vicious stifling of protest in December 1986 and a budding prospect of national autonomy, a genuine self-expression was in the air. Socialist realism had ruled for too long. From out of the shadows emerged those who had not dared to show before – or if they had attempted to do so, had been denied the chance.

Abylkhan Kasteyev (1904-1973) was perhaps the first Kazakh to have devoted his life to painting, beyond the traditional ornament – the visual language of Kazakhs. He sought to record with love, joy and grief the dearest things: faces of relatives and friends, landscapes and objects. Kasteyev created epic images of a reality where nature and man lived in harmony. Post-war, Soviet-trained Kazakh artists like Moldahmet Kenayev (born 1925), Sabur Mambeyev (born 1928) illustrated here, and Salihitdin Aitbeyev (1938-1994), also illustrated here, celebrated with varying degrees of skill and banality, themes of Kazakh life, which Sovietisation had effectively destroyed.

Abdrashit Sydykhanov (born 1937) began working with Aitbayev until the December events of 1986 when Kazakh nationalism was cruelly stifled. His subsequent works put together *tamga* – geometric signs of Kazakh tribes, and ideologies of mythology and history.

Pictorial expression was henceforth in the hands of younger performers: Bakhyt Bapishev, Askar Esdauletov, Galim Madanov, Aimagul Menlibayeva, Marat Bekeyev. Their creativity has evolved on the one hand from independent Kazakhstan, on the other from global influences. Each of them has held exhibitions abroad.

All at once in 1987 the landscape painter

Bakhyt Bapishev (born 1958) created *A Symbol of Fertility*. Despite its simplicity – a ram against a background of mountains – the image proved to be polysemantic. This ram is at once vulnerable and strong, commonplace and majestic, the support and the victim of man. It is a kind of world model, with an inherent stability and an eternal self-renewing cycle of death and life.

The motto of Aimagul Menlibayeva (born 1969) is 'Away with school, be unspoiled like a child!' The images associate experience and imagination, reality and myth, her compositions like Egyptian frescoes or Mayan friezes, and her technique essentially flat, as if drawn by a child. Askar Esdauletov (born 1962) also avoids the illusion of a three-dimensional world, his paintings saturated with mythological characters, dream phantoms, personified representation of Kazakh-dom, unfettered by rules – childlike impressions set amid adult judgments.

Galim Madanov (born 1958) has moved away from the representational. His images defy verbalisation, engaging the viewer with their texture, and a ruminative improvisation. They have built him an international reputation.

As for Marat Bekeyev (born 1964), his work lies between the national and personal, tribal and individual, collective and private, between form and formula, nature and abstraction. The main theme is the nomad, pilgrim, traveller, a person in infinite space. His drift of many years from the feeling to judgement, from the myth to life, brought him to the duality of a world of bright childhood reminiscence and the area of symbol. These worlds come into collision in, for example, *The Heaven Guest* (2003), a work of magic nonsense and penetration into the child's soul. The Kazakh artists of today are wedded to their traditional culture, but express too a powerful sense of the universal.

'Shades of Light' by Galim Madanov.

A work by Sabur Mambeyev.

The Language of Kazakh Design

This characteristic Kazakh rug was handwoven in the late 1950s. (190 x 428 cm)

*The velvet bedspread **right**, embroidered with gold, dates from the mid-19th century. (187 x 57 cm)*

Art and artistry abound in Kazakhstan. Yet the national treasure-house is Almaty's Kasteyev Museum of Fine Arts, which houses the finest collection of art in the country, including Russian and European art,

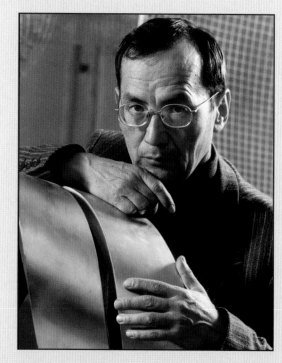

The sculptor B. Norbekov renders in polished steel his abstractions of creative unity: a perennial Kazakh theme.

and the work of artists banned during the Soviet period. Its uniqueness is perhaps in its preservation of the work of fabrication; of Kazakh carpets, wall rugs, saddlery, jewellery and wood carving.

Right: Syrmak felt carpet with mosaic pattern, early 20th century. The motif, constantly recurring in Kazakh ornament-ation, is derived from the horns of sheep, and may be said to imply fecundity. (254 x 134 cm)

The Kazakh artist Abylkhan Kasteyev (1904-73) gave his name to the Almaty museum, which contains the country's finest national art collection.

The solar splendour of the domed ceiling of Ahmed Yassavi's mausoleum (**below**) is echoed by the intricate ceramic patterning of a tile cluster (**right**) from the same site.

Nothing escapes the designer's hand – the family chest (**above**), or the trunk for bedding (**left**).

The Islamic prohibition against images of living creatures combined in the creative Kazakh mind with reverence for nature to produce a decorative style of universal application and characteristic beauty.

The flask, **below**, takes the shape of that part of the horse's stomach from which it was fabricated.

The ferocious weaponry for close combat, and mail armour of mediaeval times, called forth alike the hand and eye of the master craftsman.

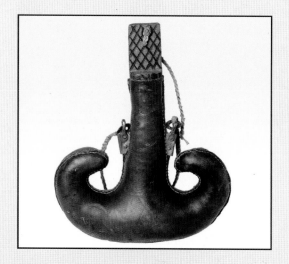

The State Museum of Fine Arts, named after Abylkhan Kasteyev, was established in 1935 as the Kazakh National Art Gallery. It has a leading role among museums of Kazakhstan. It houses a remarkable collection of the folk and crafts of the nineteenth and twentieth centuries such as rugs, carpets, masterpieces of workmanship in leather, bone, metal and wood, and ancient ceramic vessels.

The collection of the art of the Soviet period was started in 1936 with a gift from Moscow's Tretyakov Gallery; it now contains various paintings by significant artists such as Filonov, Konenkov, Sarjan and Redko. In the Russian Rooms we can follow the history of classicism, romanticism and socialist realism, while viewing works of world importance. The art of the turn of the nineteenth and twentieth centuries is reflected here in the pictures of artists such as Korovin, Serebryakov and Petrov-Vodkin.

Some 200 km north-east of Kyzylorda, there rises from the arid plain the Korkyt Monument, an aeolian sculpture in concrete which 'sings' in the wind and reflects the shape of the Kazakh stringed Kobyz. It was a gift of the Hurricane Oil Company.

*Kazakh motifs are ubiquitous – in a wayside bus shelter near Taldy-Korgan (**left**), a batik shawl (**right**), and a collage of metal and leather (**below, left**).*

The collection given to the museum in 1935-36 by the Hermitage of St Petersburg and the Pushkin Museum of Fine Arts in Moscow have provided the base for a collection of European and Eastern art. Chinese, Tibetan, Indian, Japanese and Korean art is represented here as well as works of Uighur and Dungan art. The museum is still buying works from private collections. Furthermore, it serves as a commercial gallery, exhibiting and selling the works of local and foreign artists of our own time.

*In the fabrication of amulets, a 200-year-old design (**below, left**) informs the style of today (**below, right**).*

Traditional Costume

Kazakhs lose no opportunity on festive occasions to deck themselves out in the striking and highly distinctive clothing of the recent past. Traditional Kazakh costume precisely suited life on the Steppe: its very hot summers, strong winds and the bitter cold of winter. Clothing was made of woollen, cotton, silk or velvet fabrics, and outer garments were usually lined with fur.

The men wore shirts, quilted jackets, tunics and a distinctive long, loose coat: the chapan. Winter clothing consisted of quilted garments with an interlining of camel hair or sheep's wool, coats of fur or of leather with the fleece inside, and on top of these, wide cloaks made of

thick, impermeable cloth. For winter their wide trousers were sewn from leather with the fleece inside, and for summer from either goat hide or Steppe antelope hide without fur.

The headwear of Kazakh men was a sharply pointed hat, trimmed with fox-fur, sable or mink. In summer these were replaced by tall caps of thin felt. Typical nomad footwear was high-

A ceremonial chapan, *front and back.*

heeled boots which widened above the knees, and in summer light boots with a curled toe (ichigs) or sandals.

The quality and ornamentation of a woman's clothes reflected her position in society. Unmarried girls wore conical hats trimmed with fur and decorated with eagle-owl feathers or small hats adorned with beads and precious stones. Dresses of silk, cotton or velvet were worn under a bodice or sleeveless jacket of woollen cloth, the borders often richly embroidered in gold or silver thread. Over this they wore a velvet or leather belt with silver clasps and decorative plaques. Older women wore jackets over free-flowing dresses, and on their heads a large kerchief or shawl wound in various ways (the kimeshek, jaulyk, sulama).

Another garment was the beldemshe, *a wrap-around skirt of velvet or thin cloth, gathered at the waist on a wide belt of the same material, fastened with buttons or a buckle.*

Adorned for marriage a bride might be caparisoned as opposite in her conical soukele, bearing its complex symbols, and contrasting with the magnificently

brocaded Khan's headgear, top left. Or she could wear white, as in the model middle right, beside her groom in his gold brocaded chapan.

Three everyday styles of female headwear are demonstrated.

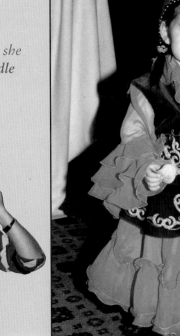

Kazakh Silver of the 19th-20th Century

A pectoral ornament, from western Kazakhstan, of embossed and filigree silver, with gilt and glass. 20th century.

From Turkestan, in southern Kazakhstan, a belt clasp of silver and enamel. 19th century.

From the ethnically Kazakh Karakalpak region of neighbouring Turkmenistan, a temple pendant of silver fretwork and cornelian. 19th century.

From Semey, eastern Kazakhstan, the breastcollar, crupper and girth of a harness in notched, stamped and engraved metal, gilt, and leather. 19th century.

The jeweller's art in Kazakhstan derives from ancient times. The Sak gold culture of the first millennium BC was inherited by the Hun era, evolving a polychromic style, and thence to the Turkic peoples' mastery of silver-smithing, down through the vicissitudes of history to a wondrous flowering in inventive hands of the zergers of the nineteenth and early twentieth centuries. In peaceful times nothing escaped their decorative

A saddle from north-eastern Kazakhstan of cut-out metal, stamped and engraved, backed with velvet over a wooden base 19th c.

A saddle of wood and leather from Semey, emblazoned with gilt, agate, chalcedony and cornelian. 19th century.

The back of the belt's clasp illustrated opposite.

An amulet from the Karatau region of southern Kazakhstan, of embossed and engraved silver, gilt and enamel. 19th century.

mastery of moulding, inlaying, engraving, filigree, enamel and niello – brooches, rings, amulets, pendants, belts, charms, sheaths, scabbards, hilts, saddlery and harness… The examples on these pages are from the collection lovingly amassed by Imangali Tasmagambetov, recorded by the photographer N. Postnikov and others at the behest of the Ministry of Culture and Information.

A clasp of stamped and embossed silver and cornelian, from western Kazakhstan. 19th century.

A leather belt, decorated with silver, gilt and enamel buckles and bosses, from southern Kazakhstan. 20th century.

A matchmaker's finger-ring from Mangistau, of engraved, stamped and embossed silver, gilt and glass. 19th century.

A pair of bracelets of stamped and engraved silver, with inset cornelian, from western Kazakhstan. 19th century.

The Timurid Legacy

A bronze lamp holder.

A ewer of cast bronze.

Timur the Lame, or Tamerlane as he was known in the West, claimed descent from Genghis Khan and ascended to the throne of Samarkand in 1369 at the age of 33. He spent his life in military campaigns. Inheriting the Jeti-Su of Kazakhstan, he subdued Persia and Georgia, turned north in 1390 to conquer the Tatars and the eastern Kipchaks, pursued the western Kipchaks and overran Damascus, and defeating the Turks on the plains of Ankara before turning back towards China, three years prior to his death – in Obrar – in 1405.

Yet he was an enlightened ruler, uniting clemency with justice, fostering learning, religious devotion, and the arts which flourished, above all on his home ground, today's Kazakhstan, on which he lavished the architectural glories of Taraz and Turkestan. Trade with China and the Mediterranean brought wealth and a continual flow of artistic influences. The surviving relics of his era preserved in museums throughout Kazakhstan, speak his name.

A stand for a multiplicity of candles.

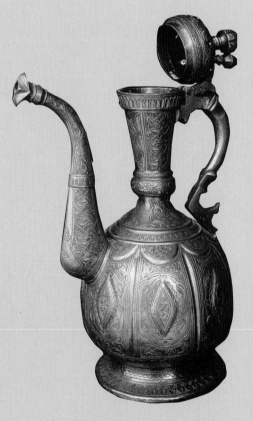

A pitcher used for washing.

Right, the tip of a ritual halberd.

Below, a door of the Timurid mosque at Turkestan.

A metre across, this magnificent bowl provided water for those cleansing themselves before worship at Ahmed Yassavi's Mausoleum, built on Timur's orders and with his detailed approval. Koranic verses decorate the outer rim.

Below, a stand of polished bronze for lighted candles, the product of an early 15th century Timurid foundry, probably in Obrar.

One of the wonders of
the world, the
mausoleum built to
honour the name and
remains of the mediaeval
saint and scholar Ahmed
Yassavi, at his home site
of the town of
Turkestan, is preserved
today in all its glory.

Below and **right**, the baths
of the architectural complex.

Architecture

The architecture of Kazakhstan is organically bound up with the nature of this mainly Steppe country, and with the way of life of the tribes and people who have settled in it. Constant mobility was a vital necessity for the nomadic majority of its population.

Starting in the Bronze Age, however, settled villages emerged in the river valleys with a nexus of agriculture. The Bronze Age left us with impressive constructions in central Kazakhstan, such as Begaza, Landybai and Tasmola. These are original places of ancestor worship. Composed of many-tinted stone slabs and blocks, they crown the hilltops and mountain ridges, representing points of orientation in the unbounded expanse of the Steppe. They were a symbol of the authority of the tribes and their leaders.

At that time adobe mausoleums appeared in the south of Kazakhstan, in the valley of the Syrdarya. These memorial buildings, similar in plan to the graves or 'kurgans' of central Kazakhstan, became prototypes for later religious structures of Central Asia and Kazakhstan. They are distinguished by the fact that the architectural mass comes out of the earth's surface and is covered by domes. The mausoleum in Tagisken (dating from the

ninth to eighth century BC) of a central cupola composition with a tent-shaped dome, made up of wooden beams, is probably the first structure of its kind in central Asia.

Eurasian nomadic existence acquired its classical image around the middle of the first millennium BC in the time of the Saks and the Scythians. It was then that the trappings of this nomadic life developed : a light collapsible dwelling, the prototype of the future yurt, a moving home on a cart, a type of equipment and horse harness, and also typical riding gear – the prototype of contemporary European costume.

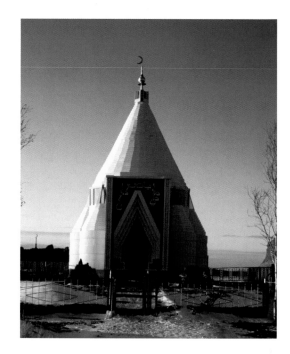

The successors of the Bronze Age cattle breeders and metallurgists – the Saks – continued to erect grandiose graves for their dead chiefs made in the form of stone or earth barrows reaching hundreds of metres in diameter and tens of metres in height. Some of the Saks tribes led a half-settled way of life. It was these tribes in particular, living along the old river beds of Syrdarya, who preserved and developed the adobe building traditions. The Balanda mausoleum, dating from the fourth to second centuries BC, is a shining example of the fruitful development of the central cupola composition theme. The academic S.P. Tolstov, who has researched this monument, considers it to be the first cupola building in Central Asia. The building is round in plan, composed of

*The mausoleum of Aristan Baba, the teacher of Ahmed Yassavi (**top picture, opposite**) is a work of the early twentieth century, following the classic lines of mediaeval mosque architecture of dome and arch, as exemplified in Yassavi's own mausoleum at Turkestan, and his mother's burial site at Ipsijab (Sairan), **opposite lower right**.*

*The influence of the Steppe yurt is evident in the design of the recent private mausoleum built to honour the memory of the head of a family in the Caspian region, and Atyrau's mosque rebuilt in modern times, pictured **above**.*

a central burial chamber covered in a clay dome and enclosed by a round gallery. In this monument the builders employed the basic architectural constructions characteristic of dry and poorly wooded regions of Asia: cupola, vaults and arches. Architectural successes were also achieved in the living quarters and fortified buildings of the Saks of the Syrdarya valley. They would later be assimilated by the successors to the Saks: the Usuns, the Huns and the Turks.

The Turkish tribes not only assimilated the habits of building out of adobe, but also learnt how to make fired brick, and also perfected nomadic mobile accommodation. In about the middle of the first millennium AD the yurt acquired its basic structural parts: a collapsible and folding wooden framework and the system of felt covers.

The spread of Islam in Kazakhstan brought with it new types of buildings: the mosque, *medresseh*, *khanaka*. Islam took root most successfully in the south of Kazakhstan, in the agricultural towns and villages along the trade routes. The towns along the Great Silk Route – Ispijab, Taraz, Otrar – had the three part structure typical of the medieaval East: citadel (*ark*), the town itself (*shakristan*), and the suburbs (*abad*). They had a system of water supply, and defensive buildings. The basic mass of inhabited buildings were built closely adjoining one another, single storey houses out of adobe with flat roofs. Above them rose the bulk of religious and courtly structures, and communal buildings. Made out of fired brick and decorated with colourful glazed ceramics and moulded terracotta tiles, they stood out against the background of the monotone residential dwellings.

Although the Mongol invasion held up the development of towns and agriculture, it did not change the course of the development of architecture taking shape in the early Middle Ages. The descendants of Genghis Khan and their retinue adopted Islam, mastered Turkish culture and by the beginning of the fourteenth century were Mongols only in name. They began to erect mausoleums over the graves of the khans, sultans and family members similar to those over the graves of the legendary and real preachers of Islam. Examples of such buildings are the mausoleum of Joshi Khan and Timur Kutluk in central Kazakstan, Kok-kesen and Syrly-tam in the Syrdarya valley. The leading works of mediaeval architecture are the *khanaka*, built over the grave of the beloved Kazakh preacher Sufi Ahmed Yassavi at the behest of Timur. It absorbed and perfected all the attainments of the architecture of the Islamic east, both in its construction and decoration.

Among the mausoleums erected over the graves of the Kazakh khans, the mausoleum of Alasha-khan – that is a general Kazakh khan exerting influence on neighbouring tribes and people – stands out due to its scale and decoration. Built not far from the mausoleum of Joshi Khan – the founder of the dynasty of Deshti-Kipchak – in terms of its architecture it is recognisably the tomb of a descendant of Genghis Khan, but significantly exceeds it in scale. It seems to announce the birth of a new dynasty – the dynasty of Kazakh khans. Recent investigations of the monument, undertaken in the process of its restoration, have allowed it to be dated to the sixteenth century, and for the moment the most suitable 'candidate' for the title might be Khaknazar.

The faceted cupola above the entrance to the Neimatbai mosque of Taraz dates from the 19th century.

Above, the onion domes of St Nicholas' Cathedral dominate the skyline at Shymkent, and (above, right) the same saint's cathedral in Almaty, built in 1909.

Domes and Cupolas

The dome and the cupola have been favoured in Kazakh architecture, from antiquity to this very day. Their appeal to the eye and the spirit surely derive from the implicit peace and totality of the earliest Steppe dwellings and all that is implied by the sacred cycle of life and the Dome of the Heavens.

Mastery of dome construction was a West Asian attainment – most manifestly of the Byzantine empire as in Constantinople's Hagia Sophia, then boosted by Islam to achieve such wonders as Jerusalem's Dome of the Rock, Kazakhstan's Turkestan mosque for Yassavi, and Agra's Mogul (i.e. Mongol) Taj Mahal, Shah Jahan's memorial to his beloved (1630).

Astana's impressive National Museum, a treasure house of Kazakh artefacts and historic records, is a domed edifice for our own time.

The dome had spread to Christian Europe – as evidenced by Brunelleschi's Florence cathedral (c.1430), Bramante's dome at St Peter's in Rome, and Wren's St Paul's of London (1675). Meanwhile, the characteristically Muscovite onion dome had entered Russia by the inventiveness of Venetian designers brought across from Baghdad... and from Orthodox St Basil's, reappearing across Kazakhstan.

*The cathedral dedicated to Christ the Saviour in Almaty's Panfilov Park (**above**), designed by A.P. Zenkov in 1904, was built entirely of wood and without a nail – virtually the only building to survive the 1911 earthquake intact.*

Below, the remarkable 'draped' dome of Pavlodar's modern mosque recalls both yurt and veiled womanhood.

Below, left, it is once again the dome that lends authority to the Presidential headquarters in modern Astana.

Tsarist and Soviet Architecture

The joiner's craft of a century or so ago remains evident in a number of surviving buildings in Almaty (as **left**) and a few in Astana (as **above top**). The gemütlich *charm of a few stucco survivors of pre-revolutionary Kazakhstan, like the little museum in Almaty (**lower left**) catch the visitor's eye. **Above**, the post-War Academy of Sciences in Almaty, has an air of pleasing confidence.

When the Russians began to build in colonised Kazakhstan from the mid-nineteenth century, they brought with them a skill and a style in the use of wood which made for a homeliness and warmth in domestic building well suited to long and snowbound winters. Some fine examples survive, and are preserved today with tenderness and pride. Other dwellings of brick and brightly painted plaster, often with arched windows, were held to a single storey in regions – like Almaty – subject to earthquakes.

*Imperial Russian baroque is exemplified by the frontage of the Ishyn Hotel at Astana, **below**; and a Graeco-Roman touch is visible in Karagandy's wintered theatre (**right**). **Above**, Almaty's college students' 'Palace' recalls the stylistic brutalism of the post-War era.*

Formal or public buildings, like those for government, or hotels, tended towards the grandiose, yet could often present a façade of classical dignity. Of an ornate charm unique to Tsarist 'Turkestan' (of which today's Kazakhstan is a part) were the stations and premises of the 'Turk-Sib' (Turkestan-Siberian) railway. Soviet rule, with the apotheosis of the role of the State, brought a portentousness to official buildings, while the homes of the citizens were either wooden tenements or, more conveniently, faceless blocks of high-rise flats.

Flat-dwelling remains today the favoured form of residence for the majority, above all for convenience and warmth, as ordinary folk escape the trouble and expense of the three- or four-room wooden

The egalitarian anonymity of high-rise apartment blocks in Almaty are relieved by trees, in leaf in summertime and snow-bloomed in winter. The former capital's unfinished stadium in the foreground aimed at proving that reinforced concrete can fly.

bungalows with asphalt roofing, subject to rotting and leakages and inefficient for heating. Today's newly rich build their dachas in clusters in the countryside, inclined to compete – in the view of those with a sense of architectural probity – in being that much swankier than the neighbours'. Yet in the field of independent Kazakhstan's new public buildings, as we shall see, are arising some new buildings which are fine by any standard.

Astana, a Capital for the Future

One of the symbols of the new Kazakhstan is the tower named Astana-Baiterek – 97 metres high, to reflect the fact that it was in 1997 that the decision to move the capital began to take effect. Baiterek is the name of a holy tree, in the crown of which the mythological bird the Simurgh or Samuruk laid a shining egg each day. Each night a wicked dragon raided the nest and ate it. People killed the dragon; and so the Sun of Kazakhstan came to be eternally shining, reflecting the eternity of creation. This sublime conception was the work of architect Akmyrza Rustambekov.

Called in by Kazakhstan's Government as their consultant was Kisho Kurokawa, born in Japan in 1934, city planner and architect extraordinaire. The grace and confidence of Kazakhstan's new capital stems in high measure from him.

Architect Kaldybai Montakheyev's buildings are the Residence of the President, the Central

Moving the capital to Astana (from Almaty) set the architectural imagination alight. The decision was taken in 1995; the actuality began in December 1997. The Government consulted one of the finest architects/ town planners in the world. With impressive speed the quite provincial township – albeit centrally sited and well-linked, on the sweeping curve of a river – once known as

The city's premier superstore dominates the river spanned by the main bridge and its dramatic arch symbolising the three-Juz. As for the Ishym itself, a skater's paradise in winter, it becomes a bather's spa in high summer.

Square of Astana, the buildings of the Council of Ministers, and of Parliament, and the waterfront of

the Ishym. Major contributors include the architects Sultan Baimagambetov and Timur Suleimenov.

The appropriately soaring Ministry of Transport and Communications is framed by the arch of the Ministry of Energy and Mineral Resources, seen **further left**, which handles the exploitation and sale of the nation's hydrocarbons.

Geometric grace, greensward, and the majestic curve characterise Astana's planned development (left).

Akmola, then as Tselinograd, had acquired an array of impressive and harmonious public buildings and thousands upon thousands of offices and flats, on a city plan of generous proportions.

The plan anticipated growth to a million souls within three decades. Yet within its first six years as capital, that prospect looked like an underestimation.

The Ministry of Finance, the wits like to observe, bears a resemblance to the sign for a dollar (**above**). To the Sports Centre (**below**) there unquestionably belongs an athletic grace.

Chapter 7

The eyes of those in the world most alert to the geo-politics of world economy are on Kazakhstan. For here they see a country brimming with potential, yet up to the present date still tantalisingly at one remove from the realisation of that potential. The promise is, of course, of truly significant expansion and national prosperity as the country's natural resources – first and foremost in hydrocarbons – find their international markets. The great finds of oil and gas are relatively recent: their full exploitation on, or in, the ground tomorrow, not today. The reaching of the global market is the parallel conundrum – at this very moment on the brink of resolution. And as the world awaits, so do the people of Kazakhstan.

Economy

Global consortia have joined hands with Kazakhstan to exploit the hidden treasures of hydrocarbons beneath or beside the Caspian, already bringing employment to thousands and giving the young country a glowing dawn.

The Economic Challenge

A significant feature of the Communist philosophy of the Soviet Union was its pre-occupation with material (and human) resources. Truckloads of coal, bushels of wheat, ingots of steel, megawatts of electricity: these were what measured and confirmed Soviet power, and impressed bureaucrats. In that respect Kazakhstan must have appeared to be multiply blessed. Of all the sixteen republics in the former Soviet Union, Kazakhstan almost certainly possessed the greatest amount of resources per capita. The country had seemingly

exported thousands of tons of fish from the Aral Sea and Lake Balkhash. And relatively speaking, Kazakhstan had a tiny, but well educated population, with over 95 per cent being functionally literate. A virtual 'Land of Plenty'. At first sight, the prospects for an independent Kazakhstan must have seemed boundless.

In Soviet times Kazakhstan was therefore almost certainly a net exporter of wealth, and could demonstrate a very positive rate of return on investment. It had the resources and the space. And because of its size, pollution was not an issue that exercised anyone's conscience to any extent. With its

Promise however was one matter. Turning that promise into prosperity was quite another. Two things made it difficult. Firstly, Kazakhstan had developed a solid machine-building industry based on its mining and metal processing. With the demise of the Soviet Union, the market for Kazakhstan's machines was suddenly reduced by 90 per cent. The railway wagon manufacturing plant at Kazalinsk close to the Aral Sea used to supply the entire Soviet railway network serving over 220 million people with railway wagons. In a matter of two years the factory had lost virtually all of its market outside the country and was

*Not all industry is on a mega-scale. Shopping malls, like that in Astana, **left**, rent out their premises to aspiring retailers... offering the products of the manufacturers of fashionable winter-wear (**right**).*

endless land resources producing temperate and semi-tropical crops (everything from barley to watermelons) which were exported all over the Soviet Union and beyond. Geologists found virtually every element in the Periodic Table on its land surface. Kazakhstan mined and processed gold, silver, lead, zinc, copper, uranium, coal, iron ore, bauxite and phosphorite ores. In addition it had wolfram, molybdenum, barites, tungsten, beryllium, titanium and cadmium in plenty. It had one third of the world's resources of chromium and manganese and a quarter of the world's uranium. Kazakhstan was thus an industrial giant in its own right. Despite being a landlocked country thousands of miles from the open sea, the country even

bountiful resources it could afford to import skilled labour from the western part of the Soviet Union to develop its industry and to attract young pioneers from all over the Soviet Union to harness the Virgin Lands and produce record grain harvests. This very wealth of space and paucity of people also allowed the development of the Baikonur Space Launching station and, alas, the Semipalatinsk Nuclear Testing Site. Both needed all the space they could get.

At Independence Kazakhstan was not the richest of the Soviet republics. That distinction fell to the Baltic republics and particularly the thrifty Estonians, close to European markets. However, while Kazakhstan may not have had the actual riches, it certainly had the promise.

now reduced to servicing the Kazakhstan Railways network which served under 15 million people. Kazalinsk Railway Works had over 5,000 employees at the time of Independence. Despite some ingenious attempts to diversify production to meet the new realities, this factory and hundreds others like it soon had to cut production and staff drastically. In Kyzylorda, also in southern Kazakhstan, the Soviet planners had sited a factory for manufacturing rice harvesting equipment. It had sold its highly specialised equipment to collective farms all over the Central Asian and Caucasus republics. However with Independence its market was reduced to a few rice farms along the nearby Syrdarya River. Now its main buyers were in foreign countries sheltering behind high tariff walls. The outcome was inevitable. Such factories had difficulties in maintaining production and revenues, in paying utility bills and in purchasing raw materials. The result was an unemployment rate in excess of 12 per cent in the late 1990s, and disenchantment and disillusionment with the elusive fruits of independence.

Secondly, freed from what many regarded as the rigid yoke of State Socialism, Kazakhstan then plunged

promptly into a wave of what often proved to be untimely privatisation. Most of it was well-intentioned. However several factors combined to complicate the picture. In the first place foreign investors had to be courted and won. Kazakhstan did not have a lot on offer apart from its dilapidated Soviet infrastructure, and because few investors knew the country or its people, it was immediately labelled as a high-risk investment site. The first investors were not willing to risk too much capital, nor to share it with local people. Investors needed to maximise profits, to slash staff numbers and staff

benefits and to repatriate funds as quickly as possible. This in its turn engendered a righteous indignation on the Kazakh side, that foreign investors were not serious, that they were out to make a quick buck and to strip the country of its huge assets. Although Kazakhstan had taken bold steps to move away from its grim Soviet past by trying to modernise and privatise its mineral-based industry, the period from 1994 to 1997 was an unhappy one. Several disputes between the Government and foreign investors ended in acrimonious debate in the courts. This hardly improved Kazakhstan's reputation as a safe haven for

The barracks wall depicts the President amid the waving corn as generator of bounty, but the country's serious wealth is sourced in the Caspian west, where a floating drill rig probes for hydrocarbon treasure.

reputable investors. The chief architect of the privatisation policy, Prime Minister Akezhan Kazhegeldin retired because of ill health, and eventually slipped out of the country in 1997 after an acrimonious dispute with President Nazarbayev. In 2001 Kazhegeldin was sentenced *in absentia* to ten years imprisonment for economic crimes.

One of the investors who did stick around was the giant Indian steel producer ISPAT (part of the LNM Group). This took over operations of the Karaganda Metallurgical Combinat (KARMET) in Temirtau in November 1995. Between 1990 and 1994 production had fallen from 6.2 million to 2.0 million tons of ingot steel. This was largely because of the loss

of the all-Soviet market. By rationalising production at a very inefficient facility, ISPAT-KARMET was able to increase production to 3.5 million tons. In taking over the KARMET facility ISPAT also took on over 60,000 workers and responsibility for all manner of social services and an entire public tramway system. ISPAT also operates numerous coal mines in Karagandy Oblast and has recently acquired the Lisakovsk Iron Ore Processing Plant in Kostanai Oblast close to the border with Russia. ISPAT KARMET is a good example of how foreign investors and Kazakhstani

industry can get along together to increase employment and production.

The first three to four years of Independence were therefore difficult ones, with little durable foreign investment, high inflation, stagnating industry and negative rates of growth. Annual inflation rates in 1993-1994 were over 1,500 per cent. The Gross Domestic Product (GDP) was falling at over ten per cent per annum and the official unemployment rate rose from 0.6 per cent in 1993 to 13 per cent in 1995.

However from about 1996 onwards things began to change. This was largely due to the adoption of more cautious economic reform policies and the attraction of increased foreign direct investment (FDI). Of the former

Communist countries, only Hungary has been able to attract more FDI per capita than Kazakhstan. In the ten years from 1993 to 2002 Kazakhstan attracted almost 13 billion US dollars or about 1,000 dollars per capita. In 2001 it attracted almost three billion dollars of foreign investment. The United States accounted for about half of this. Among the major foreign investors have been the Samsung Group of South Korea who have revived the fortunes of the giant Kazakhmys copper plant at Jezkazgan in the centre of the country and the Mitsubishi Corporation of Japan who are also involved in various metals projects.

*Even the wise K.A. Satpaev, father of Kazakhstan's geology, could not have foreseen the impact of his prospections on the Caspian coast, where the port of Aktau (**right**) is the country's fastest growing city.*

These are apart from the numerous multinational oil companies like BP, AGIP, Chevron, Texaco and British Gas working in the petroleum sector. However, oil and gas accounted for over 80 per cent of the FDI in Kazakhstan in 1999.

It is a bizarre reflection that the global investors of the twenty-first century in Kazakhstan's minerals were in fact following a path in Kazakhstan first trodden by a British engineer businessman, Philip Ridder. After coming upon a huge lode of zinc and lead, he started lucrative mining operations in the remote Altai Mountains in eastern Kazakhstan in the late eighteenth century. A town was built in 1786 and named after Ridder and it has been engaged in mining operations for zinc, lead, gold and silver ever since. The

city was renamed Leninogorsk, or 'Lenin's Mountains', by the Soviet administration, but in 2001 the city council decided to revert to the original name of Ridder.

Another interesting foreign investor is Turkey. It is estimated that Turkish entrepreneurs have invested well over one billion dollars in Kazakhstan since Independence. Their presence can hardly be overlooked with the giant hyper-modern 'RAMSTOR' supermarkets in

Astana and Almaty. These help to bring Turkish consumer goods to the notice of the rising Kazakhstani middle classes. The fact that Turkey is the second most important foreign investor in Kazakhstan after the United States is not surprising. In global terms, Ankara, only four hours away by air, is close to the markets of Kazakhstan. Because of the bonds of the Turkic languages, Turkish businessmen also feel a special affinity with Kazakhstan, and can communicate without too much

difficulty in Kazakh-speaking areas of the country. Even far-flung towns like Uralsk or Kyzylorda now have their own Turkish-owned supermarkets and hotels.

By the late 1990s Kazakhstan was beginning to model itself on the Asian 'Tiger' economies with a liberal and largely reformed economic system. It had reformed its tax and foreign investment systems, and by the end of 1997 the large majority of businesses and housing stock

had been privatised. However this was before the financial crash in south Asia in 1997 and the financial crisis in Russia of 1998. This brought Kazakhstan up with a start. It did not, however, take Kazakhstan long to recover, and the important Foreign Investors Council which has had a major influence on policy was established in June 1998.

In many ways, as it entered the new millennium, Kazakhstan had luck on its side. Gross Domestic Product grew at 9.6

per cent per annum in 2000 and at 13.5 per cent in 2001 whereas rates for the first five years of independence had been largely negative. And these levels of growth seemed set to continue. A whole concatenation of fortunate circumstances was behind this growth. The weather and harvests had been good for a number of years in a row. Wheat and wool production, for example, began to recover although they were still far below pre-

macro-economic management, economic reform and rationalisation of the tax system also did their bit to encourage investor confidence in the country and to push the country's international credit ratings up. At the beginning of 2001 the Government had established a National Oil Fund, modelled on Norway's, to manage and invest Kazakhstan's oil and gas reserves for future generations.

Having been launched – almost against

present but was clearly receding. Old people could depend on getting their pensions in time. Foreign investors were beginning to feel that they could trust the Government with their money. The huge open-air bazaars were full of local food and goods. Small businesses and services were flourishing as never before.

Kazakhstan had met the economic challenge of Independence head-on and was now beginning to enjoy it.

Independence levels. Kazakhstan's oil and gas production was booming, especially with the discovery and development of the giant Kashagan and Karachaganak fields in the west of the country. Foreign investors were now flocking to Kazakhstan as never before, partly in response to the development of the petroleum and mining sectors and partly in response to enlightened and informed investment policies formulated by a sympathetic Government and National Bank. Firm

its better judgement – into Independence it was perhaps inevitable that the country's economy would be bedevilled by a measure of confusion, at least for the first few years. No one had had any experience of the dramatic transition which took place at the end of 1991, and no one had any experience of how to handle the effects. However by the time Kazakhstan had entered its second decade of independence things were looking very much better. Agriculture was slowly getting to its feet, poverty was still

With estimated reserves of 100 billion barrels of oil and 2.4 trillion cubic metres of gas, both onshore and offshore along its Caspian coast, Kazakhstan is one of the world's largest unexplored hydrocarbon countries. Nazarbayev was the first Central Asian leader to conclude a deal – in 1992, with Chevron, for the Tengiz field – with a foreign oil major.

A New Oil Nation

At the beginning of the year 2000, President Nazarbayev was openly speculating whether Kazakhstan could become as big an oil producer as Saudi Arabia within fifteen years. Right up to Independence in 1991, however, oil and gas production in Kazakhstan had been overshadowed by the far larger oil business in Russia. The American company Chevron became the first foreign oil and gas operators in sovereign Kazakhstan when in 1992 they took over the Tengiz field in the Caspian Sea. Kazakhstan's hydrocarbon adventure both onshore and offshore, is thus of fairly recent initiation.

And yet it is also true that towards the end of 1999 the country also celebrated the one hundred year anniversary of its oil production. For it was in September 1899, at Karachungul close to Atyrau on Kazakhstan's Caspian coast, that the first successful oil well in Kazakhstan was drilled – in what was then Russian-controlled territory. Because the deposit was so small and so remote, it never became commercially viable. The first commercial operations did not get started until 1913 just to the east of Atyrau. From that date on, Kazakhstan was to grow into a significant producer of oil and in due course also of gas.

Even before 1899 the presence of oil was already well known in Western Kazakhstan. Nomadic Kazakhs had long been well aware of the curative properties of crude oil, especially in the treatment of skin diseases. The traditional practice was to collect oil from surface pools for spreading on affected parts of the body. This came to the attention of various Russian scientists already exploring the resources of Kazakhstan which was then in the process of being gradually incorporated into the Russian empire. In the 1890s the railway companies began to commission detailed mineral surveys of western

After the Tengiz field – whose operations are pictured here – got under way, further deals were struck with other American, Chinese, British, Italian, Japanese and Turkish companies, netting Kazakhstan between $400m and $800m annually in investment. Then came the discovery of the big new Kashagan field.

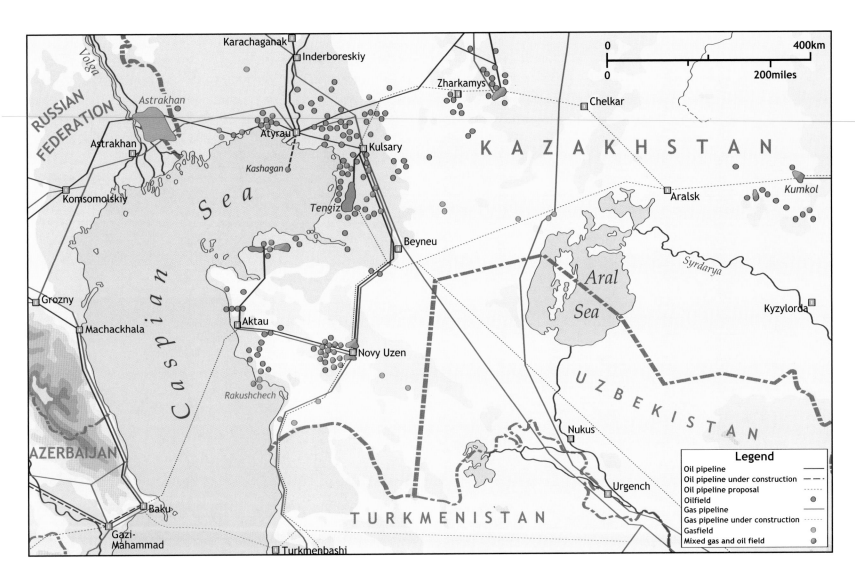

Kazakhstan, and this led to the drilling of the first wells at Karachungul by a Russian-German consortium.

Oil resources continued to be identified and exploited throughout the Soviet period in Western Kazakhstan. By 1937 proven reserves were estimated at 30 million tonnes. Thus over the whole of the twentieth century several generations of certain Kazakh families were establishing themselves in the oil production business and laying the basis for future prosperity. After the Second World War one of Kazakhstan's greatest scientists and President of the Kazakh Academy of Scientists, K.A.Satpaev, began to take an active part in the exploitation of Western Kazakhstan's oil resources.

It was only after 1980, however, that Kazakhstan's oil industry began to assume international dimensions. The Tengiz field was discovered in the north-east Caspian in 1979; today it is estimated to contain six to nine billion barrels. This is about half of what the North Sea oilfields are thought to contain. The Kashagan field, north of Tengiz, discovered in 1997, is thought to be the biggest oilfield in the world to have been revealed since 1970. It is said to contain anything between eight billion and 50 billion barrels. Kashagan will not be an easy field to develop. It covers an area of 85 kilometres by 25 kilometres and lies five kilometres below the surface of the northern Caspian Sea. In winter the operator, AGIP, has to work on the sea-ice with the ever-present danger of spills. The local geology is complex and the full exploitation of these fields is difficult to forecast.

If the higher estimates for oil reserves in Tengiz and Kashagan turn out to be accurate – and they could well be so –- Kazakhstan would have oil reserves of over 60 billion barrels (8.2 billion tonnes), greater than those of Russia and placing Kazakhstan third in the order of countries with quality hydrocarbon reserves in the world, after Saudi Arabia and Iraq. Oil production in Kazakhstan in the year 2000 was 35.3 million tonnes (700,000 barrels a day) and was growing at an annual rate of over 15 per cent. In 2003 expectations were that by the year 2015 production would have increased by over five times, attaining 200 million tonnes (or four million barrels a day). This would be approaching two-thirds of Saudi Arabia's current production, and would be greater than that of Iraq, Kuwait or Iran. At that rate of exploitation, Kazakhstan's resources would last another 41 years.

However, as a land-locked country, Kazakhstan will be more dependent than most on pipelines, and always on the goodwill of its neighbours and the good behaviour of its neighbours' inhabitants.

Kazakhstan has many neighbours whose goodwill it must court: Russia, Azerbaijan, Iran, Turkmenistan, Uzbekistan and Kyrgyzstan, and in the pipeline context also Georgia and Turkey. A complicating

Baltic outlets might seem to be via Iran to the Persian Gulf – by a pipeline beneath Kazakhstani Caspian waters and either Azerbaijan or Turkmenistan waters to an Iranian Caspian port, then overland to Iran's Gulf terminal on the Euphrates estuary. But long undersea pipelines are at hazard from seismic ructions; moreover the US is currently fixated by what it perceives as Iran's hostility and has thus subjected that country to a trade embargo.

At the beginning of the new

Caspian to Novorossiysk on the Black Sea – via, of course, exclusively Russian territory, once the frontier was crossed – was completed in 2001. It has been designed to pump five million barrels a day by 2015. Then in May 2003, agreement was reached for a new pipeline, available to Kazakh oil and gas, from the Azerbaijan Caspian port and capital at Baku via Georgia's Tbilisi and thence southwards across eastern Turkey's formidable mountains to a newly-built terminal at

*Storage of crude oil is the requirement at the Novy Uzen field (**left**), due east of the Caspian port of Aktau. The wasteful burning off of gas is progressively being reduced by the liquidisation of gas for compact transportation, or separate piping (**right**).*

factor is the interests of the West where a substantial proportion of the markets lie and whose oil and gas companies are deeply committed in Kazakhstan. Naturally the Western oil and gas 'majors' would prefer to see their pipelines routed through predictably amenable countries like Turkey, which also fronts the Mediterranean. But to reach Turkey from the Kazakhstani Caspian a pipe must pass through Azerbaijan and either Georgia or, conceivably, Armenia. A geopolitically more convenient route to a terminal sea-port alternative to Russia's Black Sea or

millennium, Kazakhstan was, inescapably, dependent on the goodwill of Russia through which the bulk of the country's oil and gas production was exported to markets further afield first by pipeline and thence by rail, either westward to the Black Sea or northward to the Baltic. It was clearly in Kazakhstan's interest to reduce its virtually total dependence on Russia for transporting its oil and gas. To do so, it embarked on the planning of a series of ambitious pipeline routes. The 1,580 km. Caspian Pipeline Consortium (CPC) pipeline from Atyrau in the

Ceyhan, on Turkey's north-eastern Mediterranean coast. Sponsored by a consortium headed by AGIP and British Gas, it was expected to be in operation by 2006, after a construction cost of some four billion dollars. A 3,000 km. pipeline carrying Kazakhstani oil or gas (or both) to China has been a further option widely canvassed, and is no less ambitious.

The Pipeline Challenge

Kazakhstan's oil and gas markets lie, for the most part, in the wider world, beyond its immediate neighbours. The exception is China; but the nearest border with China to the oilfield is some 3,000 km. to the east, and even then 2,000 km. away from the centre

of consumption. A pipeline from the Caspian to China is on the cards... but meanwhile the oil-thirsty Western markets must be reached – and not, if possible, only via Russia. Kazakhstan's first pipeline outlet is via Russia's

Novorossiysk in the Black Sea, and thence by tanker. But Turkey was ever fearful of a shipping calamity in the crowded Dardanelles. So the deal was struck in 2003 for Kazakhstan's oil to share a pipeline now being built at an estimated cost of $4 billion from Azerbaijan's Baku (to be reached from Atyrau and Aktau by Caspian

tankers) via the Georgian capital of Tblisi to the north-east Mediterranean port of Ceyhan, thus passing up the option of piping to the Persian Gulf via Iran, which the US insists in quarantining politically.

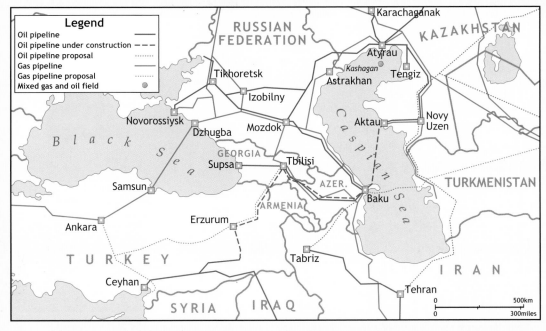

Legend
- Oil pipeline
- Oil pipeline under construction
- Oil pipeline proposal
- Gas pipeline
- Gas pipeline proposal
- Mixed gas and oil field

RUSSIAN FEDERATION · Karachaganak · KAZAKHSTAN · Atyrau · Kashagan · Tikhoretsk · Astrakhan · Tengiz · Izobilny · Novorossiysk · Dzhugba · Mozdok · Aktau · Novy Uzen · Black Sea · Caspian Sea · TURKMENISTAN · GEORGIA · Supsa · Tbilisi · Samsun · AZER. · Baku · ARMENIA · Ankara · Erzurum · TURKEY · Tabriz · IRAN · Ceyhan · Tehran · SYRIA · IRAQ

0 – 500km
0 – 300miles

Oil and gas pipelines (being laid here from the Tengiz field) need to be sunk into their trenches, serviced and cleaned, and constantly policed and protected, as do the pumping stations. The amortisation of their cost can take many years.

With such extensive production in prospect, Kazakhstan has naturally sought to expand its own refining capacity so as to add greater value to its products. By the year 2000 the country had three oil refineries, namely at Pavlodar, Atyrau and Shymkent, with a combined refining capacity of 427,000 barrels per day or about 60 per cent of the country's crude oil production at the time. A gas-oil separation plant was planned for Aksai. There would still remain the task of getting the refined product to its international markets. Meanwhile because of the availability of cheap refined imports, together with the smuggling of petrol from Russia and Uzbekistan and an inability to process all types of crude oil, Kazakhstan may experience at least temporarily an over-capacity in the refining sector.

By the year 2000 Kazakhstan was already earning of over five billion dollars from its oil and gas exports. This meant that oil and gas had already come to account for more than one quarter of the country's total production of wealth. If production and exports from the sector were to increase, as anticipated, by five times by the year 2015, then Kazakhstan's income from oil and gas would amount to 25 billion dollars a year – a sum amounting to more than the country's total Gross National Product of 21 million dollars at the start of the century.

As in other countries with rapidly expanding oil and gas production, the question was: how could Kazakhstan absorb these huge oil revenues? Several states have experienced the 'Dutch disease' where huge oil and gas revenues have generated inflationary pressures which have a negative impact on the rest of the economy (as happened with the expansion of gas production in the Netherlands in the 1990s). Kazakhstan has created a so-called 'Oil Fund' of which the purpose is to invest oil and gas revenues for the long-term benefit of the nation in the form of increased pensions and other social

benefits. It is too early to determine how successfully this will meet the challenge and opportunity of increased revenues. What is already certain, however, is that Kazakhstan will be required to muster wisdom, decisiveness and political tact to a high degree so as to maximise the potential benefits of its burgeoning oil and gas industry for the best interests of the people as a whole.

Mining

Kazakhstan has been described as the 'ultimate mining and metallurgical country'. It possesses huge reserves of all the basic minerals essential for industrial development. They are: gold, silver, lead, zinc, coal, iron, copper, chromium, manganese, bauxite, wolfram, molybdenum, titanium, barites and uranium. All of them are being exploited, to different degrees. The mining and metals industry production is valued at 2.7 billion

dollars of which 75 per cent is exported. The industry employs over 200,000 persons.

Gold

Kazakh gold from the Altai Mountains has been known for centuries and is a feature of the glorious traditional Scythian jewellery to be viewed in the National Museum in Astana (*see* Chapter 6). The country's gold reserves are put at

At Karagandy coal has been king for generations, and its heroes colliers to whom monuments (above) are erected. The coal fuels the local steel mills.

800 tonnes and about 20 tonnes a year are mined. The Vasilkovskoye mine in North Kazakhstan Oblast (close to the border with Russia) is estimated to be the fourth largest gold mine in the world. The Government plans to expand production, but this will require foreign investment which so far has not been forthcoming. The main production takes place in East Kazakhstan near Oskemen. Most of the gold itself is processed at Balkhash. Canada is the principal foreign investor in the gold business in Kazakhstan.

Coal

Although some of Kazakhstan's coal is low-grade anthracite, the country's reserves amount to 30,000 million tonnes. Current production is 60 million tonnes a year so that reserves will last 500 years at current levels of exploitation. This is less than half Kazakhstan's coal production at Independence when the country was the third largest coal producer in the Soviet Union. Coal production declined largely because of non-payment of debts. Most of the coal is used for generating power, so that the decline in production has had an effect on energy production in the country too. Almost a third of Kazakhstan's coal is exported, mainly to Russia and the Ukraine, but a large proportion is exported elsewhere. Most coal is produced in a series of mining towns around Karagandy and at Ekibastuz in Pavlodar Oblast. New ventures into open-cast mining are expected to increase production to almost 100 million tonnes a year. As it is, the Bogatyr open-cast mine near Ekibastuz produces almost half of the country's coal output. This is expected to have a commensurate impact on the energy situation in the country.

Chromium

Chromium is very important for Kazakhstan as the country possesses almost one quarter of the world's reserves, and there is no substitute for chromium in the production of stainless steel. It produces about 2.4 million tonnes a year which amounts to about 20 per cent of the world production.

Copper

Copper is one of Kazakhstan's most important mineral products, as it is known to have the third largest reserves in the world. Recent output has been about 370,000 tonnes a year and it is expected that this is sufficient for 30-40 years production. Mining of copper is divided between the centre and the north of the country whilst the refining is undertaken at Jezkazgan and at Balkhash in Karagandy Oblast. The main copper producing company is Kazakhmys in which South Korea's Samsung has a major share.

Bauxite/Aluminium

Bauxite is mined in large open-cast mines in Kostanai Oblasat in northern Kazakhstan and alumina is produced in the country's only alumina processing plant at Pavlodar. Kazakhstan produces about 3.6 million tonnes of bauxite and just over one million tonnes of alumina a year which are exported to Russia for smelting. There are plans for constructing Kazakhstan's first aluminium smelter for producing refined aluminium.

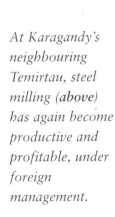

At Karagandy's neighbouring Temirtau, steel milling (above) has again become productive and profitable, under foreign management.

Overleaf: copper mining at Jezkazgan.

Lead/Zinc Production

Lead and zinc have been mined for over a century in Ridder (formerly Leninogorsk) (*see* 'Economic Challenge' on page 234) in the foothills of the Altai mountains. A newer plant exploiting ores from the Karatau mountains in South Kazakhstan is located in Shymkent. A Swiss company, Glencore, has invested heavily in Kazzink, the country's main zinc producer and has opened new mines in East Kazakhstan. Kazakhstan produces about 200,000 tonnes of zinc and 160,000 tonnes of lead annually.

Iron Ore and Steel

Kazakhstan's iron ore resources and steel production are the basis for the country's industrial production, as it is self-sufficient in iron and steel. The country has reserves of about 12 billion tonnes of iron ore, and has recently produced about ten million tonnes of iron ore a year. However it is likely that this will stabilise at around 12 million tonnes a year. The main mines are at Rudny in Kostanai Oblast close to the Russian border. The principal steel works is at Temirtau in Karagandy Oblast.

Annual steel production is in the region of four million tonnes.

Kazakhstan's steelmaking operation at Temirtau, under the management of a London-based Pakistani group, is one of the most efficient and profitable in the world.

Kazakhstan is still one of the largest wheat exporters in the world, and only Australia has more arable land per head of population. Cotton and sunflower oil is also widely grown.

Agriculture

It has been said that Kazakhstan could feed a billion people, if its agricultural potential were to be fully exploited. Even despite its widely dispersed population, Kazakhstan is an important agricultural producer. It is one of the world's largest wheat producers and it exports about four million tonnes a year from an annual production of about 18 million tonnes a year. It used to produce over 30 million tonnes in Soviet times, and still produces more wheat per capita than any other country in the world.

Only Australia has more arable land (2.68 hectares) per person than Kazakhstan (2.04 hectares per person). But in much of the north of the country, the ratio is nearer ten hectares per person, so that Kazakhstan has more agricultural land than almost anywhere else on earth. However, lack of people and agricultural infrastructure make its potential difficult to realise fully.

In February 1954, looking to make his mark after the death of Stalin in 1953, the emerging leader of the Soviet Union, Nikita Krushchev coined the term 'Virgin Lands' (Tselinny Kray). These were the great Steppes and prairies to the east of the Urals in Siberia and Kazakhstan, where young pioneers were exhorted to settle, to open up the Soviet Union's new grain fields. Over 350,000 young pioneers moved east from European Russia, Ukraine and Belarus to find a new life. Over fifty years

on, many of them, or their descendants, are still there, although the majority have probably by now returned to the west. One strange relic of this exodus are the weekly scheduled flights from Pavlodar and Kostanai in northern Kazakhstan to western Russia, the Ukraine and Germany.

As much as 200,000 sq. km., or more than one-tenth of the country, was set aside in Kostanai, Akmolinsk, North Kazakhstan and Pavlodar Oblasts for large-scale collective agriculture. These areas were sparsely settled by indigenous Kazakhs so that there was little resistance from that quarter to the ploughing up of the grasslands and Steppes. Northern Kazakhstan had also been used as a

dumping ground by the Soviets for inconvenient national minorities like the Chechens or the Volga Germans. Thousands of them are still to be found in the small country towns built in the 1950s to service the Virgin Lands. And more than 800,000 people arrived from the rest of the Soviet Union to take up the challenge of the Virgin Lands.

Since 1991 and the coming of independence agricultural production on the Virgin Lands has fallen. The amount of land under wheat fell from 140,000 sq. km. in 1991 to 103,000 sq. km. in the year 2000. Productivity, too, has fallen. The reasons for this fall are complex. It can mainly be attributed to the break-up of the

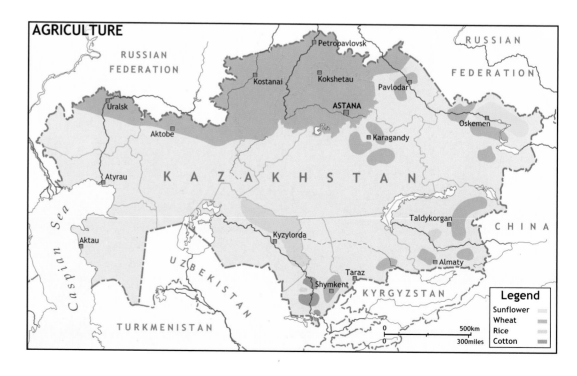

*The truest product of the fragile ecology of the Steppe is livestock – best of all the karakul sheep, **below**, or camels or goats. Yet deer farms flourish, for venison and the antlers' velvet; and so does the honey bee.*

collective farms. This meant that agriculture was starved of new investment in machinery and infrastructure. The areas and distances in the Virgin Lands are so great that a high degree of mechanisation is essential for efficient operations. At the same time the original grassland ecology of northern Kazakhstan is fragile and subject to drought. This clashed with the industrial approach to agriculture adopted by the Soviet pioneers. The result was extensive ploughing, over-utilisation of resources, soil erosion and land degradation. The humus content of the soil has been reduced between five per cent and 20 per cent because of over-ploughing. Soil fertility has been reduced because of compaction by tractors.

There are, however, signs of new life in the Virgin Lands as more land transfers to private hands and as more small businesses emerge in the towns to serve agricultural production. A major new grain terminal has been constructed on the Caspian Sea, and an increasing number of foreign investors are beginning to eye up Kazakhstan's wide open spaces and to appreciate the potential which these offer in a world which will always need wheat.

Yet of course grain production is only one aspect of Kazakhstan's agriculture and a relatively new one. Livestock rearing is a much more traditional occupation in Kazakhstan and one which has been the basis for the country's nomadic culture for many centuries. Even today over 40 per cent of the value of agriculture production comes from livestock production. It has been estimated that three quarters of Kazakhstan's agricultural land is suitable for livestock rearing. Horses, camels and sheep are the most important animals being reared. Indigenous sheep are particularly well suited to the Steppe and semi-desert conditions of central Kazakhstan. The *karakul* industry which produces 'Persian' lamb furs, which can fetch up to 5,000 dollars for a coat, has been a particularly productive aspect of livestock rearing.

Kazakhstan also has a small but significant production of semi-tropical fruit, rice and cotton under irrigated conditions along the Syrdarya River before it enters the Aral Sea. Considerable effort has been made in recent years to impove the hydraulic conditions on the Syrdarya River to make better use of the scarce river water.

Mention also has to be made of privatisation. This has been an important aspect of agricultural development since Independence. It has been estimated that over 70,000 farms have been turned over to private farmers and most of the unwieldy collective farms have been broken up and the land distributed to small farmers. A recurrent problem of course has been the need to provide new farmers with sufficient capital and credit to be able to

Fisheries; New Hope for the Aral

Surprisingly for a land-locked country, fish has often been an important part of the diet in Kazakhstan. This is because there are many hundreds of fresh and salt water lakes throughout the country. The Caspian Sea, the Aral Sea and Lake Balkhash have all supported important fisheries. In 1960 no less than 60,000 tonnes of assorted fish were landed and processed in Kazakhstan and Uzbekistan and sold in markets throughout the Soviet Union. By 1975 the fisheries existed no longer; the canning and freezing plants had closed; and the fishermen had rolled up their nets and moved elsewhere or sought other means of livelihood. A combination of drying-out, pollution from fertilisers and salinisation had put paid to an industry and pattern of life centuries old. By 1980 only three-fifths of the original Aral Sea remained, its ancient ports stranded miles inland.

The Caspian Sea had been significant for fishing for centuries and Atyrau a centre for catching the Caspian Sturgeon (*Acipenser imdirentris*) in the Sea and the Ural River for over eighty years. Widespread poaching and illegal fishing have reduced stocks dramatically and the Caspian caviar industry remains under serious threat. The authorities have established several sturgeon breeding facilities around Atyrau in order to safeguard one of the country's most important economic assets.

The Aral Sea, too, was an important fisheries reource producing over 40,000 tonnes of fish a year, before it began to dry out.

In 1979, however, Soviet scientists began to experiment with introducing to what was left of the Sea a species of flounder, *Kambala glossa*, which it was thought could adapt to the increased salinity in the Aral. Local fishermen began to start catching the fish in the mid-1980s and by 1990 it appeared that the flounder was well established and might even have some commercial value.

As chance had it a Danish environmentalist, Kurt Christensen, happened to be visiting Kazakhstan in 1991. Denmark had a traditional expertise of seine netting for flounder. The Danes provided equipment, training and financial credits. By 2003 over 600 Aral

The Caspian Sturgeon, a source of fish flesh and of caviar, is being protected from poaching, and bred at Atyrau.

fishermen had been organised in co-operatives, and the fisheries had began to provide a livelihood and sustenance to several thousand people around the north Aral Sea.

*Resourceful Kazakhs have immemorially supplemented a winter diet with fish caught on a bait hook through holes in the ice. **Below**, the Mayor of Aralsk gives company to a stranded buoy.*

Electricity

At Independence Kazakhstan's electricity generation and distribution system was closely tied into the highly inefficient and wasteful Soviet system of electrical energy, with close links to the Russian system to the north and to the Central Asian system to the south.

Kazakhstan has now built up an independent electrical power infrastructure. At Independence, generating capacity was about 17,000 megawatts but this fell to about 10,000 within a few years. Similarly power consumption fell from about 85 billion kilowatts to 50 billion. Demand fell as prices rose and demand adjusted itself to the new financial realities.

Because of its huge reserves of coal, Kazakhstan depends on fossil fuels for generating 85 per cent of its electricity. Another 14 per cent comes from hydropower schemes in the Tien Shan and Altai Mountains. The final one per cent is from a small nuclear power plant at Aktau on the Caspian Sea. At least 70 per cent of Kazakhstan's power is used by heavy and processing industry. As most of the country's coal and industry is located in the east of the country in East Kazakhstan and Karagandy Oblasts, the majority of

Kazakhstan's power plants are located there. The largest one, the 4,000 megawatt coal-fired plant at Ekibastuz, is situated at one of the country's largest coal-fields.

By the year 2000 more than 90 per cent of the electricity sector was in private hands, and one major US company AES was responsible for 30 per cent of the country's power generation. Britain and Israel have

With its indigenous fossil fuels, Kazakhstan's now privatised power generating industry can provide electricity inexpensively and profitably.

also been involved in the privatisation process.

Because of the physical size of the country, Kazakhstan has been provided a series of decentralised transmission networks. The country is served by 15 main transmission networks and these have been privatised.

The transition from a highly subsidised, highly inefficient supply system to a market-based one where prices reflect real costs has not been easy for the consumer. Pensioners and people on low incomes have experienced difficulties with increased electricity bills and the Government has had to introduce measures to assist vulnerable social groups.

Banking and Financial Services

At the beginning of the twenty-first century Kazakhstan had the highest annual economic growth rate (over 13 per cent) of any of the former Soviet republics. Inflation had been reduced to six per cent per annum. To some extent this was due to the orderly way the country's banking and financial services had been developed. The National Bank of Kazakhstan has taken a leading role in regulating the sector.

A small number of banks account for almost three-quarters of deposits. There is also growing competition from foreign banks as the limit for foreign equity in the banking system is 50 per cent. Lending was expected to increase considerably in the first decade of the new century as people got used to the concept of banking and as more foreign banks entered the market. Because of firm regulation by the National Bank of Kazakhstan and because of its interventions in the market, banking in Kazakhstan has attained a good international reputation. The public is showing an increasing confidence in home-grown banking although there is still a long way to go. The Government has established a Stock Exchange with a view to raising more capital on the open market for investment in the country.

In the early 1990s there was widespread recognition throughout the world that the best aid was 'help to self-help', that is financing to start small and medium scale enterprises (SMEs). In many cases people did not need more than a few hundred dollars (to buy some camels, for example) to be able to start a business. In other cases they needed a lot more.

Much of the initiative for SME development came from the United States which has been active in stimulating private development to create jobs and entrepreneurs. For example USAID established a Kazakhstan Community Loan Fund in Taldy-Korgan and

*A handful of well-trusted banks headquartered in Almaty (as **above**) and Astana, plus the EBRD and USAID, are capitalising small businesses.*

Shymkent. It disbursed 12,000 loans of an average of $200 each. Over 80 per cent of the borrowers were women. The Government of Kazakhstan also established a huge Micro-Credit agency which disbursed over 20,000 loans. The European Bank for Reconstruction and Development (EBRD) lent over 70 million dollars million through local banks to start up small businesses all over Kazakhstan. The average loan size was about 10,000 dollars. Such credits and loans enable small businessmen to set up all sorts of local businesses, from simple sewing shops to bakeries, breweries and food processing factories.

By 2003, new economic sprouts were breaking through the soil.

Tourism and Transport

Kazakhstan has a myriad of tourist attractions, and it now has excellent air connections (through Lufthansa, British Airways, KLM and others) to the rest of the world. It is as yet by no means a major tourist destination. It still receives less than half a million foreign visitors a year which is a tiny number compared with the 70 million who visit France and the 20 million who visit Russia every year. And most foreigners visiting Kazakhstan come for business. Only 50,000 people (mainly from Germany and western Europe) come first and foremost as tourists.

Before Independence Kazakhstan was regarded as an exotic (and therefore little known) appendage to tours to the Soviet Union, and the numbers who visited were minuscule. Since Independence the Government has sought to build up its tourist infrastructure before embarking on a wholesale marketing programme. There are now excellent hotels of international standard in Almaty and Astana. There are daily flights from Moscow, Frankfurt, London and Amsterdam. There is a good network of domestic flights within the country which is vital in a country as big as Kazakhstan. The rail network is comprehensive, but still represents something of an adventure for foreign tourists.

The country's tourist attractions are not well known overseas. The Islamic monuments of Turkestan and Taraz in southern Kazakhstan rival those in Uzbekistan. The Tien Shan and the Altai Mountains, ranging from 4,000 to 7,000 metres are every bit as challenging and picturesque as the Himalayas. And the skiing facilities, as at Shimbulak, are fast expanding.

For those in the know, Kazakhstan is a tourist paradise. Specialist travel companies in Europe and America arrange increasing numbers of climbing/mountaineering, hunting, botanical, ornithological and fishing excursions to the Steppes and the mountains. These are surprisingly reasonable in price despite the small numbers involved. A ten-day walking trip in the pristine Tien Shan Mountains will cost less than 2,500 dollars from Europe.

Cultural tours, to sites of great antiquity, unfolding the astonishing history of Central Asia over several millenia, are surely an enterprise of the coming period.

Kazakhstan's internal transport system suffers from the fact that it was built in Soviet times as a Russian-centred one, and all transport routes, roads and railways were directed to Russian cities and processing plants. To get from one Kazakhstani city to another it is often easiest to cross the Russian border. With the collapse of the Soviet Union and the slow-down in economic activity, goods and passenger traffic in Kazakhstan fell by 60 per cent between 1990 and 2000.

Over half the freight in Kazakhstan is moved by rail, so that the country's 14,300 kilometre railway network is vital for the country's prosperity. After ten years of independence, the railways were badly in need of rehabilitation, and various schemes to privatise and upgrade the network have been introduced.

The country's road system, which was inherited from the Soviet Union, will also need upgrading and various international financing institutions are helping Kazakhstan with this task. A perennial problem is the fierce winter conditions on the Steppe. Air connections are increasingly replacing road and rail for passenger transport. A road or rail trip from Almaty to Astana will take the best part of 24 hours whilst the flight takes one and a half hours. Several private air companies have sprung up to meet the growing market, and they look set to gain an increasing share of the business and tourist travel market.

RAILWAYS AND AIRPORTS

*Mountain resorts like Chimbulak above Almaty (**opposite, top picture**) are attracting the visitor – for ski-ing, walking or mountaineering. Remoter regions may be reached by helicopter (**opposite**). Modern hotels (**left** and **above**) serve Astana and Almaty. The success of Air Astana in competition with the longer established Kazakair has boosted standards of internal air travel. But the country's rail system (**right**) is efficient and indispensable.*

INDEX

'You should love learning for its own sake.' - Abai